PRAIRIE STATE BOOKS

In conjunction with the Illinois Center for the Book, the University of Illinois Press is reissuing in paperback works of fiction and nonfiction that are, by virtue of authorship and/or subject matter, of particular interest to the general reader in the state of Illinois.

A list of books in the series appears at the end of this volume.

CARL SANDBURG

CARL SANDBURG

by Harry Golden

Foreword by Joseph Wershba

Preface by Penelope Niven

University of Illinois Press

Urbana and Chicago

© 1961 by Harry Golden
Foreword and Preface © 1988 by the Board of Trustees
of the University of Illinois
Published by arrangement with Harper & Row, Publishers. All rights reserved.
Manufactured in the United States of America
P 5 4 3 2 1

This book is printed on acid-free paper.

First published in 1961 by The World Publishing Company

Library of Congress Cataloging-in-Publication Data

Golden, Harry, 1902–
  Carl Sandburg / by Harry Golden ; foreword by Joseph Wershba ; preface by
Penelope Niven.
    p. cm. — (Prairie State books)
  Bibliography: p.
  Includes index.
  ISBN 0-252-06006-7
  1. Sandburg, Carl, 1878–1967—Biography.   2. Poets, American—20th century—
Biography.   I. Title.   II. Series.
PS3537.A618Z58 1988
811'.52—dc19
[B]   88-14416
                                                                                    CIP

For Danny and Mike, Barney and Rex

Our Grandchildren

in the hope that they

and grandchildren everywhere

will continue to live

in a free world

Contents

FOREWORD 5

PREFACE 11

INTRODUCTION 17

1. The Incredible Height 23

2. A Vastly Larger Home 45

3. American Minstrel 79

4. From Each According To His Ability
   To Each According To His Work 115

5. Street and Prairie 149

6. The Babe, Big Bill, and the Pre-eminent Hearst 187

7. In Prose You Say What You Mean 221

8. Strange Friend and Friendly Stranger 239

9. A Final Lilt of Song 263

WORKS OF CARL SANDBURG 275

INDEX 277

Foreword

Harry Golden liked to say: "Hey! Me and Carl have a non-aggression treaty going. Carl talks for half an hour, then *I* talk the *next* half hour." Malarkey. If Carl Sandburg wanted to talk for a couple of hours—and he could—Harry Golden would sit by dutifully with a beatific smile on his full-moon face. Harry was no different from the rest of us who basked—literally *basked*—in Carl's presence. Lucky were they who had Carl Sandburg look at them with that intensity of his and hear him say: "A precious face . . . good to look at." You knew you'd never get a compliment bigger than that for the rest of your life. Like all of us, Harry loved to imitate Carl's low-throated way with words, words like "ac-com-mo-date . . . la-ti-tu-di-nous . . . se-pul-chral," joke words whose reverberations made you feel that Carl had never left the room. We wanted him to stay forever. He was bigger than life. He was humanity. He was America.

And that was what Harry needed when he went South after a spell in the federal pen. He needed an anchor. Harry cleansed himself in Carl's healing waters. Carl brought Harry back to his nourishing rootholds—to Harry's own youthful idealism and socialist yearnings. Of course, Harry could belabor the point at times. "Why does he keep talking 'socialism,' 'socialism'?" Mrs. Sandburg once asked me. Carl toned down some of the hyperbole in Harry's manuscript, but when Carl was nearing the end of the road and was asked by a reporter, "Which side are you on?" he gave that wondrous grin of his and let the words roll out: "With the radicals."

When it came to facts, Carl was implacable. Friendship never stood in the way. Harry's manuscript for this book originally said that William Randolph Hearst, the newspaper mogul, offered Carl a job for $75,000—truly a princely sum in those days but incorrect. Carl changed it to $30,000—still a princely sum, but accurate. (Anyway, Carl turned it down.) In another place Harry wrote that when Carl addressed the Congress on Lincoln's 150th birthday—February 12, 1959—"Sandburg spoke briefly." Maybe briefly for Carl's usual stint, but we're talking historical fact here! Carl emended the text to read: "Sandburg spoke 20 minutes. . . ." (That speech is on records and you'll be twice blessed for listening to it.) A statement that Carl was unable to make West Point because he was deficient in mathematics and grammar prompted him to point out in his vigorous handwriting in the margin, "'Twasn't math, 'twas arithmetic." Carl was sufficiently flustered to spell it arith-ma-tic.

This book is anecdotal and mostly about Carl Sandburg. Let me tell you about Harry Golden when I first met him—in Charlotte, North Carolina, near the end of 1960. He was at the peak of his career, and I had gone down to do a series on him for the *New York Post*. I remember Harry . . . in red suspenders, fancy vest, and glowing smile. He looked at the activity swirling around him in his office home, waved his cigar in the direction of all nine rooms, shrugged his shoulders and pronounced with joyous bewilderment: "The whole thing's a bonus. I'm living on borrowed time!"

Success, by then, had come to Harry Golden, publisher of the *Carolina Israelite* and author of three consecutive best-sellers: *Only in America, For 2¢ Plain*, and *Enjoy, Enjoy*. And like most of the things that appealed to Harry, his success made him laugh till he cried. "I remember going down to the tax office here in Charlotte," he said. "I owed the government $480. I begged and pleaded with them. They were nice to me. We made an agreement I could pay $15 a week. And still I fell behind. So what happens last year? I gave the government $77,000 in taxes. Can you believe it? And I just sat there in the same chair in which I had begged the year before—and I laughed and laughed!

"Success? I needed it like a hole in the head. But at least it didn't knock me over. Maybe that's because it hit me when I was *fifty*-seven, not *twenty*-seven." Harry nodded toward his small but comfortable book-lined office and living room, his record collection of symphonies and Italian opera, his easy chair and his ever-present box of cigars. "Know something? If this whole success disappeared, it wouldn't make a bit of difference. I have my books, my phonograph, my house—and the newspaper gives me a living. Before I got rich, my suit wasn't pressed. Now, I press my suit. The whole thing's a bonus. Know what I mean?"

Irony always had an appeal for this short, round, laughing man. His life was full of it. He was a New Yorker who decided along about 1940 to make the South his permanent home. His newspaper, the *Carolina Israelite*, was published in a sturdy Presbyterian milieu and dealt nostalgically with Jewish life on the Lower East Side fifty years before. He was one of the foremost proponents of Jewish self-identity—and he was married to an Irish Catholic.

Harry Golden was a man of encyclopedic scholarship, yet he had become a master of the great American tradition of vernacular humor. He was roly-poly, even funny-looking, yet there were few speakers on the American lecture platform of his day who were more magnetic and spellbinding when talking about intellect and human rights. He had wheeled and dealt with the money crowd on Wall Street during the Great Prosperity of the 1920s, and he had taken a three-year prison rap to protect one of the most famous political church figures of the time— Bishop James Cannon of the Southern Methodist church, whom Harry was advising financially.

Thus it was that Harry was resurrected in the South. When people asked what a fat little Jew was doing preaching to Southern Christians, his answer was typical: "What if Jesus came back, and came back to North Carolina? Who better than I could explain to that Jewish lad of two thousand years ago just what a *Presbyterian* is?"

Born Herschel Leibel Goldhirsch on May 6, 1902, in Eastern Galicia, Harry was brought to America when he was two years old and grew up in the Jewish ghetto of New York City. His father was "a freelance everything": Hebrew teacher, music critic, philosopher, marriage clerk—a man who regarded intellect as the only status worth the chase; a man at home with Kant, Hegel, and Henry George. "My father," Harry said, "was in the typical Socialist tradition of those who belonged to the school who thought the victory of the proletariat would solve the 'Jewish Problem'—as well as all other problems—and, of course, none of those folks lived long enough to find out how wrong they were."

Harry's father was also a Darwinian rationalist. Once, when Harry kidded him about his strict observance of the Sabbath and of every holiday and ritual, his father replied: "A people cannot exist without form or ritual or without memory." Indeed, it was Harry's Jewishness that kept him "alive" during his years in the wilderness. "I'm not a synagogue-goer," he said, "but the thing that has fascinated me about Judaism is that Moses was not permitted to become a god. How many lesser men became gods! But not Moses. The reason, I think, is that Jews were so intent on creating and maintaining Judaism. They wanted the idea to live."

Some southern rabbis were not happy with Harry's sermonizing in the *Carolina Israelite*. He was a trouble-maker, they said. He was against segregation before being against segregation was cool. "They used to hold meetings about me," he chuckled in his growl-throated voice. "'What's he up to now?' they'd ask. 'How do we get rid of this guy? Why is he putting us in an exposed position?' They didn't understand that *their* rights depend on the black man getting *his* rights." In his last days Harry said, "I didn't do it for the 'Negroes,' I did it for America." And he did it with the weapon he knew best: humor.

First came the "Golden Vertical Negro Plan." Harry pointed out that the industrialization of the South all but eliminated "vertical" segregation. Blacks and whites *stood* at the same grocery, supermarket, department store, and bank counters. So, he reasoned, why should there be any trouble with blacks and whites attending the same classes in school—if you took out the seats and had all the students stand at their desks? The plan was received with a whoop and a holler across the country. It was regarded as a big joke. But in later years it was actually adopted by department stores in many cities of the South. When black sit-ins began in 1954 at luncheon counters, at least one large chain ordered the chairs removed from the counter so that unsegregated business could go on—on a standing-only basis.

There was also the "Golden White Baby Plan." Black people had no trouble going to white theaters so long as they were accompanied by white children. Now, said Golden craftily, if white mothers would lend their babies to black people, then blacks could go to the theaters *and* at the same time solve the white mothers' baby-sitting problems!

The "Golden Out-of-Order Plan" worked this way: Harry prevailed on a North Carolina department store owner to shut off the water in the "White Only" water fountain and put up an "Out of Order" sign. Within three days, he reported gleefully, whites were drinking "segregated water" out of the "Negro" fountain. And not a single complaint.

The "Negro Turban Plan": white hotels in Charlotte accepted black guests if assurance was given that the blacks were Hindus. All they needed were turbans! "Now, this gave me an idea," Harry chortled, "particularly with the bad conditions in the textile industry in the

South. If we manufactured, say, 12,000,000 turbans and gave each Negro a turban—it would solve the problem!"

This kind of stuff drew hearty guffaws from a neighbor down the road—Carl Sandburg. Harry regarded Carl as his greatest friend, a poet, Lincoln biographer, first-generation Swede, Lutheran, onetime Socialist organizer, child of uneducated immigrant parents. He was terrified, however, that once he became successful the news would break that he was the Harry L. Goldhurst who had gone to prison. Instead, when Carl found out he said, "this story ties me closer to him."

The prison sentence burned Harry Golden like a scarlet letter—he didn't talk about it until years later. Carl Sandburg's hand of brotherhood was his redemption. And this book was Harry's prayer offering to his friend. As Carl would have said of Harry, "He ain't what's wrong with the country!" And neither was Carl.

JOSEPH WERSHBA

Preface

Harry Golden did not intend to write a definitive biography of Carl Sandburg, as he makes clear in his introduction. There can be no mistaking his method: "My research, such as it was, was my love for Carl Sandburg." The resulting portrait is engaging and human, although not accurate in every detail. Golden did not pretend to do exhaustive research, and he was right about how much time and patience would be exacted of biographers who immerse themselves in Sandburg's papers at the University of Illinois and elsewhere. Besides, until 1983, thousands of Sandburg's papers were not fully accessible for study, and other materials have come to light in the years since Sandburg's death in 1967 and Golden's in 1981.

In his autobiography *The Right Time*, Golden calls his friendship with Sandburg the most rewarding of his life. "If Carl was your friend and your son was sick," he wrote, "Carl worried as much as you. If you were depressed, Carl wanted to share your depression as he wanted to share your exhilaration when you were happy. Carl, as a friend, accepted your entire universe, every star, jungle, and person in it." Golden had vast affection and admiration for Sandburg, twenty-four years his senior. "I have no intentions of writing an objective book," he declared. Instead, he wanted "a *Carolina Israelite* type book, the subject of every essay—Carl Sandburg." Golden's anecdotal biography is both a portrait of Sandburg and a mirror of their friendship.

Sandburg supported the project and aided and abetted Golden in it, sharing papers, letters, photographs, and memories, often on brisk walks over the mountain trails at Connemara, or in long talks on the spacious front porch, or by long-distance telephone. He read the manuscript and marked galley proofs for Golden, pointing out errors—"I never brought a guitar to [Clarence] Darrow's office and sang. . . . you are nearly as fantastic as Ben Hecht in having me in Chicago in 1910 and reporting the garment strike and bringing a guitar to Darrow's office and singing for him . . ."—and sometimes rewriting passages.

Eighty-three at the time and overburdened with work, Sandburg was living in Hollywood, working as creative consultant to his friend George Stevens, who was filming his epic life of Jesus Christ, *The Greatest Story Ever Told*. Not only was he reading proofs for Golden, he was also reading proofs for Norman Corwin's *The World of Carl Sandburg*, working on texts for a Christmas feature in *Good Housekeeping*, and writing prefaces for books by S. L. A. Marshall and President John F. Kennedy. Yet he pored over the Golden text, and the galleys survive with his careful handwritten notes and corrections.

Sandburg was lavish with praise as well as criticism: some of Golden's ideas were superb, he said, but he took umbrage with some of the sources Golden chose to quote. "This is hogwash 55 years after the event," he complained of one story Golden repeated. "This is a case of a cipher looking back 55 years and seeing himself as a Big Number." Golden kept that story but deleted one he borrowed from Ben Hecht, that Sandburg failed to meet his newspaper deadlines as a reporter for the *Chicago Daily News*. Sandburg protested, calling the charge "a goddam lie"—and he had articles with his byline to prove it. When Golden defended Sandburg against the critical disdain of a well-known literary historian, Sandburg urged him to go a step further, scrawling in the margin of the galley: "In a recital . . . Sandburg said, 'As I look at the icily cold purity of ——— I get an impression he is one of the early products of artificial insemination.'" Golden declined to make that addition.

This was, after all, Golden's very personal portrait of his friend, and so he heeded some of Sandburg's suggestions and ignored others. Sandburg respected Golden's rights as the author of the book and in the end deferred to his judgment, giving him the prerogative to be wrong about this fact or that. "To show you that I may have a thicker skin than you have, I am willing, if you say so, to go to print with the whole kit and kaboodle as it now stands in gold print on the galley proofs," Sandburg wrote in July 1961 from Hollywood. And go to print it did. While there are errors here and there, Golden is true to his vision of Sandburg, giving us a unique and valuable portrait, with its own kind of veracity and durability.

When Carl Sandburg died on July 22, 1967, his wife, Paula, telephoned trusted family friend Joseph Wershba of CBS to ask him to announce the news. Joe and Shirley Wershba and their children were welcome at the Sandburgs' Carolina mountain home as if they were part of the family. So was Harry Golden. Wershba knew and loved both men, who held him in "ancient and loving regard." They were three of a kind, coming from different places and generations to a kindred vision of the great human family. Sandburg, Golden, and Wershba, all sons of immigrants, have enriched our culture because they fed as children on the great hungers that brought their parents to this country.

Wershba has had a long, distinguished career as a print and broadcast journalist. He worked with Edward R. Murrow on "Hear It Now" and "See It Now" and has been a producer at "60 Minutes" since the show's first broadcast in 1968. For six years he was a reporter and columnist for the *New York Post*, capturing in print the essences of character and personality he conveys adroitly in his "60 Minutes" profiles. Wershba interviewed Sandburg for CBS, recorded Sandburg's resonant baritone voice singing the American folk songs he had collected since the turn of the century, and produced the CBS News tribute to Sandburg, broadcast the day after the poet's death. He has written about his friends Sandburg and Golden, paying homage to their lives and work with the candid affection and humor that made him a favorite companion, their "Brudder" Wershba.

Despite numerous honors (two Emmy Awards, a Pulitzer nomination, the Golden Gavel Award, a Hillman Foundation Award, alumni honors at Brooklyn College where he was a student in the late 1930s), Wershba has what Sandburg called a rare, rye bread humility. He protests when a biographer tells him he was part of an intimate fraternity of Sandburg's adopted brothers and sons, a member along with novelist Kenneth Dodson, Norman Corwin, Ralph McGill, Edward R. Murrow, and Harry Golden.

"Your book is going to be a nice hayride," Sandburg told Golden in 1961. It is fitting that Joe Wershba should write a foreword to this new edition of the Sandburg-Golden hayride. Golden called Wershba "a brilliant and perspicacious friend and interpreter." "Dearest Joe Washboard," Sandburg greeted him in a letter. "Alliteratively I believe in poetry, propaganda, persiflage and please pass the pickles, and pertinently, peacocks alone cannot propagate unless peahens. . . ."

"We have a debt to pay," Wershba wrote to Sandburg in 1954, when the nation was grappling with McCarthyism. "This air we breathe does not come free. . . . The word is fight. The meaning is self-respect. The philosophy is: inasmuch as ye have done this unto the least of these, ye have done this unto me." That, succinctly, is the fundamental vision these three friends shared.

PENELOPE NIVEN

Acknowledgments

My eldest son, Richard Goldhurst, associate editor of *The Carolina Israelite*, helped in the preparation of the chapter on Sandburg's poetry as well as with the editing of the final manuscript; Dr. Joseph L. Morrison, of the School of Journalism at the University of North Carolina, examined the Socialist papers at Duke University for me; Joseph Wershba, of the *New York Post*, gave me all his notes about Carl Sandburg which he had compiled both as a reporter and as a close friend of the poet, and Ralph G. Newman, of the Abraham Lincoln Book Shop, Chicago, loaned me photostats of several hundred of Mr. Sandburg's columns for the Chicago *Daily News*.

Introduction

I want to write about Carl Sandburg, but this will not be the definitive biography. To begin with, anyone who wants to write the definitive biography will have to spend six years at the University of Illinois perusing and cataloguing the Sandburg papers. Also, I am too old and too fat and perhaps too impatient to spend time with all those sources "without whose help this book would not have been possible."

For if it takes two years to write the definitive biography of a leading world businessman, it will take twenty-two years to write the definitive biography of a leading world poet.

My research, such as it was, was my love for Carl Sandburg. I consider him my closest friend, and while I respect the men of critical acumen who have sometimes tried to diminish the importance of his work, I do not believe them.

Curiously enough, the book was not so difficult a task as I first imagined. As the idea of presenting Carl Sandburg on the American scene germinated in my mind, I realized that all I would have to do was write a biographical sketch of the United States of America through the past half century and use Carl Sandburg as a reference point.

For this poet came to the American scene as a journalist, writing newspaper stories for radical magazines in Wisconsin and Illinois. He was a reporter who followed the strikes and the picket lines and the race riots, a man who wrote all about the Molly Maguires, the Pinkertons, the I.W.W.'s, and the incipiently growing labor unions. From such early conflict, this silver-thatched poet now strums a guitar for a national television audience while a motion-picture star dances and tells jokes. In his spare time, he makes records for children. Here is the span not only of a literary man but of a great country. For this is the symbol not only of our experience but our experiments in the last fifty years.

The words of Carl Sandburg are read in the high school class-

17

rooms of America more than the words of any other living American writer. One guesses this from the universally anthologized poems, "Chicago," "Grass," and "Fog" in the schoolboy textbooks, and from any examination of Carl's correspondence. Stretching back for fifteen years, there are literally hundreds of thick brown envelopes from high school teachers enclosing forty or fifty handwritten essays . . . "I asked my class to write an essay on the meaning of your poem, 'Grass,' and I hope the enclosed essays will interest you . . ."

Not ignoring Sandburg's critics, I feel he is still the one American writer who has distinguished himself in five fields—poetry, history, biography, fiction, and music—and I do not write this assessment merely to add to his laurels. For, quite frankly, the assessment is made daily, made by millions of Americans of every age and of every race, creed, and nationality—millions of Americans who know and love Carl Sandburg.

HARRY GOLDEN

Charlotte, North Carolina
August 1, 1961

What a wee part of a person's life
are his acts and his words. His real
life is led in his head, and is known
to none but himself.

Mark Twain, *Autobiography*

PART 1

The Incredible Height

"This here phizzog"

The two most impressive things about Carl Sandburg when you first meet him are his face and his incredible height. Yet he does not quite measure six feet. The impression of height results, I think, because Sandburg so much resembles an American Indian—the reddish skin over the craggy face, the high cheekbones, the narrow hips, and the broad shoulders. He is a man you think must be tall because he ought to be tall. Someone remarked of him once that when he was young and dark he looked like a Sioux brave—all shoulders and alert eyes. Once his hair turned white, he began to look more like an Osage chief—with oil wells.

Since most faces conform now to our mass-media impression of beauty, Sandburg's face is a unique phenomenon. No matter what the picture or photograph—or even, for that matter, sculpture, the expression is never the same. He has no set pose yet remains recognizably—Carl.

In *Bitter Summer Thoughts,* his poem "Phizzog" asked:

> This here phizzog—somebody handed it
> to you—am I right?
> Somebody said, "Here's yours, now go see
> what you can do with it."

Mrs. Sandburg tells me that during all these fifty-three years she's known him, Carl has always had the same unruly shock of hair over his forehead, and the same habit of leaning forward like a fast-ball pitcher winding up and pulling the string on the batter.

A joint session of Congress

The *Congressional Record* says, "Applause," the members rising as the Honorable Sam Rayburn, Speaker of the House of Representatives, says, "And now it becomes my great pleasure, and I

23

deem it a high privilege, to be able to present to you the man who in all probability knows more about the life, the times, the hopes and the aspirations of Abraham Lincoln than any other human being. He has studied and has put on paper his conceptions of the towering figure of this great and this good man. I take pleasure and I deem it an honor to be able to present to you this great writer, this great historian, Carl Sandburg."

The occasion was the result of a resolution by the House of Representatives, the Senate concurring ". . . that in commemoration of the one hundred and fiftieth anniversary of the birth of Abraham Lincoln, the two Houses of Congress shall assemble in the Hall of the House of Representatives at 11 o'clock antemeridian, on Thursday, February 12, 1959 . . ."

This was the wording of a House Concurrent Resolution, No. 57. It was the hope of the Congress that the joint session commemorating the 150th year of Lincoln's birth would be the forerunner of "wisely spaced kindred events that strike a powerful respect deep in the heart of the American people."

The actor, Fredric March, read the Gettysburg Address, then members of both Houses of Congress, the nine justices of the Supreme Court, the members of President Eisenhower's Cabinet, members of Washington's diplomatic corps, and other guests rose for an ovation to Carl Sandburg.

Sandburg spoke twenty minutes, his opening and closing paragraphs as follows:

> Not often in the story of mankind does a man arrive on earth who is both steel and velvet, who is as hard as rock and soft as drifting fog, who holds in his heart and mind the paradox of terrible storm and peace unspeakable and perfect. Here and there across centuries come reports of men alleged to have these contrasts. And the incomparable Abraham Lincoln, born one hundred and fifty years ago this day, is an approach if not a perfect realization of this character. . . .
>
> And how did Lincoln say he would like to be remembered? Something of it is in this present occasion, the atmosphere of this room. His beloved friend, Representative Owen Lovejoy, of Illinois, had died in May of 1864, and friends wrote to

Lincoln and he replied that the pressure of duties kept him from joining them in efforts for a marble monument to Lovejoy, the last sentence of Lincoln's letter saying:

"Let him have the marble monument along with the well-assured and more enduring one in the hearts of those who love liberty, unselfishly, for all men."

Today we may say, perhaps, that the well-assured and most enduring memorial to Lincoln is invisibly there, today, tomorrow, and for a long time yet to come. It is there in the hearts of lovers of liberty, men and women—this country has always had them in crisis—men and women who understand that wherever there is freedom there have been those who fought, toiled and sacrificed for it.

Tell your feet the alphabet

A few months later this venerable Lincoln scholar, poet, historian, fairy-tale writer, guitarist, and novelist was on television, reciting his poetry while Gene Kelly, the Hollywood star, danced across the set.

Sandburg strummed his guitar and directed the dancer:

> Tell your feet the alphabet.
> Tell your feet the multiplication table.
> Tell your feet where to go, and watch 'em go
> and come back.

It did not seem at all inappropriate or even extreme to hear Carl Sandburg entertain a national television audience with a poem that lent itself to rhythm and visual interpretation.

The solemn has always been mixed in this man, but along with it is a great sense of fun. If it was a different experience for Sandburg devotees, so was it a different (and infinitely better) experience for television addicts.

The first two duties of the poet are to find his voice and his listeners. What happier unity for him than television? It was altogether proper to see the first of the modern poets on a television screen reciting his poetry through a modern medium:

Can you dance a question mark?
Can you dance an exclamation point?
Can you dance a couple of commas?
And bring it to a finish with a period?

"Sometime they'll give a war and nobody will come"

The little girl saw her first troop parade and asked,
    "What are those?"
"Soldiers."
"What are soldiers?"
"They are for war. They fight and each tries to kill
    as many of the other side as he can."
The girl held still and studied.
"Do you know . . . I know something?"
"Yes, what is it you know?"
"Sometime they'll give a war and nobody will come."

and:

Pile the bodies high at Austerlitz and Waterloo.
Shovel them under and let me work—
    I am the grass; I cover all.

and:

Lincoln said, "Get into the game; your nation takes you."
And I drove a wagon and a team and I had my arm shot off
At Spottsylvania Court House.
I am an ancient reluctant conscript.

These are pacifist poems, the poems school children read when
their teacher asks them, "What is the meaning here? What does
the poem say?" These are obvious messages for children. They
learn they can think when they read poetry. Children understand
easily the historic futility of war. Sandburg has written many such
poems.

Robert Frost, who has good naturedly criticized Sandburg's political views from time to time, once referred to Carl as "a pacifist
between wars." Sandburg offers no demurrer, because for all his

pacifism he has indeed responded to every war and to every crisis involving America in his lifetime. The day after war was declared against Spain, Carl enlisted in the Army and went through the Puerto Rican campaign of the Spanish-American War. A few years afterward, he tried his luck at the Military Academy at West Point but was found deficient in arithmetic and grammar. In 1917 and in 1941, he gave the war effort everything of his talents and skills he could.

On October 11, 1917, he wrote a news story for the Chicago *Daily News* which clearly indicated his break with his fellow Socialists over supporting the war effort against Germany. It is important to remember that during World War I Socialists the world over hoped to convince each of the different national parties that it was a "capitalists' war." It didn't work, but the American Socialists were the last to give up the myth. The American Socialists were having an annual convention when the war in Europe broke out in August 1914. The Socialist leaders decided to send a cable to their colleagues of England, Germany, Austria, France, and Russia. They said that the American Socialists had decided to ask their fellow Socialists in the belligerent countries not to take up arms in a war for the capitalists. The European Socialists who bothered to reply at all said, in effect: "*Deutschland über alles*"; "There'll always be an England"; and "We are fighting for our beloved La Belle France."

Sandburg was not so naive. In a newspaper story, he discussed his aversion toward the alleged sabotage of the American war effort as advocated by some of the radicals of the day.

> The word sabotage is getting up front. Sabotage is a word that a Standard Oil Company lawyer would say exists in the twilight zone. The doctrine of sabotage was formally repudiated by the Socialist Party at the time the Socialists expelled W. D. Haywood, the IWW organizer. Last June, however, the Socialist Party at its convention in St. Louis formally opened the doors to sabotage through the elimination from its constitution of the anti-sabotage clause. *Victor Berger and other German members of the Party had previously been opposed to sabotage* (italics mine).

Notice the cold formality with which Sandburg now refers to his friend and former employer, the Socialist leader Victor Berger.

In 1940 Carl began lecturing to help support the American stand against the Fascists and Nazis in Europe. He gave a speech called, "What Lincoln Would Have Done," and his summation—"What Lincoln would have done is just what Roosevelt is doing."

Writers and writer figures

Unlike Vachel Lindsay, Ezra Pound, T. S. Eliot, Edgar Lee Masters, and Robert Frost, Carl Sandburg has dipped his spoon in every dish from proletarian poetry to the classic biography of Abraham Lincoln and to an identity as the "voice of America singing." He sings his way across the country, and I believe that in many respects he is much closer to Mark Twain than to Walt Whitman.

I believe that the only writers America has accepted as personalities have been Mark Twain and Carl Sandburg. It is a harder struggle for a native American writer to gain recognition as a personality than it is to gain publication. This is because Americans expect writers to be celebrities. A celebrity does not have to come from a certain time or a specific place. Nor does he even need something definite to say. A celebrity needs only the ability or the luck to occupy the public's attention. A celebrity does this, sometimes in spite of himself, by satisfying a certain stereotype. He becomes, in short, a writer figure instead of a writer.

Woe betide the writer who does not lend himself to the popular image! "I sat down by the wayside of life," wrote Hawthorne, "like a man under enchantment, and a shrubbery sprang up around me, and the bushes grew to be saplings, and the saplings became trees, until no exit appeared possible, through the tangling depths of my obscurity."

American writers—Melville, Whitman, Thoreau, to name a few —work in a solitude that becomes a virtual prison. Seldom do American men of letters realize they are part of a literary movement. Carl Sandburg says he had no idea he was part of a renaissance called the Chicago Movement until years later. But living in this solitude has consequences. One of them is that the public enforces a division between what a man writes and what a man is. Most American writers have grown used to being two distinct units: one as a man, the other as a writer.

Charles Dickens exerted a powerful and direct influence on English workhouses and George Bernard Shaw helped to make the modern Labour Party in England.

American writers have rarely been that successful. They have found it hard to direct a personal influence even on belles-lettres.

Yet Sandburg and Twain succeeded as personalities because in their writings and in their persons they grasped something essentially American. I think it is that Twain celebrated the vigor of a rural America rushing to close the frontier and Sandburg embodies the last of the Lincoln ideas.

Neither Sandburg nor Twain was a personality with an influence because he was a representative of an age past and gone, although this is part of it. America is an urban and highly materialistic culture today and the Lincoln ideas have long been submerged by the exigencies of crisis government and politics by advertising. While Sandburg embodies that part of the past, he also embodies the victory won by the union men in the bitter labor wars and the successful fight the immigrant waged against entrenched privilege. This is a fight not completely over. When Congress applauds Sandburg on Lincoln's birthday, the Representatives and Senators may be trying to convince themselves they are applauding what they *were*, but down deep perhaps they know they are also applauding what they are. It is not for nothing that Sandburg's parents were immigrants and that Sandburg, long before he undertook the Lincoln biography, described in eloquent poetry the terrible adjustments of immigrants and farmers to an industrial society.

So, too, did people revere Mark Twain as the first native American humorist who gained world stature, the writer who revealed to us the American language. But at the same time they could not help but realize that this voice was warning them of the dire moral consequences of racial segregation and of the hidden violence that waits within the American breast.

Americans have always been in love with their essential innocence—which is why they had to be forced into the role of leader of the free world by elimination rather than by choice. But they are also aware that that innocence has long been dissipated.

Both Twain and Sandburg had the one quality an American writer must have to become a personality: popular appeal, the ability to reach a wide audience. There have been writers of infinitely more sophistication than either Twain or Sandburg, stylists with infinitely more control, and writers with a deeper quality of mind, but just as often these writers were afflicted with a deep parochialism.

Sandburg and Twain realized that American unity was not a unity of optimism and sentimentality, but of optimism and violence. They are both optimistic writers with a profound understanding of the violent and dark side of American life.

Gustatory audience

Sandburg has made it clear to me that, until 1960, he never had an agent actively handling his poems. Scores of his poems undoubtedly could have been placed in magazines but he could not take time from his writing and other work to go through the monotony of sending manuscripts around.

In 1960 he met Lucy Kroll who became agent for his current writings, and for TV, radio, and miscellaneous engagements. She took something over one hundred poems and, instead of sending out manuscripts, she invited editors to her office and a quiet corner where they could read.

Editors of *Playboy* paid $3,600 for six poems and a parable. Sandburg remarked, "It was fun to be read by the most gustatory audience of readers in America, all of them definitely opposed to artificial insemination."

Carl's history of labor 1904–1961

"At first the labor leader was thrown out and taken to jail. Later the labor leader was let in, but they searched him first. Now the labor leader is met by a butler and is led to where he puts his feet under the table."

Fifty-two years of evolution

When Sandburg read the Democratic Party platform adopted in the national convention in Los Angeles in 1960, he said, "That's a very good imitation of the national Socialist Party platform adopted in Chicago in 1908 when my future wife and I were in sparking attendance."

Who reads Sandburg?

Sandburg once wrote, "A man writes the best he can about what moves him deeply. Once his writing gets published as a book he loses control over it. Time and the human family do what they want to with it. It may have periods of wide reading and acclamation, other periods of condemnation, decline, neglect—then a complete fadeout—or maybe a revival. And what revives in later years is often what was neglected when new. This happens. In literature and other arts—it happens . . ."

The head of the St. Louis Public Library, Mr. Charles Compton, once made a survey around the question, "Who reads Sandburg?" and found that beyond a certain array of intellectuals, persons who socially and professionally are strong for Culture with a capital "C," there were policemen, taxi drivers, stenographers, beauty parlor workers, machinists, and a wide range of plain people who could not afford to buy books but were regularly drawing out "the Sandburg poetry books" from the public library and finding in those books something close to their lives, something that sang to them.

"To eat regular"

On each of Carl's birthdays for the last fifteen years the reporters usually ask him what he wants out of life. So I asked him, too:

"I guess I can say mainly five things. To be out of jail, first of all—to be out of jail. This is a free country. Something pretty nice about being out of jail. I know—Bunyan, he wrote a pretty good book in jail, but I'm not sure I could.

"Second, to eat regular. Why not?

"Third, to get what I write printed.

"And fourth, let's say a little love at home and a little nice affection hither and yon over the American landscape. I don't need Asia or Europe for affection. Mexico? Yeah, I'd like a little affection from Mexico. The longer I live, the better I like Mexico and Mexicans.

"And then, maybe the fifth thing I need. It seems like every day when I'm at all in health, I've got to sing and I go to it for a half-hour or hour."

What do you miss at eighty?

On January 6, 1958, the State of North Carolina celebrated Sandburg Day. There was a big dinner in Raleigh and Governor Luther Hodges made Carl an "Honorary Ambassador" of the Tar Heel State.

I asked Carl what he missed most, touching eighty, of what he had when he was fifty.

"What do I miss at eighty? Most? At fifty I could still run fifty yards at a fair speed and I could run up most any stairs. Now I take my time and walk slow up the stairs. Not that I got any heart condition. But I am cagey, I remember a dear and long-time friend, Meyer Kestnbaum, having no history of a heart condition suddenly passing away in his office.

"I remember at forty years of age how I decided that never again would I run at top speed to first base or second and third and then the home plate.

"I interviewed Babe Ruth in Florida in 1928 and I asked him this and that, and somehow he was all of a sudden saying: 'I'm thirty-four now; at thirty-five, a ballplayer's legs and eyes begin to give out—they are not what they used to be.' The Chicago *Daily News* syndicated this to twenty-two newspapers and sport pages all over the country crackled with the latest word from the home-run monarch.

"But there are compensations. Seneca, the Roman philosopher, wrote about the serenities and contemplations possible in 'Old Age.' The late Frank Lloyd Wright and I had agreed that we did some of our best work in our seventies and he did some of his best work in his eighties.

"I remember the first time I heard a bellhop in a hotel point me out to another bellhop in connection with something or other, as 'that elderly gentleman over there.' Elderly gentleman! Yeah!

"I know plenty of young people whose hearts are too old and their outlook on life too old, as though they have lived more years than their birth certificates report. I feel myself as having direct kinship with all true child hearts. I have had two books of poems and two books of stories published that have been read and welcomed by millions of children. I believe if I should ever enter what is known as the second childhood I will in those years have fun and peace of mind."

So says Carl.

The basic question

In an offhand way, Sandburg told me once, "I missed getting into *The People, Yes* one little item, a question and answer I thought I ought to include."

"Let me hear the question," I said.

"What was it the last man on earth said?"

"Tell me."

"Where is everybody?"

High diving with Mary Magdalene and Judas

"Why ain't I got a right to write for movies? That's a header; that's a high dive I haven't made. Why ain't I got a right to take a dive in the Twentieth Century lot?"

So in July 1960 Carl Sandburg headed for Hollywood to work for George Stevens on Fulton Oursler's *The Greatest Story Ever Told*.

George Stevens, the producer, said emphatically that it was not a question of Carl lending his name to the production. "He will make a complete contribution in all creative areas of the production," said Stevens, "and will devote his full time to working with us from the start to the finish of this dramatic undertaking." No contract and no word on salary. "A handshake is all that's needed," said Stevens.

They gave Carl Marilyn Monroe's dressing room—her "undressing room" he called it. He was high on Stevens because of the producer's previous productions of *Shane, Giant, A Place in the Sun,* and *The Diary of Anne Frank,* but not on Miss Monroe's "undressing room" which he found a little too fancy: "Can't stand the silks here." They transferred him immediately to a less pretentious room. He also insisted on being transferred from a forty-five-dollar-a-day hotel suite to a twenty-five-dollar one—even though he wasn't paying the rent. The suite was too gaudy for his taste.

Carl had previously had some experience with Hollywood. The late D. W. Griffith wanted to do a Lincoln movie based on Sandburg's writings. "I told Griffith that I wanted $30,000 and he offered me $10,000," Sandburg said. "He got Stevie Benét for the job. Stevie was good. I forget the name of the picture."

Before Stevens went into the armed services in World War II his pictures were interesting though not portentous. He became a colonel in the war and was among the first officers to see the concentration camps.

Dreiser's novel *An American Tragedy* which Stevens directed under the title *A Place in the Sun* is a true and graphic interpretation, and Sandburg says that Dreiser would have had pride in it. Sandburg also feels that Stevens was wonderfully true to the actual diary of Anne Frank. The picture opens with white birds flying over the scene, whirling and beautifully alive, using their wings in a perfect freedom, no laws restraining them from going up, down, and around howsoever they please, birds having a freedom not known at all to the persons penned and hiding in a small upstairs room whose quiet is interrupted occasionally by the clang and clamor of Nazi storm troopers marching in the street below.

Stevens says plainly, "Sandburg thinks he will learn from me, and I think I will learn from him." Sandburg told a reporter, "We have a scene in *The Greatest Story Ever Told* that has a conversation between Mary Magdalene and Judas Iscariot. And," says Sandburg, half in mischief and half in truth, "I believe this scene is more portentous than anything in Shakespeare."

Sheboygan, Wisconsin

When Jack Kennedy was campaigning in the Wisconsin primary in 1960, the newspapers reported one day that he had toured Sheboygan, Kiel, Manitowoc, Two Rivers, and Sheboygan Falls. Carl Sandburg, in Philadelphia taping a show for CBS, picked up the telephone and called his wife, Paula, and read her the clippings. These were Carl Sandburg's towns fifty years ago. They comprised his district when he was a labor organizer. Paula remembered each one of the towns. Sandburg said, "Times have changed. Sheboygan was 15,000 when we used to canvass it. For Jack Kennedy, the newspapers call it a city of 45,000."

"Break the factories and cathedrals . . ."

Although Carl has never met Mr. William Zeckendorf of the New York realty firm Webb and Knapp, Sandburg assures me he hates him.

Zeckendorf directed the acquisition of the block where Harcourt, Brace, Carl's publishers, had the fifth floor of 383 Madison Avenue. Carl went in and out at No. 383 for thirty years. Suddenly Zeckendorf took over. He put in air conditioning and sent the rents up. He threw out a familiar news-and-cigar stand on the ground floor where Sandburg had made thousands of purchases.

"He abolished the longest and nicest Childs Restaurant in the United States," Sandburg says, "running from Madison Avenue to Vanderbilt Avenue, a block long, where I had eaten and had fellowship a thousand times. He put one bank at the south end of the block and another bank at the north end of the block, with large vacant spaces and vacant tables waiting for borrowers and investors to come in and talk things over with men of the bank.

"On top of the building Zeckendorf put a cute domed penthouse," Sandburg says, "where he held dinner parties where the food served was directed by a chef flown from France. Classy, eh? To hate Zeckendorf nourishes me. I join up with George Stevens out at the Twentieth Century-Fox Studios. Zeckendorf and the clients he heads paid Twentieth Century-Fox forty million dollars for land. Buildings are to be torn down to make room for apartment buildings and a big Zeckendorf shopping center. The point I make is Zeckendorf has fun and enjoys what he is doing, just as I take this as a free country where I can do what I am doing in hating him."

But he kept on reading

During a discussion at a radical meeting in recent years, a heckler shouted that Sandburg would do well to read Karl Marx. Sandburg shouted back:

"I read Karl Marx when I was a fireman in Galesburg" (and, after that full loud laugh), "but I kept reading and reading and I'm still reading."

One of the more important jobs Carl held to support himself through college was "call man" for the Galesburg Fire Department, sleeping at the firehouse and depended upon to leave his college classroom if the fire whistle blew during the daytime. The pay was ten dollars a month. When the alarm rang during the night Sandburg stepped into his boots, pulled up his pants, buttoned them on the way to the brass pole, slid down, and on the hose cart or chemical wagon put on his coat. At half-past six in the morning Carl slid down the pole again, got on his bicycle, and rode the eight blocks home for breakfast. His mother, who, Carl says, could hardly believe one of her boys was going to college, often said: "You do the best you can, Charlie, and maybe make a name for yourself. It don't do any hurt to try."

While the other firemen were playing checkers, Carl was reading. Carl was always reading. One of the pure joys for me in writing this book has been the satisfaction in confirming a pet theory of mine: that you cannot be a writer unless you are a reader. First a child must *hear* before he can *speak*, and first a writer must *read* before he can *write*.

Carl Sandburg has read all of his life. Everything. And it began at the very beginning. A favorite book in college was A *Study of English Prose and Writers* by J. Scott Clark of Northwestern University. The book ran 879 pages and covered twenty-one English writers and five Americans. Robert Browning was an early favorite and Carl went very deeply into John Ruskin. But I am wrong to use the word "favorite" in examining Carl's lifetime reading. Everything was his "favorite"—the printed word was his "favorite." In the early days there were Daniel Defoe, Washington Irving, Joseph Addison, Nathaniel Hawthorne, and Ralph Waldo Emerson. Carl says, "I bought for ten cents a second-hand book which fitted into my hip pocket, *The Last Essays of Elia* by Charles Lamb. I still have that book and read in it five or ten minutes every once in a while. I go to it like some people who at times must have bread with nippy cheese and beer."

And during all this reading how was Carl Sandburg coming along with his own practice at writing? On February 13, 1899, he submitted a book report to his professor. Here is the last paragraph:

> In every person there is both good and evil. The writer of "Dr. Jekyll and Mr. Hyde" shows that the tendency toward evil in a person must not be acknowledged to one's self, much less indulged in. The oftener you yield, the easier you give way in the future. This truth is impressed strongly on the reader and the fact that this great moral truth is distinctly illustrated in such an interesting manner will give to "Dr. Jekyll and Mr. Hyde" a position in literature distinct and peculiar but bright and lasting.

Chicago Dynamic

Sandburg had made a speech in Chicago on October 30, 1957, in celebration of *Chicago Dynamic* held under the sponsorship of the Chicago Association of Commerce and Industry.

Westbrook Pegler, the Hearst columnist, commented on "the proletarian millionaire."

No matter what the occasion, Pegler always has the same comment to make about Carl. He says, for instance, "Sandburg is, in further fact, a shrewd vulgarian who perceives, in common with Will Rogers and Adolf Hitler, the winsomeness of the wayward forelock flopping down over the eyes . . . I reverently submit that the master might well spend $1.50 for a haircut . . . and leave 50 cents for the barber. This might come hard but he would hardly miss the money out of an income, mainly from the Lincoln El Dorado, which has exceeded the joint revenues of Twain, Tennyson, and Dickens."

Westbrook Pegler is always mad at Carl for having made money. He is, in fact, mad at all newspapermen who make money, myself included. For a newspaperman not to die broke is an affront to Pegler. Only Pegler, the ex-sportswriter, should make money.

What Pegler neglected, however, was to read the *Chicago Dynamic* speech of this "proletarian millionaire."

> If I had not seen the passing of the twelve hour workday and Benjamin Fairless and my friend, Phil Murray, at a table working out an agreement that they signed, I would not be here tonight. I like it and give it praise that the twenty-one thousand men in the Gary Steel Works have an eight hour day, a five day week, time and a half for Saturday and for Sunday.

Compromises and cranberries

Daniel Webster, the Dartmouth graduate who served as a Congressman from New Hampshire and a Senator from Massachu-

setts, who supported the compromise measures on slavery introduced by Henry Clay, is not one of Carl's favorite Americans. Carl
says Webster was guided by three rules: (1) Never to pay any
debt that can by any possibility be avoided; (2) Never to do anything today that can be put off till tomorrow; (3) Never to do
anything yourself which you can get anybody else to do for you.
"Webster was not as responsible a person himself as in his oratory
he wanted the people of the United States to be."

But Ralph Waldo Emerson is one of Carl's most enduring
friends and companions among men of the past. Carl quotes
Emerson's letter to Carlyle that he was "not a poet but a lover
of poetry and poets—a sort of harbinger of the poets to come."
Emerson's first published sheaf of verses hardly paid the cost of
printing. Carl says it was a small venture. "His poems did not
pay. His cranberry meadows paid much better."

The pawpaw growers

There is a ghetto proverb, "It is easier to run beside a loaded
wagon." Carl would understand this proverb because he loves to
work. I have not been able to find a single week, or day, or hour
in his entire life that he was idle—when he was not working at
something, earning something.

Often he held two jobs at the same time. The twenty-four-hour
day was not long enough. He loved to work and he loved his
earnings because he saw in these the means which would enable
him to think and to write.

Carl never said to parents or family, "Don't bother me about
some menial task—I'm a poet and must not be distracted."
Nothing of the sort. Carl made his contribution at every stage.
He quit "outside" work not a single moment too soon—only
after he had ample assurance that his writing alone could support his family.

When he was working for the Chicago *Daily News* he found
another way to increase his income. He made money reading his
own verse to audiences. He liked talking in public and so he

began making trips, none of them so far from Chicago as to interfere with his newspaper duties.

Few travelers recognized him on those jaunts and in the beginning when they asked him what his line was and he replied, "Poetry," they laughed at the joke.

Sandburg sometimes used another line, "I would answer that I was Chairman of the Board and President of North American Pawpaw Growers Association. That satisfied them, a line they could understand. The pawpaw really has its points."

He never tired

Carl does not treat criticism kindly, criticism of either his favorite authors or his own work. I sat with him when he was reading the reviews of *The World of Carl Sandburg* which had opened on Broadway with Miss Bette Davis. Said Carl: "I will put it bluntly, the intelligent reviewers find the work a joy and a delight, the slobs are bored to tears."

Carl read the slobs, then looked up, his small eyes hard, his jaw outthrust, those lips of his now tightly clenched, the muscles working in his face, and made only one remark: "I've been a critic myself. I *know* when a man has become tired of his job."

The SSIIP

Early in 1961, Carl went to Chapman College in Orange County, California, probably the most Republican area in all of the Far West. He made a speech in which he started off by reading all of President John F. Kennedy's Inaugural Address. After every incisive phrase, he would pause and say, "This is Lincolnesque." Later on, to the auditorium filled with Daughters of the American Revolution, he described a recent conversation he had had with Frank Sinatra in which these two had decided to form the SSIIP—the Society of Sons of Illiterate Immigrant Parents.

Second-best bed

Mrs. Adda George, the widow of Professor John E. George of Northwestern University, is an enthusiastic admirer of Sandburg. She thought the preservation of his birthplace in Galesburg a fitting memorial.

With the help of Mary Sandburg, Carl's sister, she found the home located near the railroad yards where August Sandburg, Carl's father, worked in the blacksmith shop as a helper. It was in dilapidated condition; it had changed hands many times and was in near collapse.

The house was owned by a stubborn Italian lady who offered great protest before she let Mrs. George hang a plaque on the door and put a boulder between the sidewalk and street commemorating the house as Sandburg's birthplace. The Italian woman often hid the plaque and more than once tried to roll away the boulder.

In 1945, the Italian woman's son offered a sixty-day option to buy. Mrs. George formed a Carl Sandburg Association, incorporated as a nonprofit educational institution under the title "Sandburg Birthplace." A fund-raising campaign realized the purchase price and restoration began.

On October 7, 1946, the three-room birthplace was formally dedicated. The Birthplace contains the Sandburg family Bible, some wooden Bishop Hill chairs, the Sandburg stereoscope, and a trundle bed with handwoven coverlets, a gift from the descendants of Galesburg pioneers. All of Carl's writings are catalogued and included in the library, as well as his phonograph recordings and the Remington 15 typewriter on which he wrote *Abraham Lincoln: The Prairie Years*.

Just inside the front door is a tribute to Sandburg from Stephen Vincent Benét:

> He came to us from the people whom Lincoln loved because there were so many of them and through all of his life, in verse and prose, he has spoken of and for the people. A great

American, we have just reason to be proud that he has lived and written in our time.

On the walls are pictures of Sandburg's father and mother, of Sandburg himself as a boy and as a grown man, and of Paula, his wife, the sister of Edward Steichen whose photographs also hang there.

Part of the Birthplace is maintained by gifts of Galesburg schoolchildren who recently contributed 43,360 pennies to the Association. These pennies were a gift for Carl on his eighty-third birthday which produced the biggest penny excitement Galesburg has ever known with special policemen carrying the bags into the bank.

Through a generous appropriation secured from the Illinois State Legislature by the late Senator Wallace Thompson of Galesburg, a Lincoln Room built around Carl's six-volume biography is completely restored with Lincoln-period pine furnishings. The fireplace and the chimney are of handsome brick salvaged from another old Galesburg house, which was one of the stations of the Underground Railroad.

In the dwelling are the kitchen utensils used by Carl's mother and some of the furniture which the Sandburgs had at the time of Carl's birth—January 6, 1878.

There is also the bed on which Carl was born. This bed, however, has rope slats to support the bedding whereas the actual bed on which Carl was born had wood slats. But Carl and I have solved the puzzle.

The Peterson house in Washington, D. C., across the street from Ford's Theatre, had a bed with rope slats. It was on this bed that Dr. Leale and the soldiers laid the dying President Abraham Lincoln. What probably happened is that a few years after Lincoln's death, the Peterson bed was shipped to Galesburg in time for Carl's birth.

PART 2

A Vastly Larger Home

Det är en pojke

These are happy words in Swedish. *Det är en pojke* means, "It's a boy!" These are the words August Sandburg heard on January 6, 1878. Eighty-three years later these words were the title of the lead editorial in the *Peoria Journal Star* celebrating the birthday of the man who made Chicago's big shoulders respectable.

I don't remember any autobiography that started so originally as Sandburg's *Always the Young Strangers:*

> A big unseen bell goes "Bong!" Knots come loose, long-woven bonds break from their folds and clutches. "It is my time now," says the mother while tugs and struggles in her womb say, "My time too has come." There is a tearing asunder of every last hold and bond, the violence of leaving the nine-month home to enter a second and vastly larger home. In the mother and the child the crashes and explosions go on, a series leading to the final expulsion. Not till then can there be a birth certificate, a name and a christening, a savage small mouth tugging at pink nipples.

It was quite a boy who came to the Sandburg home that winter morning and quite an eighty-three years.

Sandburg notes that he was born exactly one hundred years later than Thomas, the father of Abraham Lincoln, and one year earlier than Joseph Medill Patterson. This is his way of declaring the change into which he came.

While he grew to manhood, Charles Yerkes bought and sold the city of Chicago through corrupted municipal officials, but at the same time Jane Addams founded Hull House, Thorstein Veblen wrote *The Theory of the Leisure Class*, and John Dewey tried to bring education into some sort of alignment with industrial society by founding the Elementary School of Chicago University.

The story of these years up to the turn of the century is told in *Always the Young Strangers,* Sandburg's autobiography which covers the years of his boyhood through service in the Spanish-American War and ends with his matriculation at Lombard College. Ostensibly, it is the story of a boy of Swedish stock growing up in Galesburg, Illinois.

But, like most of Sandburg's works, it has a very strong grain of American social history running throughout.

It is the story of America in change; of Chicago becoming the great symbol of the new urbanization; of the workers beginning to fight for a common bread and dignity; of the land filling up with new immigrants ". . . looking two ways to the ends of the street for the new people, the young strangers, coming, coming, always coming."

It is a book which Robert Sherwood in *The New York Times* (January 4, 1953) called the greatest autobiography ever written by an American, "not forgetting Benjamin Franklin, nor Henry Adams, nor showing them disrespect," and which Gerald Johnson described in the *New Republic* (January 19, 1953) as "bearing the same relation to poetry that nacre does to pearl." While it was not poetry, it was rather "mother of poetry" and "better adapted to the common uses of life than are the gems that are too precious for every day wear."

The history of this time has always been Sandburg's subject. He has been with history more than most poets. It is not exaggerated to say you would learn more about the industrialization of America reading Sandburg's poems than you would learn about Elizabethan England reading Shakespeare's plays. I do not imply because Sandburg absorbs the social scene his poetry is necessarily better; but it is that absorption which gives his work its unique American quality.

Sandburg was the son of immigrants and he has never been an expatriate; his diction has always been closer to the spoken rather than written word. Both chronologically and spiritually, he is the first poet of America's twentieth century.

He was the son of an immigrant who could not write his name, and he wrote a biography of Lincoln whose own mother could not write her name. August Sandburg and Nancy Hanks wrote an X instead of a name. Today, this poet and biographer is the subject of my book, and my own mother could not speak a word of English.

Thus, this great continuity to the American experience of which Sandburg is a pre-eminent symbol. America is always absorbing the immigrant only to reproduce the pioneer.

College city

Knox College, the "old Siwash" of George Fitch's *Saturday Evening Post* stories, Lombard College, and Brown's Business College gave Galesburg the nickname of "the Athens of the Midwest." The poet Edgar Lee Masters studied at Knox College although Sandburg is Galesburg's only native-born poet.

Galesburg was also a city with an intimate relationship with history. It was on the campus in front of old Main of Knox College that Lincoln and Douglas held one of their debates. In October of 1896 John Huston Finley, then the head of Knox College who had known Lincoln, staged an Anniversary Celebration of the debates. Young Sandburg got away from his job on a milk wagon long enough to get out to the Knox campus and see a rostrum populated by Chauncey M. Depew, President of the New York Central Railroad who had stumped New York State for Lincoln in 1864; Robert Todd Lincoln, the son of the President; and Senator John M. Palmer.

Sandburg recalls puzzling about Robert T. Lincoln and wondering what kind of talks the son had had with his father in the White House: "What kind of Secretary of War had he been in the cabinets of Garfield and Arthur? I had read of how at one Republican National Convention after another some delegate always nominated (Robert T. Lincoln) for President and he would get one vote. I had read too that he was the lawyer for the Pullman Company and he was all for the company and against the strikers in the bloody strike of 1894."

Galesburg was also a town where the sign "Sample Room" hung on the front of saloons. Sandburg explains that traveling salesmen were able to lay out their goods and customers could go in and inspect them and also "sample the whiskey and beer."

Sandburg and his brothers and sisters were all born on corn-husk mattresses and for some years they slept on them until the family moved from South Street to a house on Berrien Street, No. 622-24, in which he grew up.

Carl was baptized Carl August. Most immigrants and sons of immigrants start to Anglicize their names in America so Carl was registered in school as "Charles A." and his father always called him "Sharley." Years later, when he went into Wisconsin as an organizer, he realized that among all those Germans up there his baptismal name of Carl would do much better. Eventually Lilian Steichen, who was to become his wife, told him she liked Carl better than Charles and that settled it.

The Sandburg family was Swedish Lutheran and regular. August Sandburg had come to America some years before from his native Sweden where he had earned a living as chore boy in a distillery. He had saved enough money for steerage passage and, because he had a cousin living in Galesburg, settled there. Sandburg says his father was "a black Swede" with straight black hair, black eyes, deep set, and somewhat below medium height. He started for work at 6:45 every morning, arriving at the Chicago, Burlington & Quincy Railroad's blacksmith shop precisely at 7:00, came home at noon, ate his dinner, walked back at 1:00, and continued on until the 6:00 o'clock whistle. "Then he stood sledge alongside anvil and walked home."

August Sandburg never learned to write. He signed his paychecks from the CB&Q with an X, "his mark." The mother, Clara Matilda (Anderson) Sandburg wrote both English and Swedish in a legible and sometimes elegant hand. She got up at 6:00 o'clock every morning, prepared breakfast for her man and seven children. She washed and ironed all the clothes, sewed and repaired many of them, and had a deep concern for the education of the youngsters. Neither parent learned English thoroughly and the father always spoke with a slow Scandinavian accent. But the father read the Bible and got great consolation from it.

The father earned fourteen cents an hour, forty dollars in good months, nineteen dollars in bad. Out of this with heroic patience he saved enough to buy the home on Berrien Street.

The town of Galesburg, when the boy Sandburg lived there,

numbered fifteen thousand, about one-sixth of its population for-
eign-born. It was a Republican town and Sandburg says when he
was six years old he could remember politics running hot in the
blood of man. He went with his father one night downtown to a
Republican rally and remembered the lighted torch parade. His
father swore that every man marching was a Republican. The
men were yelling, "Hooray for Blaine!" and "Blaine for President!" keeping time with their feet.

In 1888 the railroad engineers went out on strike, their slogan
a take-off on the abbreviation CB&Q—"Come Boys and Quit Rail-
roading."

There was wild and furious talk about the "scabs." A striking
engineer had been shot to death. On the way to school the boys
would pass the spot on the sidewalk where they said the engineer's
blood had dried on the wooden boards.

August Sandburg took no sides in all of this, either by voice or
by action. He was noncommittal by nature.

He refused to join the anti-Catholic APA (American Protective
Association), which was very popular at the time among some of
his friends and neighbors. As a matter of fact, he belonged to
only two organizations all of his life, the Lutheran Church and
the Republican Party. (The organization of railroad blacksmiths
came many years later.)

The places of the striking engineers were filled mostly by firemen and Carl remembers a string of respectable cottages off Mul-
berry Street occupied by scabs. The name of the street was
Cottage Avenue, but for years afterward strike sympathizers
called it "Scab Alley."

At fifteen Sandburg finished the eighth grade and the family
budget at the moment did not allow him to go to high school. So
he went to work.

Of all the jobs at which Sandburg worked the one he considers the plum of his boyhood was as porter and shoeshine boy
in the Humphrey Barbershop. Humphrey's was half a floor below
the street in the basement of the Union Hotel on the Public
Square of Galesburg. "By looking out a window we could see
what shoes people were wearing," says Sandburg. "A long mirror
fronted the four barber chairs. On a rack were some thirty shav-

ing mugs, each with its owner's name gilded on it." Mr. Humphrey
said to Sandburg: "The best people in Galesburg come here." The
floor was checkered tile. "I knew every check. I swept it every
day and mopped it three times a week."

Like Stephen Crane, who picked up the *Red Badge of Courage*
from the stories Civil War veterans told him on the steps of the
Trenton Court House, Sandburg began to get an essential feel of
the way men talk, and what makes them talk, and beneath all
this, the basic opinions of men un-self-consciously expressing their
deepest views about life. That these are most often expressed in
platitude and cliché none will deny, but no one who has read *The
People, Yes* will ever say they are meaningless.

One of his early jobs was peddling milk. To this day he can
remember the routes, walking six to ten blocks carrying one or
two cans of milk, the names of the housewives into whose pitchers
and crocks he measured out a quart for a pink ticket, a pint for
a green ticket.

In the brightening town of Galesburg there were two milkmen
—one a boy destined to sing of America and Lincoln, the other
a tradesman named Samuel Kossuth Barlow, formerly a farmer
near Galva who often was a fiddler at country barn dances.

From him Sandburg learned three or four songs he never
encountered elsewhere. Sometimes they discussed politics and
Sandburg confesses that once on the milk wagon he talked a
long streak to Sam about the rich being too rich, and the poor
too poor, farmers losing their farms on account of mortgages and
ten-cent-a-bushel corn, millions of workers in cities out of jobs,
and how was it all going to end?

Sam Barlow sat quiet for a spell and said, "Well, Charlie, I'll
tell you what's the matter. There's just getting to be too many
people in the world, just too many goddam people. We've got to
have a war and kill off a lot of 'em before times will get real better." Sandburg thought this a little startling from a strict
Republican.

In June of 1894 Carl Sandburg's father got him a pass to
Chicago on the CB&Q. He recounts that he put his head out and
said as he passed each town he had heard of for years, "So this is
it, well!" In Chicago he ate at Pittsburgh Joe's. Breakfast was a

stack of pancakes, molasses, oleo, and coffee with a dash of milk in it, all for a nickel. Dinner was a large bowl of meat stew, bread, and coffee, for ten cents.

In Keokuk, Iowa, heading toward the Kansas wheat harvests, he got a job on July 4 at a lunch counter, taking orders for fried eggs, "one side or over." The owner who had hired him kept going out and coming back, whiskey on his breath. In the late afternoon he vanished. Sandburg decided to vanish too. He left Keokuk in an empty boxcar, where he slept part of the night, and the next day had himself hired on a railroad section gang at Bean Lake, Missouri.

After a diet of fried potatoes and pork, while boarding with the section boss, he left without his ten days' wages and went to Kansas City and at night sold hot tamales along the sidewalks. Other jobs followed—dishwasher in a restaurant for $1.50 a week, meals, and "a cot at the end of an unswept hallway"; potato digger, window washer, carpet beater, chore boy; pitching wheat bundles to threshing-machine tables in Pawnee County, Kansas— and all of these jobs helped to teach him his America.

For Sandburg's America is a distinct America, the America of the working Midwesterner, the laborer, the union man, the scab, the Wobbly.

He came back to Galesburg. The trip changed him. "I was easier about looking people in the eye. When questions came I was quicker at answering them or turning them off. I had been a young stranger meeting many odd strangers and I had practiced at having answers. At home and among my old chums, they knew I had changed but they could no more tell how than I. A way deep in my heart I had hope as never before. Struggles lay ahead, I was sure, but whatever they were I would not be afraid of them."

At home, on the milk wagon and at the barbershop Sandburg had read several times William Jennings Bryan's "Cross of Gold" speech that so stirred the Democratic National Convention. Bryan became his hero.

When Bryan spoke at Galesburg, Sandburg went to hear him and followed him when he spoke at nearby Monmouth. "Later," Sandburg says, "I found out he was only a voice, an orator, a singer, and not much of a thinker."

At eighteen Sandburg announced to his family that he was a Bryan Democrat, a statement which led his staunchly Republican father to believe that "Sharley" would come to no good end.

"Put it on the book"

The Sandburgs bought most of their groceries two blocks from their home where a sign hung "Swan Olson & Bro." Swan Olson had marched with Sherman's army from Atlanta to the Sea.

One of the Sandburgs would go to the Olson store, buy what the mother wanted, and have Olson "put it on the book." Once a month August Sandburg would cash his CB&Q paycheck and settle accounts, getting a nickel cigar for himself and a sack of candy for the kids at home.

The value and importance of credit was taught to the Sandburg children early. Carl remembers how he learned the lesson. He had reached the age where he was entrusted with *the book* and one afternoon he was instructed to go to Olson's store to buy molasses and buckwheat pancake flour. Olson wrapped the purchases and Sandburg handed over the book. He saw Olson note the purchases and the idea suddenly burst on him that he could buy anything he wanted—as long as the grocer wrote it down. A piece of licorice caught his eye. He asked the grocer how much it was.

"Five cents," replied Will Olson.

"Put it on the book," said Carl. It was his first big personal purchase. He ate the licorice and came home with the stains surrounding his mouth and on his hands. When his mother saw them she asked what had he been eating.

"Licorice," said Carl.

"Where did you get it?" she asked.

"I told Olson to put it on the book."

Mrs. Sandburg reached out and as quick as a cobra slapped him —hard.

"I had learned what it meant to say, 'Put it on the book,' if it was the Sandburg family account book that could be carried in a man's hip pocket. I was ashamed and I learned that the book was for the family and not for me."

"A nice piece uh proputty"

Of all the investments available in the past one hundred and fifty years, the one that has withstood all tests and hazards is property—real property. The one thing to remember about owning real estate is not to owe too much money on it. Even with the great suffering and unemployment of the Depression a man who did not owe money was in good shape. Indebtedness and interest rates kill you. Take it from a man who knows.

In Sandburg's autobiography *Always the Young Strangers* he tells the story of "The Sleeping Mortgage." His father, earning a dollar and forty cents a day, put by enough money to buy a quit-claim to a lot in Galesburg. He was proud of his accomplishment. He called it "a nice piece uh proputty."

But after he'd paid for it, the executrix of the estate of a William C. Grant produced an old mortgage, signed years before August Sandburg came to America, which put a lien on the property. August Sandburg had to borrow $807.24 to redeem the mortgage: $556.40 in capital and $250.84 in interest. Sandburg says, "You couldn't say he hardened his heart to his family, his friends, and the world, though you could say that every soft spot in his heart had become less soft. He could raise his eyebrows and slit his eyes with a searching look. He had learned it from the Sleeping Mortgage."

No sober cars

Sandburg drove horses both on his milk route and for the Galesburg Fire Department, and he compared that with driving an automobile: "Driving a motor car or truck is very different from that of driving any horse-drawn vehicle in the old days. Many a drunken driver was brought home by his sober horses. Today he is brought home by the hospital ambulance or the fellows who help the coroner."

A hobo is no bum

At the age of eighteen, Sandburg first hoboed his way to the wheat fields of Kansas. A few years later, he rode in the boxcars and lived in the hobo jungles on his way East. He has hoboed a lot. During these trips he met all kinds of hobos. He met the "library stiff" who spends all his time in the town library to escape the "town clowns" (policemen) and who, because of this adventure, becomes quite erudite; and he met the hobos who followed the electric companies and built the power stations across the Northwest.

The hobo was an itinerant workman following the harvests and the building gangs. They proliferated from 1890 until 1925.

Hobos have a basic class structure: as Skeets Simmons, a famous hobo, once explained to Major Bowes, "A hobo is a man who will travel and work. A tramp will travel but not work. A bum will not travel and will not work. He is just a bum." Hobos also have an abiding distaste for hitchhikers. The hobo is on his way to work and looks upon the hitchhiker as a man who wants to save carfare the easy way.

There are several ways that the hobos ride trains. If it is a freight train and the railroad conductor is not watching, sometimes a man can ride on top of a boxcar, sometimes in a coal gondola or an empty boxcar, and sometimes when the train is watched and the boxcars have sealed doors, the one place he will try is on the bumper between two freight cars, standing. If he has been ordered off the bumpers, he can then ride the rods. That's the last desperate place. He rides with his face down, his arms and legs clutching the two parallel iron rods, and he gets his face and clothes full of dust, dirt, and grime. (Happily, the rods are gone. Only the wooden, not the steel, passenger cars had them.)

The elite among the hobos used to ride the bumpers of fast freights with perishable cargo. They risked death from rolling off while standing when sound asleep.

There were bindle stiffs who did not ride the rails at all but tramped over the countryside carrying blanket rolls and some spare clothes. These men followed the wheat harvests and were always considered excellent workmen. Sandburg says that after 1905 some of the bos were "card men"—they carried the red Industrial Workers of the World (I.W.W.) membership card with them—but the card's red color had been adopted long before Lenin and Trotsky made red suspicious.

Sandburg tells of his arrest after he hopped a freight in Philadelphia one moonlight night.

Never once did a brakeman or a switchyard cop see him or bother him as he lay stretched in comfort on top of the boxcar about midway of the train. He enjoyed the famous Altoona Horseshoe Curve in the bright moonlight. He fell asleep and awoke at seven o'clock in the morning in broad daylight and, climbing down, found he was in a suburb of Pittsburgh named Wilmerding. He walked across the town, stopping for a large and pleasant fifteen-cent breakfast.

About midafternoon, he was in the town of McKees Rocks, standing with five other hobos in a coal gondola, an all-iron car with no roof but with sides that helped conceal the riders. Suddenly two men climbed into the car wearing the badges of constables. They put all six of the hobos under arrest and marched them, handcuffed two by two, Sandburg manacled to a Negro, to a justice of the peace. They were all charged with "riding on a railroad train without a ticket."

The hobo ahead of Sandburg was a man in his sixties. He pleaded that he was a molder by trade and had come from Youngstown, Ohio, hoping to get a job in Pittsburgh. This old fellow told the judge the pension he drew from the Government for service in the Union Army during the Civil War was too slim to let him pay the ten-dollar fine.

"Serving ten days won't cost you nothing," said the judge. Sandburg stepped up and told the judge he had served with the Sixth Illinois Volunteers in the Spanish-American War and his regiment had been the first command on Puerto Rico. The judge remarked that an awful lot of veterans were in the courtroom but it was still ten dollars or ten days.

Up in the seventh tier of cells in the Allegheny County jail, Sandburg shared with two other prisoners a cell intended for one man. He made his inquiries and was informed that the sheriff was paid by the county fifty cents a day for the feeding of each prisoner, and that the sheriff got the "throw-outs and come-backs" of food from large restaurants and hotels, so Sandburg and the Union veteran cost him nothing at all.

Having served his ten days, Sandburg again went to a railroad yard at night and climbed into a boxcar half filled with hard coal, slept well in the hard coal, caught two or three more freight trains which had him in Chicago in two days.

He says he has often thought of how if there were time and he had the lawyers, he would sue Allegheny County, Pennsylvania, for false arrest: "The charge of riding on a railroad train without a ticket. The coal gondola we were in was not part of a train and it wasn't moving a foot nor an inch while we were in it, and the charge was that we were riding."

No hobo forgets his days on the road and Sandburg is no exception. In April of 1952, when Carl won the gold medal of the National Institute and American Academy of Arts and Letters for historical and biographical writing, Harvey Breit of *The New York Times* asked him what he was going to do with the award. Answered Carl: "I'll wear it on the inside of my coat and when a railroad dick stops me and flashes his badge, I'll flash my gold badge right back at him."

James Thurber, the playwright and satirist pre-eminent of *The New Yorker* magazine, has learned so much about hoboing from Carl that at a literary function in 1949 he was able to pass along the following couplets to Sandburg, the oldest hobo in the place:

> Casey Jones he was a son of a bitch.
> He went through Toledo on an open switch,
> Dropstitch stockings and low cut shoes,
> A pack of Fatimas and a bottle of booze.

The hobo experience was valuable to Sandburg. He listened and learned the lingo, which is among some of the best slang ever invented, and he memorized the songs. Many of these songs some decades later found themselves in Sandburg's *American Songbag*. He has written poems about hobos and " 'Boes" is among his best:

I waited today for a freight train to pass.
Cattle cars with steers butting their horns against
    the bars, went by.
And a half a dozen hoboes stood on bumpers
    between cars.
Well, the cattle are respectable, I thought.

Traveling the rails also gave Sandburg the opportunity to see small towns, prairie towns, wheat towns, and big cities. Above all, hoboing taught him about all kinds of work, for a hobo's life is work. One of the old hobo songs goes, "A Hobo is a Travellin' Man But He Ain't No Bum, Bum, Bum."

Moonlight excursion to Porther Ricky

After a year of hoboing, Carl Sandburg had come home to Galesburg to a job as an apprentice housepainter. On the morning of February 15, 1898, he was ready to go out and slap red paint on a barn when the news came. The battleship *Maine* had been blown up in Havana Harbor at 9:40 the night before.

Thomas Leslie McGirr, a lawyer who was captain of Company C of the Sixth Illinois Regiment of State Militia, announced that Galesburg would recruit volunteers. So Carl Sandburg enlisted and was mustered in at Camp Douglas at Springfield. He was issued a blue jacket with brass buttons, light blue trousers and cap, all of the same type as the Union soldiers wore in the Civil War.

Six companies of Carl's regiment sailed on the ship *Rita* from Charleston and arrived in Guatánamo Bay, Cuba, on the evening of July 17. The escort battleships *Oregon*, *Indiana*, and *Iowa* were welcome sights to the boys from Illinois prairies. On July 25, the *Rita* landed its troops in Puerto Rico and the Sixth marched from Guánica to Ponce. They got acquainted with intense heat and mosquitoes. "One could kill a dog and two a man," Carl recalls. The Puerto Rican natives lined streets and roads and cheered them on. At Utuado the news came that the protocol had been signed and peace declared.

Some of his military experience Sandburg recorded in a diary. It is an incomplete diary, as are most diaries of privates (only the generals have enough time or take themselves seriously enough to fill out a war diary). An August 10 entry records: "After drying out our clothes and washing, had dinner and we marched to Adjuntas where we bivouaced on one side of hill and cooked rations. The hill was divided into three shelves upon each of which a battery was placed. I slept between two ponchos as on previous nights. Some unique houses were built of ponchos and banana leaves."

The diary records only the dates between July 28 and August 12 at which time Sandburg wrote: "Washed. The camp was one grand slippery mudhole. Mounted guard at 6 p.m. A farce."

When Finley Peter Dunne had Mr. Dooley referring to "Ginral Miles' Grand Picnic and Moonlight Excursion to Porther Ricky," Sandburg gripes that Dunne had probably had a tenderloin steak garnished with onions before he took up his writings for that day. When Richard Harding Davis wrote that for the troops under General Miles Puerto Rico was a picnic, Sandburg says Davis was remembering the dry corners he slept in, the roads where he never walked carrying fifty pounds in a baking sun, the mosquitoes that never bled nor closed an eye for him, the graybacks he never picked from an inhabited shirt, and the rains he never stood in.

After the peace was declared, Sandburg sailed with the Sixth Illinois and was mustered out in Springfield, Illinois. He came home and his brother, Mart, asked, "Well, you didn't get killed, did you?"

"No, they didn't give me a chance," said Sandburg.

"Well," said Mart, "last year you were a hobo and this year a soldier, what's next with you?"

"Maybe I'll go to college," said Sandburg.

"Is there any money in this poetry business?"

Sandburg enrolled at Lombard College in Galesburg for courses in Latin, English, inorganic chemistry, elocution, drama, and public speaking in 1899.

Lombard was a Universalist college, with 17 instructors and 125 students, and had been founded simply enough in 1851 as the Illinois Liberal Institute. In those days Lombard was an innovation among colleges. It was a distinctly liberal school, but it has since closed its doors on its last graduating class, its facilities, equipment, and good will having been taken over by Knox College.

To pay his way through school Sandburg received an appointment from the mayor as a "call man" with the fire department. He slept in the firehouse at night, and in the daytime when the fire whistle blew he telephoned, and if it was a big fire bicycled to it. His pay was ten dollars a month.

"One time for about a year I drove a team of fire horses," he says, "and gave them the currycomb daily, cleaned out the stalls, and when there were no conflagrations exercised them up and down the street two hours a day."

At Lombard he discovered he would like writing and knew that he would do a lot of "fooling around with pens, pencils, and paper."

College helped him. He came to classes studying Chaucer, Browning, Shakespeare, Piers Plowman. Elbert Hubbard seemed more a good companion than a profound influence. Elbert Hubbard was to Sandburg's generation what H. L. Mencken was to mine and *The New Yorker* magazine to the present. Hubbard was called the Sage of East Aurora, New York: he went down on the *Lusitania* in 1915 and is remembered for having written "Life is just one damned thing after another" and *The Message to Garcia*.

Carl said to me, "Perhaps as long as I live I shall occasionally look into certain writings of Elbert Hubbard. When I was editor of a college paper readers took note of a fellowship I had with Elbert Hubbard. As a poseur he must be credited a genius. He wore his hair long, sort of framing his face, a rather handsome face. He wore an outlandishly wide shirt collar and his necktie was a cascade of black that fell down close to his navel. He not only lectured across all America but he took on one season on the Keith Orpheum vaudeville circuit where he was followed by another friend of mine who wrote under the name of Bugs Baer."

Sandburg became managing editor of *The Cannibal*, the college yearbook, in which he included a picture of the college janitor, Allen Harshbarger, along with photographs of faculty and famous grads. Then followed his election as editor of *The Lombard Review*: "My black-bordered editorial on the death of President McKinley in the October number had a few good sentences but was stilted and perfunctory."

Basketball was Carl's game. He played right guard and was captain of the Lombard College team for four seasons. The school paper records a game: "At no period could either side claim the game, for up until the last few seconds it was a tie with the score 10 to 10, when Captain Sandburg threw a difficult goal from under the basket and saved the day."

And he fell in love at college, "but not too deep," Carl says. "I did fall several times but always fell out." There was a particular girl: "I waltzed and two-stepped (with her) more than with any other girl at the assembly dances," says Carl, "but before it got too deep I cut out the strolling and stayed away from the assembly dances, and every time I saw the girl after that I spoke hints about my vague and uncertain future."

In May of 1899, Congressman George W. Prince notified C Company of the Sixth Illinois which had just been mustered out of the Spanish-American War that he would appoint one veteran as a candidate for West Point. The officers of the company solicited Sandburg and on May 12 Carl received communication from the Adjutant General of the War Department appointing him conditionally to the United States Military Academy.

He did well enough physically but on the written tests the Academy found him deficient in arithmetic and grammar and instructed him to leave. Had he been graduated from West Point, Sandburg would have been in the class that included Generals Douglas A. MacArthur and Ulysses S. Grant III. He went home to Galesburg, made his excuses, got into his fireman's uniform, slept at the fire station that night, and the next morning got himself a job as handyman at the Union Hotel. Every day at 4:30 A.M., including Sunday, the night policeman rapped on the brass pole to get him up. Carl slid down and went into the basement of the Union Hotel. He shook out the clinkers and got the boilers going so the guests, cooks, and dishwashers could have hot water.

Before the beginning of the fall term at Lombard, Carl also tried his hand at selling advertising for *The Lombard Review*.

The following summer Carl sold stereoscopic views to farm people. The stereoscope projected a pair of two-dimensional photos into a single three-dimensional picture. Many an American grandmother used to have one. It looked like a trombone fitted for the eyes instead of the mouth. Sandburg sold the photos which replenished the supply of farm families. Most of the photos were of piazzas in Florence and Rome, and many reproduced classical sculpture.

In June of 1901 Carl began to have trouble with his eyes. He went to Doctor Perry, the best-known eye specialist in Galesburg. After a long and thorough examination the doctor said a growth, a film called pterygium which tends to move toward the pupils, afflicted him.

The doctor told young Carl that if the film covers the pupils— you go blind. Carl went to the Cottage Hospital in Galesburg. An operation successfully removed the film. He lay in darkness for ten days except when the nurse took off the bandages momentarily to administer medicine.

Carl came out of the hospital with bloodshot eyes and wearing smoked glasses. Slowly over the weeks the surfaces cleared and a few weeks later he didn't need the smoked glasses.

Carl told me that as he lay in total darkness day after day, never seeing daylight, he did more deep thinking than ever in his entire life. He thought of what it is to go blind or to be born blind and he told me of his thoughts of the blind men and women he had heard about, so many of them heroic and lovely, making more out of life than so many of those who see and know not what they see. "I marvel," he says, "at the keen and brilliant writings of James Thurber since he lost his eyesight. I look at his mind and will and call him a hero in the finest sense of that word hero."

Carl was also devoted to Helen Keller and followed her activities across a half century. The day after a Keller appearance at the old Palace in Chicago, Carl wrote to his fellow vaudevillian a letter which is included in the recently published biography *Anne Sullivan Macy—The Touch of Magic*, by Lorena

Hickock: "Possibly the finest thing about your performance is that those who see and hear you feel that zest for living. The zest you radiate is more important than any formula about how to live life."

At Lombard he turned over many prospects. Once he wondered if he might become an advertising man and took a short correspondence course in copy writing from Witt Cochrane, advertising manager of the Lytton Store, Men's Clothes, in Chicago. About the same time he stopped in one day to talk with J. Austin Larsen, a "magnetic healer," and Larsen offered him a job advertising his healing magic in the local papers. Larsen claimed he had a magnetism that would cure diseases and make cripples walk. He was a short thin man with pink skin, a sandy Vandyke beard, and foxy, elusive eyes.

Sandburg told Larsen he did not know enough about the cures he claimed to make to be sure he wanted to write for him.

But Larsen said, "You don't have to sign your name to what you write, just sign my name, it's me you are promoting and if you don't want my money for that kind of work, I can easily find somebody else."

"This hooked me," says Sandburg. "He paid me good money for writing lies about his wonderful magnetic hands and mind. I consulted with him two or three hours a week, stuck at it three weeks and then told him it wasn't my line. The dirtiest thing I did for him was to give him an idea that he worked out. In a wide hall he had his name J. Austin Larsen spelled out with crutches of cripples who had thrown them away after he had healed them and made them able to walk. If and when I should meet Saint Peter at the gate I wouldn't be surprised if he said, 'What about your work with J. Austin Larsen back in anno Domini 1901? Do you think you belong up here or down there?' "

J. Austin Larsen kept Sandburg off Madison Avenue.

Sandburg later told his brother Mart, "I'm going to be either a writer or a bum." He had spent four years at Lombard but in the spring of his senior year, he grew restless and never stayed to be graduated. He took to the road and traveled through New Jersey, New York, Delaware. What he remembers best about his decision to become a writer was his father asking with a somber face, "Is there any money in this poetry business, Sharley?"

Sandburg waited a few seconds and all he could say was, "I guess, Papa, I haven't got any hope."

Bell ringer

During his second year at Lombard College Sandburg earned part of his tuition by ringing the school bell. The bell tolled to summon and dismiss classes and Sandburg was up there pulling the bell every hour. The bell tower had the overflow from the college library and was filled with Universalist works lining the four walls. When Sandburg didn't have a class immediately after his bell-pulling stint, he would stand reading these theological works and to this day he is perfect in all the arguments that God is good and will not send us to hell.

There is no doubt that Sandburg was influenced to a considerable degree by his father's and mother's Bible readings and his early Lutheran training. He attended Bible classes, and often sings lines from an old Swedish hymn:

> Pris och ara
> sjunga vi,
> Herren Jesus
> Som kopft oss fri
> Hosiana hosiana
> Hosiana sjunga vi Gud's namn.

> (Praise and
> sing we,
> Lord Jesus
> Who bought us free.
> Hosanna Hosanna
> Hosanna sing we God's name.)

Since his confirmation at thirteen in the Lutheran Church in Galesburg, however, Sandburg has not been on the membership rolls of any established church or religious institution. His adult allegiance went to the Social-Democratic movement. Yet his correspondence shows clergymen have been among his most ardent followers. Unitarian speakers have often included his name in the roll call of Americans of their fellowship, but so also have Quakers, Universalists, and Congregationalists, and, of course, Lutherans.

Hundreds of sermons have been delivered on Carl Sandburg in churches of every Protestant denomination in the country; a Christian scholar prepared a lengthy essay, "Christ and Carl Sandburg"; and Rabbi Emil Hirsch of Chicago called him "America's most distinguished Spinozaist."

I once asked him the direct question and he replied: "I am a Christian, a Quaker, a Moslem, a Buddhist, a Shintoist, a Confucian, and maybe a Catholic pantheist or a Joan of Arc who hears voices—I am all of these and more. Definitely I have more religions than I have time or zeal to practice in true faith." But it goes much deeper than that, and from my own observation I have come to the conclusion that those Christian clergymen who have also considered Sandburg's Socialism have not been too far off the mark. His references to Jesus have always been in terms of *"this Jesus"* after the manner of the Christian Socialists who often embraced "Comrade Jesus." Carl always says, "I like *this* Jesus," and he says it with warmth and conviction. In *Remembrance Rock*, Carl writes of Jesus: ". . . the majestic anger in his nostrils when he drove the money-changers from the Temple."

The old Socialists, in contradiction to the Communists, believed His coming and His laws were the beginning of an ever-continuing economic and social revolution. The basic fallacy of this Christian Socialist idea was, in fact, its belief that men could be what Jesus asked them to be. Not every Socialist was religious, although Socialists never denied the validity of the religious impulse, but rather tried to shape it to Socialist ends. It also explains Sandburg's lifelong devotion to several Roman Catholic priests in Chicago and in Pittsburgh who were early supporters of trade unionism and who had walked picket lines with the stockyard and steel workers.

There is no doubt that one out of every three of Sandburg's poems, in the more than one thousand he has written, makes allusion to a religious theme or motif. Sandburg is not a theological poet in the fashion of T. S. Eliot, he never argues or persuades, or for that matter constructs; but he is conscious that religion is a force and that when people say the word "God" they mean something by it. Since good poets need to know all the words and wonder at all the forces, one is not surprised to find this strong Christian orientation in Sandburg.

Yet I do not believe that any of his genuinely religious poems celebrates either God or Christianity. His most famous "religious" poem, "To a Contemporary Bunkshooter," written in 1915, is a polemic against the evangelist who would pervert the natural impulses of religion from the Socialist ethic into an apologia for Capitalist exploitation:

> You tell $6 a week department store girls
> all they need is Jesus; you take a steel
> trust wop, dead without having lived, gray
> and shrunken at forty years of age, and you
> tell him to look at Jesus on the cross and
> he'll be all right . . .

"To a Contemporary Bunkshooter" was first published in the radical magazine *The Masses*, edited by Max Eastman, in his "leftist" days. Eastman is reported to have done a high jump when he received this signal contribution, titled then "Billy Sunday." Billy Sunday was the notorious evangelist who added the phrase "hitting the sawdust trail" to our vocabulary, for his meetings were held in tents and it was down the sawdust-covered aisles his converts marched. Because of the poem, *The Masses* was banned in New Haven, Connecticut, and when "Billy Sunday" appeared as a reprint in the New York (Socialist) *Call*, the police of Lynn, Massachusetts, seized the papers on an early Sunday morning newsstand raid.

When Alfred Harcourt became enthused about Sandburg's poetry and was urging that his firm, Henry Holt and Company, publish the whole corpus, he knew this attack on evangelist Billy Sunday would disturb the highly conservative Mr. Holt. Mr. Harcourt had to exercise great persuasion to have the dignified house of Holt publish this radical and poetic innovator in the first place, let alone summon the persuasion to publish a Wobbly invective against the famous "revivalist." Before the manuscript was submitted to Mr. Holt, Mr. Harcourt had discreetly removed "Billy Sunday," but once Holt agreed to publish the book, he reinserted the poem, retitling it "To a Contemporary Bunkshooter."

What surprised Carl some years ago was an article by Henry Kolbe called "Christ and Sandburg" which appeared in *Religion and Life*, a quarterly published by Northwestern University. Mr. Kolbe had quoted scores of allusions to Christ from the 816 poems Carl had included in *Complete Poems*. "After reading the article," Carl says, "I was at last aware how often my mind had been preoccupied with the Christ tradition."

It is a mistake nevertheless to say Sandburg is religious. He is fervent, he is just, he is passionate—all Christian virtues but not uniquely Christian virtues. Although many of his poems borrow the form of hortatory prayer, such as "Prayers of Steel," they are not supplications to God but exhortations to men. And though he often addresses God it is in the generic sense that he uses His name, such as when he writes, "Bless thee, O Lord, for the living arc of the sky over me this morning." In an honestly critical sense, this not a poem about God but about nature and in it God serves as a poetic convenience; his poem "They Ask: Is God, Too, Lonely?" is a poem upon the condition of loneliness rather than the condition of God.

But the clergymen do have their point. Sandburg has an ethic, and a fervency, but what is even more significant is that in reading this vast output of a radical poet, historian, biographer, and novelist, you will not find a single line in which he has "dismissed" Christianity or even inveighed against the Christian metaphysic.

When he received the Albert Einstein Award at the Yeshiva College, he called himself a "Yeshiva bocher" (a Talmudic student), and he thought of one of his poems:

> The best preacher is the heart,
> say the Jews of faith.
> The best teacher is time.
> The best book is the world.
> The best friend is God.

I have no fears about saying that the young bell ringer in the Lombard College tower was as near to God as any of the students in the seminary.

The Poor Writers' Club

Sandburg's first books were three little paperbacks: *In Reckless Ecstasy*, 1904; *The Plaint of a Rose* and *Incidentals*, 1905. These books bore the colophon of the Asgard Press.

The Asgard Press was the property of Professor Philip Green Wright who taught English, mathematics, astronomy, and economics at Lombard College. Wright was a disciple of William Morris, the English poet, designer of the Morris chair, and an apostle of handicraft arts. Wright had the same intense regard for good printing and craftsmanship that characterized Morris and, like Morris, he was a many-sided man, almost a Renaissance figure. He was versatile enough to write passable poetry and ingenious enough to design his own home.

Wright organized the "Poor Writers' Club," a select group of budding literary talents who met with him weekly to read Kipling, Turgenev, and Mark Twain, and recite aloud their own compositions. These students were Sandburg, Athol Brown, and Howard Lauer. Wright was the sort of teacher who was always a success not because he knew so much but because his enthusiasm was contagious. Athol Brown has said, "He seemingly only sought to stir us into action in order to see what would happen."

Wright was also imbued with an intense social consciousness. A new century was beginning and with it Wright hoped to see a new social order. Sandburg, who had already been an itinerant worker, a hobo, and a soldier, knew the trials of the city and the despair of the farms. Labor and farm organizations were beginning to see what they could wrest for their members through political action. Change and optimism were in the air and Wright and Sandburg shared it. This and Wright's profound conviction about Sandburg's talent made them close friends.

Of Sandburg, Wright has written, "I do not remember that there was anything particularly distinguished in his appearance,

anything that is to suggest incipient genius. He looked like one
of the proletariat rather than one of the intellectuals . . . He had
seen a great deal of the world, some of it, I believe, from the
underside of box cars traveling via the Gorky line to literary
fame. The boys called him 'the terrible Swede': not such a bad
accusation after all; for it is a quality of this old Viking blood
that enables its possessor to land on his feet in every environ-
ment.

"My own association with him was on literary grounds. He,
together with two other incipient geniuses, Brown and Lauer,
constituted an extremely informal organization which met Sunday afternoons in my study for literary refreshment. We called
ourselves the 'Poor Writers' Club'. . . . Brown is now a pedagogue,
Lauer on the payroll of a factory, but Sandburg, true to his
Norse instincts, disdains harness."

Both teacher and student satisfied their curiosity about Socialism
by reading Karl Marx's *Das Kapital*. Wright doubted the Marxian
prophecies and believed the capitalist system had a resilience and
an adaptability toward change that would elude its violent over-
throw.

While Wright was a graduate student at Harvard, Nicolay
and Hay, Lincoln's private secretaries, published their official
biography of Abraham Lincoln in *Century Magazine*. He was
teaching at Lombard College when Nicolay and Hay brought
out their two-volume *Complete Works of Abraham Lincoln*.
Later, when Ida M. Tarbell began serializing her *Lincoln Studies*
in *McClure's*, Wright himself began formulating a historical per-
spective of Lincoln. Talking to Sandburg, Wright was spokesman for a new movement which had come to see Lincoln not
only as exemplary but as representative and prophetic, not only
a shaper of the American dream but also a product of that
dream.

John C. Weigel, Lombard '08, one of Wright's students, in
a descriptive brochure about Wright's accomplishments republished from the Knox College *Siwasher*, wrote: "Through
(Wright) I first gained a picture of the real Abraham Lincoln,
the kind of human being Carl Sandburg has given us in *Abraham*

Lincoln: The Prairie Years. And as I read it, Carl Sandburg, I wondered if even you know how much of Philip Green Wright shines through the rare beauty of your precious book!"

Wright believed in homeopathic education, the student's total involvement. A poet should print as well as compose his own works. He himself had written poetry and owned a printing press which he kept in the basement of his home. Thus was born the Asgard Press with the motto *Kunst im Kleinsten.*

Wright set, printed, and bound a book of his own poems entitled *The Dreamer* for which Carl wrote the introduction, and then set Sandburg's book of poetry, *In Reckless Ecstasy.*

Sandburg was out of college and had already been published sporadically in a little magazine called *Tomorrow,* edited by Parker H. Sercombe, about which Wright is reputed to have remarked that while the magazine was a little queer, Sandburg showed its best promise.

In Reckless Ecstasy was a brochure fifty pages long, printed on a ten by fifteen Gordon press with Caslon face type. Carl roamed the basement watching his first youthful effort set into galleys. Fifty copies were printed, bound in cardboard covers, and put together with ribbon. To come across them now is to come upon a rare collector's item valued somewhere in the neighborhood of five hundred dollars. Afterward Wright printed Sandburg's *Incidentals,* and a poem *The Plaint of the Rose* with hand-painted roses on the cover.

Some years later, Wright left Lombard College after failing in an attempt to bring about a union between Lombard and neighboring Knox College. He returned to the Harvard Graduate School to take up his studies of economics under Professor F. W. Taussig a quarter of a century after Harvard had conferred a Master of Arts degree upon him. When Woodrow Wilson appointed Taussig the first Chairman of the United States Tariff Commission, Taussig took Wright to Washington. In Washington, Wright soon distinguished himself as an outstanding economist. His researches on sugar tariffs and vegetable and mineral oils were internationally acclaimed. He was eminent enough to be included in the *Dictionary of American Biography* for which Sandburg wrote the sketch, and Sandburg also wrote the memorial brochure printed for private distribution by Wright's family after his death:

> Philip Green Wright will always be a momentous figure to me . . . I had four years of almost daily contact with him at college, for many years visited him as often as possible, and there was never a time when he did not deepen whatever of reverence I had for the human mind . . . He was at home in either the hard as nails utilitarian fields or in the realms of the ethereal and insoluble. He was a great man and a great teacher.

It was a relationship of mutual benefit. Sandburg believes that Wright was the prairie Leonardo da Vinci and Wright believed that Sandburg was a great singer who would fill men with a new hope.

When I began work on this book Sandburg sent me a short handwritten note: "The three great influences on my life—my teacher at Lombard, Philip Green Wright, my wife, Paula Steichen, and my brother-in-law, Edward Steichen."

Getting somewhere

Incidentals is a series of half-poetic, half-prose aphorisms, more usually called a prose poem, but here the intent is not absolutely poetic. It is not absolutely poetic because one can sense youth intruding on discipline.

Like many writers, particularly those who are prolific, Sandburg has an abiding neglect for his early work and has never seen fit to have any of it republished. He may well be right. Sometimes a writer's early works have only a historical interest. And sometimes, like the rest of us, the memory of youth often brings with it the memory of dismay at enthusiasm unrestrained.

Then, too, writers often respect their work in the degree that it gained them popularity, established an audience, and started a reputation. Early work, they suspect, will be used as a sort of graph which charts their progress and can often be imagined as a sort of quasi-mistake and thus be used to associate the writer with his own history rather than with his own heart.

There is no need to talk about the later Sandburg peeping through the early Sandburg work. There is no need to. *Incidentals* is a young man's credo and its value accrues from understanding it as a young man's credo.

Incidentals' basic credo is that there's enough happiness to go around and enough heroism to insure it will.

"As disasters are sudden, triumphs are unexpected. The spirit of victory is as rapid as the genius of ruin. To get up and go on when you're knocked down is to get somewhere."

In all times and in all places youth believes it can remake the world. The young poets commit themselves to the rearticulation and refabrication of this idea in the diction and style suited to their times and hopes.

Let us say charitably that youth is often wrong; or even less charitably, but more exactly, young people are just as ineffectual as their elders.

Certainly no changes can be made if youth does not cherish these ideals when it can.

Sandburg is aware of this, for his book begins with an apologia. He calls his *Incidentals* "useful impertinences." He says, "I am an idealist, I don't know where I'm going but I'm on my way."

These passages are a selection of attitudes, all of them perhaps peripheral. They are the articulation by which young men often sense rather than define the goal they will pursue.

Sandburg writes that there is no lust or perversion the human imagination can conceive that has not been practiced somewhere sometime by men and women: "Neither history nor newspapers surprise me any more." The young are always at pains to tell us they will never be surprised. They say they are hardened and skeptical but they forget that only the hardened and the skeptical are surprised.

I mean no derogation in calling Sandburg a skeptic. I remember that Santayana remarked skepticism is the chastity of the mind and one does not surrender one's chastity to the first comer, but waits to exchange it for fidelity and truth. Nor do I mean *Incidentals* is only a collection of youthful ambivalences. Indeed much of this writing combines power and metaphor:

What is shame?
Shame is the feeling you have when you agree
with the woman who loves you that you are the
man she thinks you are . . .

Truth consists of paradoxes and a paradox
is two facts that stand on opposite hilltops
and across the intervening valley call
each other liars.

Sandburg grumbles when people say that he began publishing
late in life. He grumbles because it is not true. He was for many
years a Socialist pamphleteer and a newspaperman but before
that he was a poet.

Incidentals is youthful but not sophomoric. The work stamps
the poet that will be; this was Sandburg before he was thirty
and already his genius had been recognized by his teacher, a
profound man and inspired critic. The making of a writer is an
arduous process and Sandburg's gifts and final popularity de-
scended upon him not because he was nearing forty, but because
twenty years before he had started writing and, when the public
at last recognized him, the public realized that he had been writing well.

Does clubbing a man reform him?

If Galesburg helped make Sandburg a poet, Galesburg also
helped make him a radical. Carl Sandburg, the Galesburg schoolboy, became a radical in 1893, the day Governor John P. Altgeld
of Illinois extended a pardon to the four surviving Haymarket
rioters.

Briefly, the Haymarket riot took place on the evening of May
4, 1886, at an open-air meeting in Chicago's Haymarket Square.
A wave of strikes and a spirit of revolt had swept over Chicago,
and three agitators, Albert Parsons, August Spies, and Samuel
Fielden, were crying out against police killings and clubbings of
strikers.

A small audience listened. A light rain started. The meeting was about over. Then came a troop of 176 policemen from the nearby Desplaines Street Station led by Officer "Black Jack" Bonfield, who ordered immediate dispersal.

Someone in the crowd threw a bomb. Eleven persons were killed and over one hundred injured. The police made free and wild with their revolvers; anybody was a target.

The next day, police rounded up nine anarchists, including a yeast manufacturer named Oscar Neebe who happened to be visiting one of the arrested men. Seven of these anarchists were indicted as accessories before the fact in the murder of Police Officer Matthew Degan.

When the trial began, Albert Parsons of his own will came out of hiding in Wisconsin to surrender himself to the court in Chicago. Seven of the defendants were found guilty of having conspired to murder policeman Degan. The yeast manufacturer, Neebe, was sentenced to fifteen years in prison. No one has ever discovered who threw the bomb.

While awaiting execution, the eight men were offered a commutation of sentence if they would disown their beliefs. Three, Fielden, Schwab—the editor of the *Arbeiter Zeitung*, a Socialist newspaper—and Neebe, took advantage of the offer; Louis Lingg killed himself in his cell by blowing away half his face with a smuggled blasting cap. Four, Parsons, Spies, George Engel, and Adolph Fischer, were hanged.

A bitter time it was, as the Irish say. The trial had been conducted in the midst of public hysteria. The defendants were convicted before the judge's gavel rapped. The prevailing opinion, says Sandburg, was that these anarchists boasted of dynamite as a weapon of terror and deserved their punishment. "They were not regular people and they didn't belong to the human race, for they seemed more like slimy animals who prowl, sneak, and kill after dark . . . This I believed with millions of other people reading and talking about the trial. I didn't meet or hear of anyone in our town who didn't so believe, at the time."

On November 11, 1887, the day the four men were executed, the schools let the children out early, and on his way home, Sandburg, in company with other boys, heard one man hail another with the four words Sandburg says he never forgot: "Well, they hanged

'em!" The joy with which this information was conveyed shamed
Sandburg. The statement, he says, struck him as a "glad howl"
and neither his mother's nor his father's defense of the execution
diminished his shame.

Five years later Sandburg was able to read Governor John Peter
Altgeld's sixteen-thousand-word pardon of the remaining three
prisoners.

"The jury which tried the case was a packed jury selected to
convict," wrote the Illinois Governor, who proceeded to list the
errors of the presiding jurist, Judge Gary, and reasoned that
there was no proven connection between the man who threw
the bomb and the men in prison. Altgeld concluded that the
police were just as guilty, for they had broken up a peaceful meeting and had clubbed the heads of the workers. Of these labor wars,
Altgeld asked, "Does clubbing a man reform him? Does brutal
treatment elevate his thoughts?"

"I knew as I moved through that sixteen-thousand-word message," writes Sandburg, "crammed with what I now took to be
sober facts and truth, that I wasn't the same boy as five years
before when I was glad about four men hanged. The feeling grew
on me that I had been a little crazy, 'off my nut,' along with
millions of people like myself gone somewhat crazy."

The pardons were political suicide for Altgeld. The consequences, however, were clear to him. He had declared, "If I decide
they are innocent, I will pardon them if I never hold office another day."

Altgeld left a large shadow on the American political scene.
He was not only a humanitarian but a new breed of politician.
What the newly evolving urban, industrial society needed most
was justice, strictly interpreted, for it was not force but justice
which eventually ended the labor wars and then not until Franklin
D. Roosevelt came along in 1933 with his New Deal.

That Sandburg realized the inherent justice of the pardon was
no easy decision. Altgeld was beaten when he ran for election.
It is to be remembered that when Sandburg was a boy the
Supreme Court was called the "Bulwark of Privilege" and that
few people listened to the claims the immigrants and the workers
wanted to make upon America. But these claims began a long

battle which changed the image of America and constituted a more profound application of democratic principles.

Forty-five years later Carl Sandburg was willing to pin all his hopes for America's future on the United States Supreme Court. "Earl Warren is one of us, Harry, and so is Bill Douglas, and Hugo Black, and Mr. Brennan; they will keep the track clear—in our time, at least."

Proud words wear hard boots

"How many times do you refer to me as 'a Socialist'?" Carl grumped when I showed him this manuscript. "Hell, you've got me here 'a Socialist' at least a hundred times. Why don't you change a few of them?"

"Carl," I said, "you weren't organizing for the Republican National Committee up there in Wisconsin in 1908, were you?"

"No, I wasn't. I was organizing for the Social Democratic Party but you ought to change a few of those 'a Socialist' anyway."

"What will I change them to?" I asked.

"Make a few of them 'a radical,' " Carl said.

"O.K., Carl, but remember, you're the guy who wrote when you let proud words go, it is not easy to call them back."

PART 3

American Minstrel

Sinclair Lewis wept

Since 1904 when he quit the banjo and took up the guitar, Carl Sandburg has practiced music daily.

"The guitar is a noble instrument. It takes someone who is devoted to it, like Segovia, to bring out its possibilities. If I'd gotten a prison sentence, I'd probably have become pretty good on the guitar."

Carl Sandburg's voice is heavy, but there's a haunting quality about it. I suspect his timing is what makes it great. I've heard him sing in a huge auditorium in a whisper, and yet the entire audience sat silent, spellbound.

His voice is entirely untrained. What few lessons he had came from a choirmaster in Galesburg. It seems, too, he always plays the same chord.

But his is a voice in which you can hear farm hands wailing and levee Negroes moaning.

Public singing started for Carl when he was a boy in Galesburg. Later he joined the nontouring Lombard College Glee Club. He also sang with the Berrien Street barbershop harmonizers downtown. What really developed Carl's voice and music, however, was the inspired knowledge that his guitar playing made him a much-sought-after lecturer.

Lecturing began early for Carl, as early as 1909 with that lecture, "Walt Whitman: American Vagabond."

Eleven years later, after a lecture at Cornell College, Iowa, Carl suddenly dug out a guitar from behind the lectern and said, "I will now sing a few folk songs that somehow tie into the folk quality I have tried to get into my verse. They are all authentic songs people have sung for years. If you don't care for them and want to leave the hall it will be all right with me. I'll only be doing what I'd be doing if I were at home, anyway."

The audience stayed, liking the songs as well as the poems, and since that day Carl's singing has been part of every program.

When the Republican Club of New York asked him, the author of *Abraham Lincoln: The Prairie Years,* for an address in 1927, they added, "Bring along your guitar." His platform success is due in no small part to his facility with the guitar. As he himself remarked, people like to see a poet but listening to his poems is another matter.

By the time *Smoke and Steel* was published in 1920, Sandburg was receiving yearly dozens of invitations from universities and literary groups. Some friends regretted his career as a platform singer, wishing he would spend more time writing. But they were wrong.

Carl earned a good livelihood from these appearances, which enabled him to carry on with his writing. Here is a sample poster various organizations used to advertise Carl's lectures:

AMERICAN FOLKLORE
With Readings From His Own Poems
CARL SANDBURG
Tuesday evening—March 10th
Benefit—Albany League of Women Voters
Tickets at $1.00 at 8:30 o'clock

"But the best singing Carl Sandburg ever did," wrote Lloyd Lewis, in *The Chicagoan,* on August 17, 1929, "was at the dinner Morris Fishbein gave for Sinclair Lewis upon the novelist's return to America after a 2-year absence."

Among the guests that evening were one or two fellows who had not thought so highly of *Main Street,* and the affair might have been a failure but for the presence of Carl Sandburg.

Fishbein saved the evening by asking Carl to sing. Somebody brought a guitar and the iron-jawed Swede stood up and in that soft, don't-give-a-damn way of his, sang "The Buffalo Skinners."

'Twas in the town of Jacksboro,
In the spring of '73,
A man by the name of Crego
Came stepping up to me
Saying, "How do you do, young fellow
And how would you like to go

And spend one summer pleasantly
On the range of the buffalo?"

Everything quieted. It was a great man's song—about starvation, blood, fleas, hives, entrails, thirst, Indian devils, men cheated out of their wages and killing their employers to get even—it was a novel, an epic novel boiled down to simple words and set to queer, haunting music that rises and falls like the winds on Western plains.

Lloyd Lewis continued:

"I've heard the discoverer of the song, John Lomax, of Texas, sing it, but never like Carl sang it that night. It was like a funeral song to the pioneer America that is gone. And when Carl was done Sinclair Lewis spoke up, his face streaked with tears. 'That's the America I came home to. That's it.' "

In A *Child of the Century*, Ben Hecht writes:

I was to hear this voice for many years, in the streets during long walks, in the (Chicago) *Daily News* office at the desk beside mine. To this day I remember it as the finest voice I ever heard, reading or talking, better even than the remarkable voices of Paul Muni, Jack Barrymore, and Helen Hayes. In Sandburg's voice lived all his poetry. It was a voice of pauses and undercurrents, with a hint of anger always in it, and a lift of defiance in its quiet tones. It was a voice that made words sound fresh, and clothed the simplest of sentences with mysteries. I had heard a cousin of this voice speak out of Sherwood Anderson, but Sherwood was garrulous and many-mooded. There was never garrulity in Sandburg and there was only one mood in him—a measured passion. Whether he chatted at lunch or recited from the podium he had always the same voice. He spoke always like a man slowly revealing something.

As modern as the Volstead Act

In the years Sandburg traveled meeting audiences before whom he read his verses, he always closed his program with a half-hour of songs. With each song he gave verbal footnotes. The songs Sandburg sang often reminded listeners of songs of a kindred character they knew entirely or in fragments. Often these listeners would refer Sandburg to persons who had similar ballads or ditties. In due time Sandburg was a walking thesaurus of American folk music.

After he had finished the first two volumes of his *Lincoln,* Sandburg went to work assembling a book of songs out of hobo and childhood days and from the memory of songs others had taught him. He rummaged, found composers and arrangers, collaborated on the main design and outline of harmonization with musicians, ballad singers, and musicologists.

The result was a collection of 280 songs, ballads, ditties, brought together from all regions of America, more than one hundred never before published: *The American Songbag.* Each song or ditty was prefaced by an author's note which indicated the origin and meaning of the song as well as special interest the song had, musical arrangement, and most of the chorus and verses.

The book, published in 1927, has been selling steadily ever since. As Sandburg said at the time: "It is as ancient as the medieval European ballads brought to the Appalachian Mountains, it is as modern as skyscrapers, the Volstead Act, and the latest oil well gusher."

Schopenhauer never learned

Sandburg is in constant demand as an entertainer. Two things contribute to his popularity. First, Carl respects his audience and prepares his speeches carefully. Even when he is called upon for impromptu remarks, he has notes written on the back of handy envelopes. He has his own system of shorthand, devised by abbreviations: "humility" will be "humly," "with" will be "w," and "that" will be "tt".

The second reason for his popularity is his complete spontaneity with the guitar. It is a mistake, however, to imagine that Sandburg uses the guitar as a prop. He is no dextrous-fingered college boy but rather a dedicated, humble, and bashful apostle of this instrument. At age seventy-four, he became what he shyly terms a "pupil" of Andres Segovia, the great guitarist of the Western world.

It is not easy to become Segovia's pupil. One needs high talent. Segovia has written about Carl:

> His fingers labor heavily on the strings and he asked for my help in disciplining them. I found that this precocious, grown-up boy of 74 deserved to be taught. There has long existed a brotherly affection between us, thus I accepted him as my pupil. Just as in the case of every prodigy child, we must watch for the efficacy of my teaching to show up in the future—if he should master all the strenuous exercises I inflicted on him.

> To play the guitar as he aspires will devour his three-fold energy as a historian, a poet and a singer. One cause of Schopenhauer's pessimism was the fact that he failed to learn the guitar. I am certain that Carl Sandburg will not fall into the same sad philosophy. The heart of this great poet constantly bubbles forth a generous joy of life—with or without the guitar.

The public's identification of Carl Sandburg and the guitar is no happenstance. Nor does Carl reject this identity.

He is proud of having Segovia for a friend and dedicated a poem to him titled "The Guitar."

Carl says it is the greatest poem ever written to the guitar because he has never heard of any other poem to that subtle instrument.

> A portable companion always ready to go where you go— a small friend weighing less than a freshborn infant—to be shared with few or many—just two of you in sweet meditation.

The *New York Herald Tribune*'s photographer, Ira Rosenberg, tells an anecdote about the time he wanted to take a picture of Carl playing a guitar. Carl hadn't brought his along. Mr. Rosenberg suggested that they go out and find one.

"Preferably," said Carl, "one battered and worn, such as might be found in a pawnshop."

They went to the pawnshop of Joseph Miller of 1162 Sixth Avenue.

"Mr. Miller was in the shop," the *Herald Tribune* story related, "but was reluctant to have anybody's picture taken inside, because his business was too 'confidential' for pictures.

"But after introductions he asked: 'Carl Sandburg? Well *you* can pose inside.'

"He wanted Mr. Sandburg to pose with one of the guitars he had displayed behind glass in the center of his shop, but the poet eyed this somewhat distastefully. 'Kalamazoo guitars,' he said, 'used by radio hillbilly singers.'

"He chose one from Mr. Miller's window, a plain guitar with no fancy polish. While the picture was taken, Mr. Miller's disposition to be generous to Mr. Sandburg increased to the point where he advised, 'I won't even charge you the one dollar rental fee.' "

A knowledgeable celebrity

When someone in the audience rose and asked how does it feel to be a celebrity, Carl said, "A celebrity is a fellow who eats celery with celerity."

This has always been Carl's attitude. Lloyd Lewis wrote that when he first knew Carl in 1916, Sandburg was making $27.50 a week writing features for the *Day Book* and eating sparse luncheons in one-arm restaurants. He walked home at night for two miles beyond the end of a suburban trolley.

When fame came it changed Sandburg only slightly. Lewis remembered another newspaperman asking, "Carl, have your ideas changed any since you got all these comforts?"

Carl thought the question over slowly and answered: "I know a starving man who is fed never remembers all the pangs of his starvation, I know that."

That was all he said, Lewis reports. That was all he had to say.

In answer to a *New York Times* query on what is fame ("Thoughts on Fame," October 23, 1960), Carl said: "Fame is a figment of a pigment. It comes and goes. It changes with every generation. There never were two fames alike. One fame is precious and luminous; another is a bubble of a bauble."

"Ah, did you once see Shelley plain?"

The impression you get from Carl Sandburg's home is one of laughter and happiness; and the laughter and the happiness are even more pronounced when no company is present.

Carl has been married to Paula for fifty-three years, and he has not made a single major decision without careful consideration and thorough discussion with his wife. Through all these years, Mrs. Sandburg has pointedly avoided the limelight. She has shared her husband's greatness, but only within the confines of their home; it is a dedication which began the moment she met Carl.

Mrs. Sandburg received a Phi Beta Kappa key from the University of Chicago and she was busy writing and teaching when she met Sandburg. "You are the 'Peoples' Poet' " was her appraisal in 1908, and she stopped teaching and writing to devote herself to the fulfillment of her husband's career.

She has rarely been photographed with him and, except for Carl's seventy-fifth anniversary celebration in Chicago in 1953, she has not attended the dozens of banquets, functions, public appearances, and dinners honoring him—all of this upon her insistence. Even now I will not intrude upon her except to state a few bare facts.

The only way to describe Paula Sandburg is to say she is beautiful in a Grecian sense. Her clothes, her hair, everything about her is both graceful and simple. She has small, broad, capable hands and an enormous energy.

She is not only a trained mathematician and Classicist, but a good architect. She designed and supervised the building of the Harbert, Michigan, house, most of which was constructed by one local carpenter who carried the heavy beams singly upon his shoulder. As the Sandburg goat herd increased, she also designed the barn alterations to accommodate them. When erosion threatened the foundation of their home in Harbert, Paula Sandburg planted grapevines and arranged the snow fences which helped hold the sands away.

She was born Lilian Steichen, her parents immigrants from Luxemburg. Her mother called her Paus'l, a Luxemburg endearment meaning "pussycat." Some of the children of the family could not pronounce this name and called her Paula, a soubriquet Carl liked so much she has been Paula ever since.

But neither was Lilian her baptismal name. Her parents, pious Roman Catholics, christened her Mary Anne Elizabeth Magdalene Steichen. "My mother read a book right after I was born and there was a Lilian in the book she loved and I became Lilian— and eventually I became Paula."

Lilian Steichen was an exceptional student. This family of Luxemburg immigrants, in fact, produced two exceptional children. Paula's older brother is Edward Steichen, a talented artist and, for the past half-century, one of the world's eminent photographers. (Two years ago the photography editor of Vogue magazine titled his article about Steichen, "The World's Greatest Photographer.")

By the time Lilian had been graduated from public school, her parents were doing quite well. Her mother was a good manager and established a millinery business in Milwaukee. But her father was not enthusiastic about sending young Paula to high school. "This is no place for a young girl," he said. The parents compromised, however, on a convent school and Paula went to Ursuline Academy in London, Ontario.

She was pious, too, once kneeling through the night from Holy Thursday to Good Friday, despite the protest of the nuns that this was too much for a young girl. She knelt out of reverence for having read the *Meditations* of St. Augustine.

She read everything else she could get her hands on, including an article (she thinks it was in the *Atlantic Monthly*) by Mark Twain on "White Slavery." Paula was saddened about what was happening to little girls and vowed to kneel no more in Chapel. She had come to a decision. If there was ever a thought in her mind she might devote her life to religion, it was now dispelled. "I felt that I must devote myself to the 'outside' world."

She passed the entrance examinations to the University of

Illinois, but during the year at Urbana felt more important events transpired at the University of Chicago.

"And besides, Thorstein Veblen was one of the Chicago professors."

At the University of Chicago she studied Whitman and Shelley, and became a Socialist. Socialist leaders in Milwaukee recognized her worth, not only because of her dedication but because of her fluency in German, French, and Luxemburg. She once gave a German recitation before a convention of German-language teachers in Milwaukee.

Carl and Paula met in Milwaukee in 1907 during Paula's Christmas holiday visit to her parents. Carl was still Charles A. Sandburg. He "legitimized" Paula for Lilian Steichen, and it was Paula who insisted on Carl for Charles.

Victor Berger, the panjandrum of Wisconsin Socialism and member of Congress, had asked Paula Steichen to translate some of his German editorials into English. Carl, who was stationed in Appleton, Wisconsin, organizing for the Social Democrats, was in Berger's office and made it his business to escort Paula to the streetcar. She left the next day for her teaching job at Princeton, Illinois. (After graduation from the University of Chicago, Paula taught for two years in the normal school at Valley City, North Dakota, then two years at Princeton (Illinois) Township High School.) By the time the streetcar pulled away, he had fallen in love with Paula.

A letter awaited her at Princeton. Paula says that even though Carl's letters usually began, "Dear Miss Steichen," there was an understanding from the beginning that they would become husband and wife.

Paula generously lent me one of Carl's love letters, dated February 21, 1908, Hotel Athearn, Oshkosh, Wisconsin:

> Dear Miss Steichen: It is a very good letter you send me—softens the intensity of this guerilla warfare I am carrying on up here. Never until in this work of S-D organization have I realized and felt the attitude and experience of a *Teacher*. With those outside the party, I am an Advocate. But those within the organization have so much to learn, and to show

those who have intelligence what to do, and to get the hyper-critical into constructive work, and to give cheer to the desperate and rousal to the stolid—sometimes I know just what it is to be a Teacher.

I see you employ the exclamation point as freely as I do!— You chip away at an idea in sculptor-fashion. You leave the thing unfinished and half-put, neither neat, correct, discriminative, nor scholastic! I indict you as fellow felon!

The Dream Girl is millennial—formed in the mist of an impressionist's reverie. Millennial, and at this time, impossible. But, my good girl, she is not of the leisure-class, as we know the l-c. She is a disreputable gypsy, and can walk, shoot, ride, row, hoe in the garden, wash dishes, grimace, haggle, live on half-rations, and laugh at Luck.

You remind me of two types of women—seem to sort o' blend the two in your cosmos. Actresses of the modern school of repression, Fiske, Kalish, and Ashwell. And the Russian revolutionist!

Am going to send you *The Plaint of a Rose*. It was written as and marks the half-way point on the journey "from Poetry to Economics." A protest and justification of the universe!

I shall plan to be in Milwaukee the last days in March and one or two in April and will hope to see you then. Will tell you about some of the curious and interesting phases of the work up this way. Will also make some inquiries of you, pertinent and quasi-impertinent with reference to democratic art. One can't lecture on Whitman or Shaw without attaining facts and convictions.

I will forgive you (out of inborn generosity and largeness of nature) for writing such a long letter, provided, as hereinafter stated, that you repeat the offense! And don't forget your exclamation points!

Charles Sandburg

P.S.—Am going to have the district headquarters here from now on. My permanent address will be 248 Wisconsin Ave., Oshkosh.

P.S.: P.S.:—Once in my callow days and for many years I thot Oshkosh was like Heaven, Nirvana, Sheol, the North

Pole; mythical, imaginary, fictive, and hopeless of attainment. —But here it is! bustling and populated, stern and real, a factual entity stretching away from my window with lands, bldgs, laws, and noises!

In each of his letters, Carl sent Paula a poem and occasionally a Social-Democratic pamphlet. When she wrote Carl she was coming home to Menomonee Falls, Wisconsin, from Princeton for the spring vacation of 1908, Carl immediately invited himself.

Her artist brother, Ed, liked him immediately but there were misgivings among other members of the family. When the rumor had already spread through Social-Democratic circles that Carl was a poet, one can well imagine what this accusation did to middle-class working people in the year 1908.

Strangely enough, his being a poet hurt Sandburg in his attempt to organize the factory workers and railroad men of Wisconsin. Even Victor Berger did some whispering, and to Paula too: "Do you know he's a poet?"

Paula said she knew he was a poet and twenty years before Carl became famous, she repeated to Berger the lines from Robert Browning:

> Ah, did you once see Shelley plain,
> And did he stop and speak to you,
> And did you speak to him again?
> How strange it seems and new!

They were married in June 1908, six months after their first meeting. There was no ring ceremony, the word "obey" was eliminated with a solemn agreement that one of the parties could call it quits any time he or she decided.

A few years later, after a half-serious argument, Paula wondered whether they should invoke the agreement and Carl said, "I'll be damned if I'll go through all that courtin' again."

Carl and Paula set up housekeeping in Appleton where they paid four dollars a month rent for three rooms upstairs in a one-and-a-half-story house owned by a Social-Democrat carpenter. They bought a bed, a mattress, and some bedding; Paula made muslin curtains and several store cartons served as dresser and shelves. In 1909, they moved to Milwaukee where Carl continued his organizing but earned extra money as a writer of advertisements for a local department store. Then came a regular job on the Milwaukee *Leader*, the largest Socialist paper in Wisconsin.

The first child, Margaret, was born in 1911 in Milwaukee about the time Carl became secretary to Emil Seidel, the first Socialist mayor of that city. At the age of nine, totally without warning, Margaret had an epileptic spasm accompanied by convulsions. The Sandburgs had no money and were not to have any until years later, but they strained their financial resources as well as their thoughts and energies for Margaret. Nerve specialists diagnosed her case as nocturnal epilepsy as her seizures occurred only during sleep. They advised diet and drugs to relieve the number and severity of attacks.

Years later, after the Sandburgs had moved from Chicago to Michigan, Janet, the second daughter, was hit by a car while crossing the street in front of the Three Oaks High School in Harbert. She was unconscious for a week and lingered many weeks thereafter between life and death. X rays revealed innumerable fine fractures at the base of the skull. When she returned home, a many-windowed upper porch was set aside for her recuperation. After two years, she recovered enough to return to school, but has been afflicted ever since with severe recurrent headaches. Despite this handicap, Janet is an active farmer and a fervent fan of both baseball and politics.

Margaret and Janet were the "Spink" and "Skabootch" to whom *Rootabaga Stories* was dedicated.

The youngest daughter, Helga, Carl calls "Swipes." Helga writes poetry and won a short-story prize in 1958. She has also published two novels: *The Wheel of Earth* (1958) and *Measure My Love* (1959). A third, *The Owl's Roost* will be published shortly. Helga lives in Washington, D. C., with her son, John Carl, 19, and her daughter, Paula, 18.

When *The Prairie Years* was sold to the *Pictorial Review* for $30,000, the world did not know the tears Carl and Paula Sandburg shed that evening because of their concern about the future of Margaret and Janet. They felt that both girls, who would never really be able to earn their own livelihoods, would need total security provided for them, were at last assured a fair chance of happiness. This is what has concerned Carl through all his productive years, and explains his great care in handling of money.

Under the most rigid rules, daughter Margaret may be called an expert bibliophile. Newly developed medication and drugs have overcome her disability. She has inherited from both her parents a love of books and a mind capable of absorbing and analyzing great literature. Those who have worked around Carl have come to value Margaret's exceptional abilities.

I say, "Margaret, your father delivered a speech at a Socialist convention in 1910," and within the hour Margaret has brought me either a printed transcript of the speech or her own type-written version of the transcript which may have disappeared years ago.

Sandburg refuses to have his library catalogued, which numbers 15,000 volumes (this after the sale of a huge library, along with manuscripts of his Lincoln biography, to the University of Illinois).

"I know where everything is," he says, "and I don't want it touched."

I've discovered, however, that his confidence is based on Margaret who can unerringly walk to a shelf or a sealed box and pull out the book or document he is looking for.

I asked Helga, Carl's novelist daughter, to write me a letter:

> You want to hear about me and my father? Yes? What can I say? First he educated me by writing the unique *Rootabaga* tales, which run the gamut from comedy to pathos to tragedy. Later when I learned to type I did some of his manuscripts. He read stories and poems, his Lincoln biography to the family; the cook dissolved in tears when she came on the Lincoln death chapter in his typewriter as she was cleaning the attic. I was washed in a proper idiom; how could I escape it? I learned suitable prose. And not only his; he read from others, everything, even the trial of Jeanne d'Arc, night

after night. From Millet I copied for him: "Which is more beautiful, a straight tree or a crooked tree? . . . Whichever is most in place in the painting . . . the beautiful is that which is in place. . . . It were better that the things weakly said should not be said at all because in the former case they are only as it were, deflowered. . . . Let Apollo be Apollo and Socrates Socrates. . . ."

People came through—poets, admirers, photographers, newsmen, friends. At the beginning of the evening, he reached for a piece of bread—and by midnight when the group were still talking (often the one voice only pursuing the topic to an end), and I left them to go to bed—a pair of bread dough dice would be at his place, seemingly unconsciously worked, marked with fork-prongs with numbers. Clearing the table the next morning, I would discover them among the silver and glasses and linen. I kept early hours—I was a farmer! I remember coming down and finding just my parents still at table, talking, talking, talking, soft and persistent—and they sent me back to lie awake at four in the morning, waiting for them to go to bed so I could slip down and out again to the fresh out-of-doors where I wanted to be, and over to the pungent stables, while an old moon still shone.

In his very early published work he declared, "I am not a thing that hurries and worries," and this was true probably in desire at least; Whitmanesque he said, "I am careless, graceful, easy. I cultivate action without friction. . . . I never slam a door." He did slam doors, and sometimes ripped shirts and broke chairs. He wrote a poem about the shirt; "and the people will say, look at him tear his shirt." But he directed his fury not at his family, but at the large dark things that got in his way. He was vociferous that one should not read trash or listen to junk music. I heard symphonies with but part of an ear—the rest of me tuned to the outdoors where my friends ran in the sunset glow on the still-warm beaches.

A long-time ago he began calling me his own nickname: Swipes. He calls Paula my daughter Snick. He renamed John my son, who had been called Joseph at birth. As you know he had also renamed me when he returned from Sweden. I had been registered as Mary Ellen Sandburg—fortunately for me he returned and said how it would be.

Have I said enough dear Harry?   Helga

Carl Sandburg rarely spends money on himself and at the height of his career looks as unpressed as he did when he was a $27.50 newspaperman. He developed this habit saving money for his daughters. He has always labored with deep concern in some day establishing the necessary trust funds for Janet and Margaret. The Sandburgs have thought of nothing else for the past forty years, except putting aside the money to make secure the future of the two girls.

Yet Carl, despite this lifelong concern for his daughters, is a generous man. Once he cancelled four thousand dollars' worth of scheduled lectures to deliver a speech in honor of Lincoln in Springfield, Illinois.

I was with him the morning *The New York Times* reported the arrest of Dorothy Day, editor of *The Catholic Worker*, for failing to comply with the New York City air-raid practice alert. Without further word, Carl made out a check and sent it off to Dorothy Day. "She'll need bail and things," he said. He does these things all the time.

Ralph Newman of the Abraham Lincoln Book Shop in Chicago told me that Carl would walk along the street with him and suddenly say, "Ralph, whatever happened to Miss so-and-so who did a little typing for me on *The Prairie Years?*"

Ralph would reply that Miss so-and-so is an elderly widow today, looking forward each month to her social security check, "and Carl takes out a fifty-dollar bill and says, 'Ralph, take this to her as a remembrance.'" Newman says this has happened time and again in other instances and for other remembrances.

But his most extensive generosity is the hand of fellowship he extends to writers, new and established, whom he likes. His system is to buy anywhere from twenty to one hundred copies of a new book and ship them to friends. He follows this system with the writings of John Steinbeck, Justice William O. Douglas, Adlai Stevenson, General S. L. A. Marshall, Jessamyn West ("she's in the Thoreau tradition"), Admiral Hyman Rickover ("one of

America's most valuable men"), Ralph McGill, Archibald Mac-
Leish, Mark Van Doren, and the Chicago columnist Leo Lerner
(whose book contained a satire on Senator McCarthy Sandburg
liked).

If you look in the closets and other dark places of Connemara,
you will find stacks of books by many authors (the books of the
late Raymond Clapper, Nathan Leopold's memoirs, and other
volumes), leftovers after Carl had shipped out quantities to his
friends.

Mrs. Sandburg manages all the family finances. She keeps the
books, plans the budgets, and files the income-tax returns.

Carl has managed in recent years to get himself a telephone
credit card, an air travel card, and hotel credit cards, so that he
has reduced to a bare minimum the annoyance of handling any
money at all.

When he goes out to make a speech, he'll put on a white shirt
and his usual bow tie and Sunday suit, but when he is home he
wears old pants and a lumberjack shirt, his favorite costume. He
cannot get himself to throw anything away, including several
pairs of shoes ranging in age from ten to thirty years.

He calls his throat the voice box and has all sorts of mufflers
that he wraps around his neck when he goes out of the house to
take his evening walks. Of recent years he has grown accustomed
to having a blanket over his knees as he sits and writes or reads.
At eighty-three, if he has such a thing as an ailment of any kind,
perhaps his eyes are not as good as they were twenty years ago,
but he watches them carefully and rests them as often as possible. He has thirty or forty walking sticks, but for his long walks
along the mountain trails of Connemara he carries an ax and
chops away at branches and dead wood along the way.

The friends and tourists keep winding up that long trail from
the highway to the Connemara house. Sometimes he "can't see
anyone today," but on occasion Carl will sit and talk for an hour
or two with these strangers.

About a year or so ago a couple from Pennsylvania "dropped
in" on the way home from Florida. They talked, got their auto-
graphs, and as they were leaving the porch the woman impulsively
walked over to Carl and kissed him. The woman immediately

stepped back embarrassed and started to apologize to Paula, who laughed and said: "That's all right, he belongs to the world."

I have seen Carl go into a towering Viking rage if a letter or book has been misplaced. When Mrs. Sandburg or Margaret hands it to him, along with the evidence that it was exactly where he had hidden it himself, Carl always buries his face in his hands and they laugh with him as he says, "Please forgive me, please forgive me."

The second time I visited I brought along a camera seeking this opportunity to get a photograph of Sandburg and myself.

We took the usual walk down the mountain pathway at Connemara, Carl, Margaret, and I, and when we came to a clearing I handed the camera to Margaret and said, "Margaret, would you please take a picture of your father and me."

Carl smiled and leaned over to Margaret, took the camera from her, and said, "Margaret, we want *you* in the photograph, too. Would you please go and get your mother to snap us."

Unless there's a heavy rain or snow Carl, Paula, and Margaret take an evening walk. When I visit Connemara I join them. Janet, who helps her mother with the goat herd, keeps the regular hours of a farmer; she is at the barns at sunrise and usually says good-night after supper. The three Sandburgs walk a measured mile along the dark path, each one armed with a flashlight. The return is slower because it is uphill and they stop every few yards to look at the stars and talk. To avoid using the flashlight unless it is absolutely necessary, they always walk holding hands, "a good habit to get into," says Carl.

When Sandburg is home his laughter rings through the entire house; and when he is off on a trip, Mrs. Sandburg and the girls laugh at every letter he writes. Since they have three telephone extensions, all join in laughing during his daily telephone call.

"I'll be home in February," he wrote from Hollywood to Paula, "we'll take our walks again, holding hands."

Sand dunes and sapphire hills

The Sandburgs lived at 331 South York Street, Elmhurst, Illinois, from 1919 to 1928. The main part of this home, which the Sandburgs called "Happiness House," had been built in 1857 and was one of the oldest buildings in that Chicago suburb. While he lived there Carl worked for the *Day Book* and the Chicago *Daily News*. At Elmhurst Carl wrote many of his poems, the *Rootabaga* stories, and most of *Abraham Lincoln: The Prairie Years*.

In the twenties the Chicago suburbs expanded. Carl and his family had enjoyed isolation granted by unpaved roads, privacy insured by trees, and rustic beauty of pastures stretching behind the house. Carl often propped himself against the old barn to read or write.

Roads, sewers, and electric lights came; soon the barn was gone and a housing development mushroomed in its place; folks kept coming by the thousands from the big city. It was time for Carl and Paula and the three girls, Margaret, Janet, and Helga, to move on.

Carl had known the sand dune country on Lake Michigan where he loved to walk the long stretches of white soft sand on the Michigan side. After discussing it with Paula, Carl took the money from the *Pictorial Review* serial sale for the rights to *The Prairie Years* and the first royalties paid by Harcourt, Brace and bought a cottage at Harbert, Michigan, where the Sandburgs had spent summers. Harbert was a prosperous summer resort with cottages bordering along the lake, but the Sandburgs had decided to make it their home. They began to build a year-round residence.

Most important were Carl's workrooms. A large study was designed for the upstairs section of the house opening on a sun deck. Carl always had the idea of the self-sustaining home and the success of his books did not change his thinking. He had watched his father become a carpenter and a bricklayer and do everything around the house, and he had been raised on the folklore that a farmer can never starve. During the great depressions of the 1890s and the early 1900s the young boys, the sons of immigrants, kept telling this to themselves. The farmer can never starve. He can live on what he raises. He is his own boss. And he can never be fired from his job. He is independent.

As soon as they had settled at Harbert, Sandburg began writing *The War Years*. There was a barn on the property which soon became one of the great Lincoln libraries in the country. Around its walls were piled biographies of men prominent in the administration, war diaries, histories, archives. Part of this library was dispersed when Sandburg finished the four volumes because he lent them to other Lincoln students, and, as he says, he needed the space for other topics more current.

In the early 1940s the Sandburgs began to think about moving on. They wanted an area with less winter and a place more suitable for their expanding goat herd.

After the outbreak of the war in 1941 they knew that they could not make a move, but kept it in mind. In 1943 Mrs. Sandburg, Helga, and the late Mrs. Steichen took a trip South. They had decided that they could not live on the West Coast because Carl's work, his friends, his publisher, and his attention were drawn to the East. They would have to settle somewhere along the Appalachian range between Virginia and Florida. On this long trip the three women journeyed from Michigan down through Virginia, through Tennessee and the Carolinas.

When they came to the mountains of North Carolina, Paula said she felt like Brigham Young, the Mormon leader, coming to the Salt Lake Valley saying, "This is the place." A real-estate agent showed them several places and one of them was Connemara Farm located in Flat Rock, in western North Carolina, a few miles south of Hendersonville and twenty miles south of Asheville, 2,300 feet above sea level.

From the porch of the house you can see the Appalachian Range of the Great Smokies, and bordering on the Sandburg property is Big Glassy—a smooth upward slope rising perpendicularly five hundred feet.

The house itself is the typical Southern house of the early nineteenth century: two stories and an attic—and a large ground floor.

Connemara was originally named "Rock Hill" by Christopher G. Memminger, later Confederate Secretary of Treasury, who purchased the land and built the home in 1838. It was to Rock Hill, sheltered by the watchful mountain crags, that Memminger fled for refuge during the last tumultuous days of the Confederacy. "Rock Hill" was changed to "Connemara" by Captain Ellington Adger Smythe, from whose estate the Sandburgs bought the 240-acre farm.

When Paula explained what she had seen to Carl, he told her, "It was I who had picked the dunes and now you shall pick the next place: I leave it entirely to you."

Paula insisted Carl come to North Carolina. When he stood on the porch, looking at the sapphire hills, Carl, too, said, "This is the place."

It is a place of such haunting beauty that there are days he stuffs wrapped sandwiches in his pocket and disappears into the woods to experience silence and loneliness—and wonder.

The Sandburgs purchased Connemara. Right after the war, in 1945, the Sandburgs began their move from Harbert to North Carolina, shipping the goats by express, and because of the shortage of materials, shipping all their bookcases and as much lumber as they could.

The family's move to North Carolina was the first break with Chicago. Even on the sand dunes of Lake Michigan Carl was still part of the Chicago scene, but when he left, Robert M. Hutchins, then President of the University of Chicago, wrote, "When Carl Sandburg left Chicago, the city became intolerable."

I first met Carl at Connemara in 1948 when I went with other newspapermen for an interview and to escort him to a speech and guitar session at Davidson College, the famous Presbyterian school a few miles from Charlotte.

I did not tell Carl I had read *Chicago Poems* when I was a kid in public school on the Lower East Side of New York. I felt everybody tells him a similar story. But I had joined the Socialist Club at the University Settlement House in those days and a famous Socialist leader by the name of Algernon Lee (who later became head of the Rand School) read the poems to us. It was part of our course in Socialism.

When I stood alone with Carl on his porch at Connemara and looked over this wonderful sight and the beautiful old building, I said to him, "Victor Berger would turn over in his grave if he saw this."

Carl threw his head back and roared in laughter and yelled in through the screen door to his wife, "Paula, Paula, he says Victor Berger would turn over in his grave if he saw this place."

We became close friends that afternoon.

Goat's milk every day

There's a "poet," a retired Boston builder, who lives in Hendersonville and drinks goat's milk like mad. He drinks goat's milk for no other reason than to be able to visit Connemara to buy his supply. He hopes eventually to see Carl Sandburg so he can show him his verse. Goat's milk?, he hates the stuff.

The books at Connemara

The books keep piling up. Friends and authors and publishers send Carl books hoping he will have a comment to make.

Newspapermen and writers he's known during the last sixty years send him books as fast as they come off the press and Carl reads many of them and "dips" into the rest.

Like other men who've spent a lifetime reading, he can dip into a book and get a quick idea of what the writer has to say. He marks passages that interest him with paper bookmarks which he always has at hand cut from newspapers into strips a half-inch wide and about eight inches long.

You go through Carl's books and you'll see hundreds and hundreds of volumes with paper bookmarks bristling, many of them faded now after the years.

Doing research on Carl Sandburg becomes a comparatively simple matter. You gather up his books and just turn to the pages he marked off and read what interested him. Often you see a comment in the margin and nearly always a pencil marking of a paragraph which struck his fancy. And here and there the word "good" or "great."

Thousands of books are stacked on shelves in every room from the ground floor to the attic. While there is no system of any kind and the books are not alphabetized, there is some form to their arrangement.

On the ground floor are shelves filled with books on labor, trade unionism, novels, essays, and biographies. Upstairs, poetry, criticism, belles-lettres. And everywhere American history.

In all the rooms on the main floor, except the kitchen, the books reach to the ceiling. In Carl's study are shelves of all his writings—his twenty-nine books and their translations into a dozen foreign languages. Here also are shelves of books on the folk music of America, the books used in researching *The American Songbag*.

"Why don't you put all the Emerson books together?" his family asks.

"I want Emerson in every room. I know exactly where to lay my hand on anything I want," says Carl.

Paula, Margaret, and Janet laugh.

The tables in every room are loaded with books. While he's away, dozens of packages from publishers are left unopened. And always on the table near the door are the stacks of the telltale brown envelopes from the high schools, with their forty or fifty essays on "Grass," "Fog," or on "Carl Sandburg."

Nearly every day while he's home Carl will winnow books from the shelves in his study and on the main floor. If he places the book on the second step leading up to the bedrooms, the book is to be stored on the shelves on the ground floor; if he places the book on top of a dresser in the hallway, it means the book goes upstairs out of the way. Upstairs there are four rooms and a large center hall, and in every one book shelves cover the walls up to the ceiling.

Finally, there is an oversize carpetbag someone gave Carl as a souvenir. Into the carpetbag goes a special book once in a while, a manuscript, a set of galley proofs, or a letter. At times the carpetbag is emptied, the material sent to a bank vault.

Carl has learned to saunter

I felt better when I learned everybody else complained they could not keep up with Carl's endurance in walking—Robert Sherwood, Ed Murrow, that fine actress with the delightful figure Arlene Francis, all gave up after the first go-round. Like Thoreau, Carl has a genius for walking. The secret is his saunter. Sandburg knows how to pace it. Thoreau first wrote about the saunter, a word which comes from the French. In the Middle Ages thousands of people roamed the countryside asking for charity under the pretenses of going on a crusade, "à la Sainte Terre" (to the Holy Land). And so when the children saw another beggar coming along, they yelled, "Here comes another Sainte Terrer."

Sandburg spends a half-hour starting the day with a series of calisthenic exercises adapted from various systems. He may use one of the heavy porch chairs, which he slowly lifts above his head and just as slowly returns it to the floor. This is repeated six times. This conditioning makes him a champion saunterer.

Robert Sherwood has written an essay about a walk with Carl:

> The walk had been conducted in almost total silence when I heard Carl start talking in his wonderful, measured tones, in which there was not the slightest evidence of breathlessness . . . He was discussing the subject of life after death . . . "On that assumption," he said, "let us suppose that the immortal spirit of Abraham Lincoln is hovering over the two of us . . ."
>
> We continued for a while in silence and then I asked, "Still assuming that the immortal spirit of Abraham Lincoln is hovering over us, what do you think he would say to the proposition that you and I stop in some place and have a drink? . . ."
>
> Carl Sandburg weighed this proposition . . . "I think he would approve."

For a man who walks so fast, he is unhurried in other ways. He spent five years writing *Remembrance Rock*. A Californian sent him a manuscript for appraisal and received no answer for six months. The man wrote to inquire and still no answer. A half-year later he sent another letter, enclosing a stamped self-addressed envelope. No answer. Two years went by without reply. The final letter from the Californian was sent to the postmaster at Flat Rock, asking him to please place the enclosed letter in Mr. Sandburg's hand. The postmaster delivered it and waited until Sandburg had read it.

"Well, I guess we'll just have to send this young man's work back to him," said the poet to the postmaster, "I guess he's in too much of a hurry."

Carl doesn't come down from his bedroom until noon and he is wide awake and full of pep at two A.M. This makes it a little tough on us early risers.

He paces himself like an athlete. He has stamina. It seems to me that his grip in 1961 at the age of eighty-three is as strong and firm as it was in 1948 when I first met him.

When you invite him to lunch or dinner at a fancy hotel, he will say, "Don't you think we will be served quicker at the coffee shop?"

After a while you learn that Carl is seeking his own comfort, and his own comfort is to be in a hamburger joint frequented by truck drivers; but when he wants real gentility, he goes to the counter of the hotel coffee shop or bar.

"The luncheonette for me is a warm and human place," he says, "the dining room of a hotel is a place of loneliness and excessive cleanliness."

He is a restrained eater. His plate is never loaded. Though he likes simple food, he can become ecstatic over a new culinary adventure.

For breakfast Carl has orange juice and then a glass of goat's milk. He eats a luncheon of vegetables and fruit which vary according to the time of the year. He has meat once a day for dinner. The Sandburgs put to pasture one or two steers a year, slaughter them, and use them for meat.

Sandburg gave up smoking in 1956. He had smoked cigars for

nearly a half century, although in the early days he smoked a ciga-rette now and then. He liked his cigars long and thin and he al-ways cut them in half with great care. One half he put in his pocket and smoked the other. I never met anyone anywhere in the world who ever smoked a cigar down as completely as Carl Sandburg did eight or ten times a day. At the last puff you could hardly tell that there was a cigar between his lips.

For a year or so after giving up his cigars he chewed licorice, and gave that up when he convinced himself that the tobacco cure was complete. But he still retains an affection for cigars. He takes those that are given to him and saves them for me. Often, after a long trip he brings out six or seven cigars and counts them off; "this is Milton Berle's, this is the University of Missouri's dinner," and so forth. (About a year ago Carl did go back to smoking, but he insists that he has won the battle since he carefully restricts himself to one half cigar every twenty-four hours.)

The penknife has also played an important role in Carl's life. He has penknives all over the house and carries at least two of them with him wherever he goes. When he sets up in some home or in a hotel as an overnight guest, the penknife goes out on the night table beside him.

Over the years he's developed a habit of looking into the win-dows of pawnshops always looking for interesting penknives.

I was with him in Hollywood and we were sitting around the hotel room talking about this and that when he took out a new penknife, held it in the palm of his hand, and said, "Fifty cents."

I've given some thought to Carl Sandburg's love for the pen-knife; how he opens his mail with it and otherwise handles the little knife at every other possible opportunity. The original jack-knife must have been a great comfort to the pioneer and I be-lieve it is a peculiarly American invention, probably our very first gadget.

Mail

Carl has his own system for answering the two hundred to four hundred letters he receives every week. In recent years there has been a large volume of mail during the first part of January when the press marks his birthday on January 6.

When I said Carl rarely throws anything away, including shoes and trousers, this also goes for the packing cases and cartons which arrive from publishers. He uses these for a filing system to keep track of his mail. The boxes are marked "F" (friendship or fan letters), "No reply needed," "Later," "Hi fi" (to be looked over and answered).

Sandburg knows that hundreds of people who write to him, particularly high school and college students, are after his signature —an autograph. He generously answers all this mail. It is usually gathered by a secretary, who comes in and works four or five days every month, and Carl sends off a little note, a line or two, thanking the writer for his good wishes or for fellowship and perhaps a greeting such as "May luck stars guide you," followed by "Carl Sandburg."

In answer to inquiries and requests for advice from budding writers and students, Carl replies: "Specific advice on writing is worth very little. A fellow does the best that he can."

To lengthy letters from people who pour out their hearts telling him of their experiences or what his books have meant, or who even enter into a discussion or take issue with him on some point in his Lincoln, Carl responds, "Your letter is worth saving." But occasionally he will answer a question when he deems it pertinent.

In reply to the many Lincoln letters asking for further information or clarification, Carl writes: "Please look in the Index."

In answer to "hate" letters or those of strong criticism, Carl sends a form:

> Dear Mrs. Jones:
>> Thank you for your letter.
>> I shall try to do better.

Goat's milk—straight

The second time I visited Carl I brought him a bottle of whiskey.

I wrote about that visit in *The Carolina Israelite* and there's a chapter on it in my book *Only in America*. I told about the bottle of whiskey and now everybody who visits him brings him a bottle of whiskey.

When I say everybody I do not mean tourists on the way from Florida to New York who stop off to wave, or the high school kids. I refer to the newspapermen and the interviewers and television crews. Carl greets his guests and stands the bottle on the table in front of him. He proceeds to chat while everybody looks at that bottle which remains tightly sealed. Finally Carl will call out either to Mrs. Sandburg or Margaret, "Bring us three glasses—I'm sure these gentlemen would like some *good delicious* goat's milk."

The first reaction is your stomach will turn; but after you drink it, you realize goat's milk doesn't taste too different from cow's milk. As a matter of fact, it tastes better.

I became a goat's milk man after spending time at the Sandburgs'. I haven't been home for any long stretches in the last few years to order it regularly but I manage a bottle now and then around the country.

It was while at Harbert the Sandburgs established their goat farm. The inspiration came when their daughter Helga wanted to be a farmer and asked for a cow. Carl suggested a goat and the family has had a herd ever since.

Goats, according to Carl, have many virtues: intelligence, friendliness, frugality; moreover they provide the family table with milk, butter, cheese, and meat; thus if it came to the worst, the Sandburg family with their goat herd could forever be self-sustaining.

Paula, like her brother, Ed Steichen, is a geneticist, a breeder who knows genes and chromosomes. She breeds for high milk production and has produced Jenifer II, the North American champion who in ten months of the year 1960 produced 5,750 pounds of milk. "Each week she gave nearly her own weight in milk," says Paula.

Equally important, Paula breeds for looks and beauty. The most beautiful goat in the Sandburg herd today is a Nubian with long ears, a coat of tan with splashes and dots of white, and here and there a tint of burnt wood and umber.

Early in 1961 this doe, named Brocade, dropped four kids, each as lovely as the mother. "These four beautiful kids," says Paula, "are the result of inbreeding. The father of the sweet new arrivals is a son of Brocade."

Today the fine herds of Nubians and Toggenburgs furnish ample milk, cheese, and butter for the family with enough left over to supply a dairy at nearby Hendersonville, and Paula has long been a director and vice-president of the American Milk Goat Record Association.

One of these occasions when goat's milk was ordered for the guests while the bottle of whiskey stood majestically unopened on the table involved the Edward R. Murrow television crew. They had all been trained to use the sonorous tone Ed Murrow reserves for the word "*This* . . ." (as in "*This* is London. . . ."), and so each of the staff members said in turn, "*This* is superb, *this* is great, *this* is magnificent"—meaning the goat's milk, of course.

Carl Sandburg looked them all over, his eyes growing smaller all the while—a look that usually goes right through you. After a while he said slowly: "You remind me of the reporter on the Louisville *Courier* walking down the streets of town early one morning with that thick edition of the Sunday *New York Times* under his arm, saying over and over to himself: 'I'll read this sonofabitch paper if it kills me!!'"

That unopened bottle of whiskey which Carl left standing in sight of Ed Murrow's television people may have had its origin during a visit when Sandburg himself was the victim. Adlai Stevenson tells us the story in the "Tribute to Carl Sandburg" (*Journal of the Illinois State Historical Society*, Winter, 1952):

In the long trek that Carl Sandburg made in gathering material for his *Prairie Years*, I well recall his stopover in Bloomington, where he interviewed my father, Lewis Green Stevenson. Among others whom he wished especially to meet in Bloomington was ex-Governor Joseph W. Fifer, who bore —and not without some pride—the nickname "Private Joe," because of gallant but unpretending service in the Civil War. Joe Fifer loved good whiskey, and, having arranged a meeting with him, my father went to the cellar and brought up a pint of red Bourbon, which he had kept under lock and key for many years.

Armed with the whiskey, Carl and my father set forth for Governor Fifer's, confident that it would stir his recollections, and assured that he would share it with them. Sight of the whiskey added to the warmth of Fifer's greeting, but when Father presented him with the bottle, he placed it, uncorked, on his desk, where Father and Sandburg cast frustrated glances at it throughout the interview.

While we're through for the moment talking about goat's milk and whiskey, I believe it is worth adding a few sentences of Ambassador Stevenson's recollection:

> My acquaintance with Carl Sandburg now extends through many years. Among my most pleasant recollections are parties in Chicago in the twenties and thirties when I listened to him sing to the inimitable accompaniment of his guitar, and happy evenings with him, and the late Lloyd Lewis, where anecdotes, Lincoln, and music took us far into the night.

Carl's affection for Adlai Stevenson is part of the love he has for the State of Illinois: "I rejoice in its democratic spirit . . . that its three great Governors were of the Catholic, Jewish, and Protestant faiths, Altgeld, Horner, and Stevenson, in order of their service."

At Adlai Stevenson's inauguration as Governor of Illinois in 1948, Sandburg gave a fifteen-minute speech before the inaugural address: "I am one of the host that love Adlai with a respect bordering on reverence." Two years later, and long before Governor Stevenson became known to the general public outside of Illinois, Carl wrote: "History will remember this Adlai Stevenson."

One secretary he would like to outlive

The name of the library at Asheville, North Carolina, is Pack Memorial Public Library and I'm afraid the word "memorial" confused one of the secretaries to the late Senator Tom Connally of Texas, Chairman of the Committee on Foreign Relations and a stalwart champion of the Roosevelt era and the United Nations.

Pack Memorial Library at Asheville, in celebrating the arrival of Carl Sandburg and his family to Connemara Farm, decided to hold an exhibit of all of Carl's works and works about him.

Miss Margaret H. Ligon of the library conducted a vast correspondence with friends of Carl throughout the country as well as leading figures in the political and cultural life of the country in which she requested an expression of their esteem or idea of the white-haired poet.

January 19, 1951

My dear Sirs:

The entire nation mourns the recent passing of our beloved poet, Carl Sandburg, who illuminated for us the rich heritage of our American past and the living spirit of freedom which sets our people apart in the world.

While no words of mine can add lustre to his immortal fame, I am glad to join with you people of Asheville, North Carolina, in paying personal tribute to your late neighbor and friend, Carl Sandburg, both for his genius as a writer and for his warm humanity as a man.

Sincerely,
/s/ Tom Connally

The public mourning of the Senator as expressed by his secretary was news to Carl.

All the other one hundred and fifty-two letters sent to Miss Ligon, however, were in a more joyous mood.

Eric Sevareid wrote, "I want to say that Carl is the strongest and most enduring force in American letters today." And from George Jean Nathan, "This Carl is a great and noble soul, and I am proud to call him friend." Brooks Atkinson—but a single line, "Carl Sandburg—Yes." And from Edward R. Murrow, "I have, by accident and design, had occasion over the last twenty years to meet a not inconsiderable number of men whose names make headlines, as well as a few scholars and writers. It is part of a reporter's duty to be no man's disciple and to inoculate himself frequently against the disease known as hero-worship. So far as Sandburg is concerned I am a disciple with the disease and regard my lot as most fortunate."

James Thurber, "Carl may seem as easy to describe as a face carved on a mountain, but there are vast and complex reaches between the cat feet of 'Fog' and *Remembrance Rock*."

Sad beyond words

I have often thought that Carl is one of the kindest men I've ever known. The only sign of hatred I have seen or heard him express is directed at anti-Semites and racial segregationists.

When the Associated Press carried his statement on December 29, 1958, after the arrest of several swastika painters in Cologne, Germany, "I believe that every swastika painter deserves the death penalty," liberals accused Sandburg of compromising his stand against capital punishment. The statement annoyed some of his closest friends, others saying, "Shoot to kill."

Most of the Gentile liberals I have met stand on their detestation of all prejudice and let it go at that. For Carl Sandburg the fight against anti-Semitism and Negrophobia has been a special project. He admits to me anti-Semitism has puzzled him as much as it angers him. "I came across anti-Semitism in the union halls among my fellow Socialists, and I've heard it among the I.W.W.'s, and I've had it expressed to me by some of my dearest friends, and I find it sad beyond words, beyond words."

In answer to the rash of criticism his public statement provoked Sandburg answered the question was he serious about the swastika painters with:

"Yes. The swastika stands not for the murder of an individual or for a few individuals but for the death of a race. It is the symbol of race murder; it is the ghastliest graphic symbol in the story of mankind."

"Biographer of a photographer" is a test of sobriety

"Now," said Carl, handing me a large folder, "you have to put this essay I've written in your book. It is about my brother-in-law, Ed Steichen."

"Carl," I said, trying to avoid the proffered typescript, "how can I put in my book a whole section by you about somebody else? The book is about Carl Sandburg."

"It is a must," said Carl. "Edward Steichen is one of the great influences in my life. We have to tell the people something about him."

"Important people have to speak for themselves sometimes," I answered.

Carl's expression changed. "Harry, I'm an old man. I have always wanted to write *in extenso* about this wonderful artist and American. If you don't give me the chance, I'll never get it written."

I took the typescript. Carl had that glint of mischief in his eye. But I have to admit he is right.

It has always been my belief that we each live by and for each other. This was confirmed to me when, as a schoolboy, I read *Robinson Crusoe*. Later I realized that there would have been no story at all without Good Man Friday.

Carl wrote:

> I have known Edward Steichen now for fifty-three years. There can be no such thing as measuring the depth of his influence on my life. Like his sister whom I married he has a mind definitely superior to mine in several areas.
>
> He has been rated by good authorities as "the world's greatest photographer." For those who wish to read of his life up through the year 1929 I can refer them to a book by me titled *Steichen the Photographer* published in that year. I could make a list of scores of photographs by Steichen each and every one a poem, a document or a vivid high moment. Often when a news photographer is shooting me I ask him, "Do you realize that you are photographing America's first

biographer of a photographer?" Sometimes I add, "If you can say distinctly 'biographer of a photographer' you are definitely sober."

A nice little volume could be written about Steichen as a plant breeder and geneticist. His first garden experiments were in the village of Voulangis near Paris. He was 3 years President of the American Delphinium Society. He put on an exhibition at the Museum of Modern Art of delphiniums that represented a creative mind producing new delphinium forms.

Since my 1929 biography, Steichen has gone on with vivid and forthright living. He had come out of World War I with the rank of Colonel, directing a thousand photographers and as a close friend of Billy Mitchell he testified at the trial of Mitchell, holding to Mitchell's viewpoint.

Came 1941, Pearl Harbor, and America entered World War II. Steichen, 62 years of age, plowed under 100,000 delphinium plants, went to Washington and with the approval of Admirals A. W. Radford and Felix Stump entered the Navy as a Lieutenant-Commander directing some 4,000 photographers in the Pacific. Two years later when he was 64 he was automatically retired and two weeks later re-enlisted for the duration.

I am going into all of this about Steichen because in a definite way he embodies the American Dream. Property is nothing. Toils, hardships, and dangers are little or nothing to him alongside of the American Dream. He is no particular hand at patriotic speeches but he has some mystic concept of this country and its flag. What he said to the photographers in his command always had the suggestion or instruction, "Get faces! Get the men's faces!" He came out of the war with the rank of Captain; the United States Senate has voted him an Admiral and the House has yet to vote on it.

The United States Department of State has shown Steichen's photographic exhibit *The Family of Man* to more than 6,000,000 people over the earth and the book made from it has sold somewhat over 2,000,000 copies. One peculiar feature of the exhibition is that it has meanings for the illiterate, for those who can't read or write. On the second day of the exhibition as part of the American exposition in Moscow in the summer of 1959, a reporter on Radio Moscow said, "*The Family of Man* seemed to draw a larger attendance than any other exhibition. Many of those who went in to view it came out saying it was like they had seen people rather than pictures." The Department of State reported that in the city of Guatemala on a Sunday afternoon ending 6 weeks of the exhibition more than a thousand barefoot, illiterate Indians came down from the hills "to see people and not pictures."

Harry, I conceived the biography of Steichen, the only one of him ever done, that came out in 1929 . . . I have an idea I'll never be able to do a biography that will carry on from the 1929 biography.

I have other books in the going that I hope to finish. I cannot pause for a continuation of the 1929 biography and because Steichen has been so tremendous an influence on my life and because he embodies the American Dream in so graphic a way, this perhaps of importance in the present hour of American history, I must report to you, Harry, that this chapter which has the best part of it written by Steichen, belongs in your book. If you call this ungracious interference I will knock the hat off your head. You and I know well enough that Henry Wadsworth Longfellow wrote "Life is short and time is fleeting." It will be a dark day when our fellowship goes bust.

And what does Edward Steichen think of Carl Sandburg? At the 75th anniversary dinner in Chicago in 1953 Steichen introduced his brother-in-law: "On the day that God made Carl He didn't do anything else that day but sit around and feel good."

PART 4

From Each According To His Ability To Each According To His Work

Passion, poetry, and politics

Lucy Robbins Lang, for many years private secretary to the late Samuel Gompers, told me that the early organizers of the American Federation of Labor carried *Chicago Poems* in their kits: "At nearly every organizing meeting we had group singing followed by a reading of one of Sandburg's poems."

As I made note of this conversation in the Beverly Hills home of my friends Harry and Lucy Lang, I thought of an idea Thomas Hardy had noted in his Journal (1896): "If Galileo had said in verse that the world moved, the Inquisition might have let him alone."

Fred Beal, who attempted to organize the cotton mills of Gastonia, North Carolina, in the late 1920s, reprinted Sandburg's poem "Mill-Doors" on the back of the member application cards:

> You never come back.
> I say good-by when I see you going in the doors,
> The hopeless open doors that call and wait
> And take you then for—how many cents a day?
> How many cents for the sleepy eyes and fingers?
>
> I say good-by because I know they tap your wrists,
> In the dark, in the silence, day by day,
> And all the blood of you drop by drop,
> And you are old before you are young.
> You never come back.

No reactionaries or radicals were ever as successful as Sandburg and his contemporaries. Elsewhere in history, radicals and reactionaries have achieved great power, but by and large the society they wrought was no real improvement over the one they abolished, considered in terms of everyday living. Armies may have been stronger, industry established, and new systems of jurisprudence introduced. But rather than alleviate the troubles of the common man they have intensified misery.

The radicals who organized and propelled the labor movement which began in America in 1880 and continues, in fact, to the present, not only saw to it that the worker got his fair share of the pie, but they made it a bigger pie.

Sandburg was the first American poet able to use and exploit slang in his diction. He was the first poet to incorporate concrete political and social images into his poems; both radical innovations.

His most noted works, *The Prairie Years* and *The War Years*, the biography of Lincoln, were also radical. For the truth is that with the exception of Lincoln's own writings, the Civil War did not produce a great literature. It was not until Stephen Crane published *The Red Badge of Courage*, Stephen Vincent Benét his *John Brown's Body*, and Sandburg his six volumes totaling over a million words on Lincoln that a substantial literature about the Civil War existed. That Sandburg made literature from the Civil War is also a radical vision.

A Socialist organizer

Carl Sandburg went into the Social Democratic movement in Wisconsin because, he says, it had a dream and he wanted a share of that dream. He became one of the party organizers and traveled throughout the State making speeches and soliciting memberships.

He earned an average of twenty-five dollars a month, but he was not on a payroll. He came into a Wisconsin town by appointment and received room and board at the home of the local Social Democratic leader, who would do the promotion and hire a hall. After Carl's lecture, to which anyone was admitted free, followed by the pitch for new members, the host would explain that the Party had no funds with which to pay their organizers and that he would now pass the hat. Into the hat came quarters, dimes, and an occasional half dollar. These collections were the main source of Carl's income during the years 1907 to 1909— which included nearly two years of married life.

Carl also earned about six or seven dollars a month from the sale of his pamphlets and occasionally an extra ten dollars for an article in *La Follette's Weekly*.

The requests for literary lectures had already begun, and as early as 1908 Carl gave lectures in Michigan, Wisconsin, Illinois, and Pennsylvania. His lecture was "Walt Whitman, An American Vagabond." After one of these meetings before a group of workers in Pennsylvania, a miner shouted, "Hoorah for Walt Whitman!"

On his organizing trips in Wisconsin, he would wear white shirts with the stiff detachable collar. In the summer, he would tuck in the collar band, thus anticipating the sports shirt that came along forty years later. Just before departing, Carl would hand over to his hostess a shirt, a pair of socks, and two white handkerchiefs for her to launder. On the next trip, he would pick them up. Wherever he went, he found laundry waiting for him. Thus, he had to carry no baggage—only the pamphlets and the membership applications, and of course his Shakespeare, Whitman, and Emerson.

And what did Carl Sandburg, the Social Democratic organizer of 1907–1909 tell his audiences in those days? Read the speeches today and they sound vaguely familiar; not only because of the famous Fireside Chats of the late Franklin D. Roosevelt, but also because we remember the more recent speeches of conservative Republicans like Dwight D. Eisenhower and Richard M. Nixon.

Here was the Sandburg pitch to get new members into the Social Democratic Party: "Labor is beginning to realize its power. We no longer beg, we demand old-age pensions; we demand a minimum wage; we demand industrial accident insurance; we demand unemployment insurance; and we demand the eight-hour day which must become the basic law of the land."

Millions and more millions

"Quite an argument could be made out that Jim Hill who was a millionaire was a reformer," says Sandburg. "He was a railroad builder in territory that never had a railroad. But Jay Gould, Jim Fiske, and Averill Harriman's father—they were gamblers, speculators. The Socialists of my day saw this very clearly and we tried to get this idea across in simple language. As the years go by and the longer I live, the more I feel sorry for those who have a few millions and gotta have more millions."

"When the wedding din subsides organizer takes collection"

A faded clipping from the Chicago *Daily Socialist*, July 7, 1908:

"Menominee Springs, Wis., July 6—There was a 'charivari' the other night at a farm house near this town, where Charles Sandburg, one of the organizers for the Social Democratic Party of Wisconsin is living with his bride, who till a week or so ago was Miss Lilian Steichen. According to custom the young men of the neighborhood, all farmers and 'hired men,' gathered at night with all the cowbells, horns, tin cans, and the like they could get hold of and made night hideous with discord. They wanted the bridegroom to hand out money for beer and cigars. Instead of paying the required tribute Sandburg made a Socialist speech and took up a collection for the party.

"Shortly after the din started, two of the huskiest young farmers went to the door and demanded that Sandburg come out and 'set 'em up' to the crowd.

"A motley chorus greeted him when he appeared. Tin horns and cowbells were used with the utmost efficiency. There was a hush of expectation when Sandburg put his hands in his pockets and stood facing the crowd.

" 'Boys,' he began.

" 'Hurrah!' came a cry from the crowd. 'We'll have a drink on that!'

" 'You work hard all your lives,' resumed Sandburg.

" 'That's why we're dry,' shouted a voice from the crowd.

" 'How about those cigars, Charlie?' cried a friend.

" 'We Social Democrats are fighting for a better system. If I had a million dollars—'

"Cries of 'We wish you had!'

"'I would not give you a cent for beer and cigars. A Social Democrat gives his money to the cause he is fighting for. The Social Democratic Party of Wisconsin has no traction companies to support it. A little from each man will help. We depend on the workingman for support.'

"Then he passed the hat. Some paid and others walked away. They gave one last grand chorus of noise—a sort of infernal finale—and then a cheer for the Social Democracy."

The Socialists and Buck Duke

Where would you look for the official papers of the American Socialist Party? At the Rand School, maybe? At the New School for Social Research? Or the New York Public Library? Or perhaps in the private library of Norman Thomas?

Not at all. The official papers of the American Socialist Party are in the library of Duke University, formerly Trinity College, at Durham, North Carolina, a university endowed with the millions of James B. Duke's tobacco fortune. Only a few steps from the depository of the Socialist Party papers stands the statue of a cigar-clenching Buck Duke, symbol of the big business buccaneers the Socialists fought. Buck lies buried only a few yards farther, in the Gothic splendor of the Duke Chapel, and you might think he'd turn over in his grave at such unseemly neighbors.

Yet both have an honorable place in the American picture, and it was the scholars at Duke University who shelled out the tobacco magnate's good money to buy up all the Socialist papers once they had been rescued from the incinerator by the well-known dealer in manuscripts, Leon Kramer.

The Socialist papers at Duke University include a complete set of the proceedings of the Unity Conference of 1901 when Eugene V. Debs and his Social Democrats merged with elements of the Socialist Labor Party to form the new Socialist Party of America.

Five volumes of transcript and notes record the trial of Victor Berger for obstructing the draft before the redoubtable Judge Kenesaw Mountain Landis in 1918. Victor Berger of Wisconsin was the first Socialist Congressman and the editor of the The

Leader of Milwaukee on which Carl Sandburg worked during his Wisconsin days, after having served in the office of Emil Seidel, Milwaukee's Socialist mayor from 1910 to 1912, as his secretary. Seidel was Debs's vice-presidential running mate in the national elections of 1912. The Debs-Seidel ticket polled almost 19 per cent of the popular vote (nearly 900,000 out of 17,500,000) but no electoral votes.

And what did the Socialists Seidel and Sandburg do when they finally won the control of the city of Milwaukee? The Socialist papers at Duke show drafts for legislative bills in those years: first, the establishment of wash-houses for workers; second, municipal building inspection; third, a series of bills to safeguard factory workers; and finally—free textbooks for the public schools.

Who now recalls the names with which this collection echoes? —William English Walling, Charles Edward Russell, William J. Ghent, Bernard Shaw, George D. Herron, Gustavus Myers, Winfield R. Gaylord, Robert Hunter, J. Stitt Wilson, Allen L. Benson, H. G. Wells, Upton Sinclair. These were some of the best-known Socialists (Carl and Paula Sandburg included) who left the party in 1917 because they wanted to support America's entry into the war, differing with Debs, Hillquit, and Berger.

Even though leaving the party, Upton Sinclair wrote an eight-page letter (in the Duke collection), to President Woodrow Wilson protesting the loss of civil liberties suffered by his old Socialist friends.

The Duke papers reflect the two phenomena which led to the decline of the American Socialist Party. World War I in 1917 split the Socialists and Franklin D. Roosevelt's New Deal in 1933 made their agitation useless. The papers also show the Socialist Party's chronic indebtedness.

In the boom year of 1929, the New York Socialists opened radio station WEVD but at the same time the national office had notes of $250 and $500 it couldn't pay.

Most of the papers resound with the names of Socialists and sympathizers who form an unforgettable part of the American story: Walter Lippmann, James H. Maurer, Theodore Debs, Seymour Stedman, Kate Richards O'Hare, Otto Branstetter, Daniel W. Hoan, J. Ramsay MacDonald, Morris Hillquit, Norman

Thomas, Clarence O. Senior, Kirby Page, Sherwood Eddy, A. J. Muste, Harry W. Laidler, Howard Kester, Louis Waldman.

A 1932 letter from Fannie Hurst says she has decided to cast her vote for Franklin D. Roosevelt reflecting the attitude of the vast majority of the Socialist remnant.

Buck Duke, whose money bought the Socialist papers, had his own ups and downs too—but mostly ups. He moved up to New York City in 1884 and opened a loft factory on Rivington Street on the Lower East Side. In that same year there was a murmur of protest from former Rivington Streeters who had removed to Durham, North Carolina, to work for Buck's father in the family tobacco factory.

It seems that the factory had recruited in New York some one hundred and twenty-five Jewish immigrants who were skilled cigarette rollers. Their gripe in 1884 was against machines that threatened to displace them, and two years later they all returned to New York. Today's scholars make a big *tsimmes* about this being North Carolina's first case of resistance to technological improvements. But it wasn't that simple. The late Bernard Harris (1866–1942), one of these cigarette rollers, said he and the other Jewish workers returned because they yearned for the big city anyway.

The Republicans had too much to lose

Abraham Lincoln: The Prairie Years did one thing for Sandburg that no amount of poetry or hard work or genius or kindness could ever do. It made him respectable to Republicans. After the book had been published William Randolph Hearst offered him a job for $30,000, and to Sandburg's immense amusement the Republican Party offered him an official invitation to be the main speaker at the Lincoln Dinner of the National Republican Club of New York City. Sandburg turned down the Republicans, but at the same time he did accept an invitation to read some poetry before the Phi Beta Kappa chapter of Harvard University. His reasoning was: "Harvard has more of a reputation to lose than I have, so I'll go."

A flag no longer waving

In the period before and during World War I, Sandburg came to prominence in the Socialist labor movement as one of the contributors to the *International Socialist Review*.

The *International Socialist Review* cost ten cents. It was edited by Charles H. Kerr and published monthly. Other contributors to the *Review* were Jack London, Eugene V. Debs, William D. Haywood, and Mary Harris Jones, known as "Mother" Jones.

Whole issues of the magazine, however, were often written solely by Jack London and Sandburg, each using a series of different names. Sandburg used three names—"Jack Phillips," Carl Sandburg (or sometimes "C.S."), and the signature "Militant."

The *Review* ran ads for a railroad-style pocket watch at ninety-eight cents; and, *"Red Hot:* If you want for self or friends a paper that combats *all* religious dogmas send fifty cents for each subscriber and get the hottest paper published. Don't delay, send today for the *Agnostic."* Other ads promised, "Tobacco habit, drink habit easily conquered." Still others, "Make your own liquor at home, let us show you how, we are expert distillers," and, of course, "Genuine rupture cure. Throw away your truss."

Do not think the magazine was without worth. It printed articles about the "German Workers' Strike of 1915," "Industry and Eastern Imperialism in Japan," "Birth Control," and "Guild Socialism," as well as some of Carl Sandburg's poems, "A Million Young Workmen" and "Billy Sunday."

The *International Socialist Review* did not hesitate in proclaiming its sympathies. The cover of the January 1916 issue shows workmen carrying aloft a red banner from which radiates light. One of Carl's most widely reprinted essays was on the *Eastland* disaster.

In the summer of 1915, the Western Electric Company in Chicago wanted to stage a celebration. It decided to have a parade of employees followed by a picnic up the Chicago River. It peremptorily ordered workers to buy tickets and wear white shoes and white hats. Afterward the workers boarded the picnic steamship

Eastland. There were two thousand five hundred men, women, and children who crowded up the gangplank, whereupon the old, unseaworthy *Eastland* toppled slowly in its dock and sank to the bottom of the river, with over one thousand men, women, and children below decks trapped—and drowned.

In his column "Lookin' 'Em Over," Carl Sandburg commented angrily about this tragedy. "In the second largest city in America a passenger steamship tied to the dock toppled to the river bottom like a dead jungle monster shot through the heart.

"The foregoing piece of news sent out to American cities one Saturday was at first not believed. It was the ghastliest commentary on American efficiency so far written in international history."

Directly responsible for the certification of the steamship was William C. Redfield, Secretary of Commerce, object of Sandburg's anger. "Why didn't Redfield coordinate the human units, the high-salaried bureau heads under him so as to stop a cranky unstable ancient hoo-doo-tub like the excursion boat *Eastland* from capsizing with twenty-five hundred human lives within a few hundred yards off shore, in plain view of parents and relatives of the children who were drowning?

"There's one answer," said Sandburg. "Business required it.

"Fathead Redfield sat in his easy chair in Washington chatting with businessmen on the beauties of efficiency, his ears deaf to Andy Furuseth of the Coast Seamen's Union and his ears deaf to Victor Olander of the Lake Seamen's Union, and his ears deaf to every plea for human safety and more social efficiency on the lake steamships."

Carl's commentary on the sinking of the *Eastland* was a direct emotional appeal, a polemic delivered without courtesy. It was inspired by the confusion between business efficiency and social efficiency, a confusion still benumbing minds in the 1960s.

Actually few of Carl's radical writings were inflammatory. In "Fixing the Pay of Railroad Men," which ran in the *International Socialist Review* in three parts, starting in April of 1915, Sandburg wrote: "It is conceded on both sides that the cost of the whole job (arbitrating the demands of the railroad unions), counting expenses for experts, investigators, lawyers, printing, and reports, travel and hotel money for both railroad companies and railroad Brotherhood men will run upwards of one million dollars, possibly above that amount."

Since the arbitration itself produced a total only of $1,020,498 for the men in pay raises, Sandburg's singsong specificity speaks for itself.

A cursory comparison of Sandburg's articles with those in contemporary "left of center" magazines reveals two extremes. Sandburg was much more direct, less humorous, more concerned with facts and sources. The *International Socialist Review* was a fully documented magazine.

In a careful check of Carl's writings for the *International Socialist Review*, it is clear that he held closely to the news events, often expanding on a story which he had written for Mr. Scripps' *Day Book*. It is clear from Carl's writings then, as across the years that followed, that he went along with the basic idea of his friend and teacher Philip Green Wright of Lombard College, that capitalism has the resiliency both to survive as an institution and add to the welfare of the people. The Socialists with whom he identified himself all through those years were the Wisconsin group of Social Democrats, the Fabians of England, the Christian Socialists of France, Germany, and Italy, and the trade-union Socialists of New York.

In all of Sandburg's early prose, dated as it seems now, there are poetic touches:

> It's a workingman's world. Shovels and shovelling take more time of soldiers than guns and shooting. Twenty-one million men on the battlefields of Europe are shovelling more than shooting. Not only have they dug hundreds of miles of trenches, but around and under the trenches are tunnels and labyrinthian catacombs. All dug by shovels. Technically, in social science and economics, the soldier is a parasite and a curious louse of the master-class imposed on the working class. Yet strictly now the soldier is a worker, a toiler on and under the land. He's a sucker, a shovelman who gets board and clothes from the government that called him to the colors. A mucker-gun-man—that's what a soldier is.

I think if you reread this you will see a rhythmic scheme barely evident. Some changes and a stanzaic arrangement would make this paragraph into a poem, not as good a poem, perhaps, as most Sandburg has written, but a poem nevertheless. Its language is earthy and simple and its repetitions effectively apply the principles of prosody.

The red flag that bedecked the cover of the *International Socialist Review* has been hauled down, hauled down by Socialists (or radicals) like Carl Sandburg who chose not to march under it after the Bolshevik revolution adopted it as its official banner. The Socialists of America never recovered from the schism produced by the wide-open split on the war against Germany, and when Franklin D. Roosevelt came along, those who had waved the flag had no more battlefields on which to plant it. The first hundred days of the New Deal effectively scattered the Socialist movement in America.

Do not let any name-callers confuse you. There was a time when the men who followed these American Socialists and trade unionists were heroes one and all, and the sweets the millions of Americans now enjoy come from the victories they won.

You and Your Job

"One reason I'm a Socialist," wrote Sandburg in 1908 in his pamphlet *You and Your Job*, "is because the Socialists were the first to fight to abolish child labor, and today the Socialist Party is the only one that has dared to declare in its platform that it is unalterably opposed to child labor, and that it will do all in its power to remove all conditions that make it possible for human beings anywhere to be underfed and overworked."

The pamphlet was published in Chicago by the Charles H. Kerr Company and is signed Charles Sandburg. On its cover it displays the emblem of the Socialist Party: a circle surrounding two right hands clasped in fellowship over a globe of the world with the legend below, "Workers of the World, Unite!"

The pamphlet cost five cents and, along with its price, displays a union label. On the back cover, a single advertisement offers for $2.50 ($1.50 down) thirteen additional pamphlets ranging from Jack London's *Revolution* to Marx's *Wage, Labor and Capital*, all of which were guaranteed to make any subscriber into a well-informed, articulate, and forceful Socialist soapboxer.

Reading Carl Sandburg's agitated pamphlet fifty years later, however, removes much of the terror such emblems, titles, and union seals were calculated to incite.

It is a matter of plain and fortunate history now that the Socialist Party of America was the only political party in the world which suffered by having its opponents steal its platforms and goals. Indeed it was not American capitalism which dissipated the Socialist appeal, it was Socialism itself. Its concentration on the rights of men and the virtues of human welfare were too powerful to be ignored.

"Part of the capitalist class has done worthy work," writes Sandburg. "John D. Rockefeller, J. Pierpont Morgan, Edward Harriman have brought together interests that were fighting each other. In doing this, these men have centralized industry and transportation so that when the people are ready to assume control of them and operate them for the benefit of all, they will be ready."

Even as a pamphleteer, Sandburg maintains a certain "aesthetic distance." The pamphlet is in the form of a letter to a friend and opens with the salutation, "Dear Bill." In the course of its twenty-eight pages, Sandburg reminds Bill of the time they played baseball together and of the time when their fathers were out of work.

The letter is written to correct a complaint Bill has offered in previous correspondence. Sometimes in the past, Bill condemned out of hand men who grumble because they are out of work. To this Sandburg replies that men are out of work more usually because the industrial system puts them out of work. Society, argues Sandburg to his mythical correspondent, is a collective organism, not a collection of atomic individuals. Unemployment is rarely a willful, individual perversion but a collective circumstance.

I know all about unemployment, says Sandburg. "I was up against it in 1897 when the capitalist newspapers were full of

'Business Resuming Its Stability, Reports of Great Gains in Trade.' It was a summer and the Chicago papers said $3 a day was being paid harvest hands in Kansas. On the bumpers of freight trains and the tops of passengers, I went West from Illinois, you remember. When I got to Kansas City, the wage for harvest hands was reported at $2.50 per day. Then every mile I travelled westward, the wages dropped. And when I got to Larned, Kansas, and took a job throwing wheat on the tables of a threshing machine, I was getting $1.25 a day and board. The job lasted three weeks. So I don't blame a mechanic who is used to life in the city, and has a wife and children to care for, if he fights shy of advertised farm work."

Sandburg's argument against the capitalist system was the same argument proposed by philosophers, sociologists, and even Republican Presidents like Theodore Roosevelt. It was that the competitive capitalistic system instead of stimulating new energies, drained all energies in a daily fight for simple existence. It had produced a widespread and depressing poverty, and a strong part of Sandburg's argument in this pamphlet was that this poverty had no beneficial effects. "I think it is true," he reasoned, "that the muscles we exercise are the ones that develop, and the man who has never wrestled with problems and difficulties has never known the joy of living. But over and along with this I place the proposition that a man will grow and develop in body and brain only when employed at work that will give him some high degree of pleasure. I believe in obstacles, but I say that a system such as the capitalist system, putting such obstacles as starvation, underfeeding, overwork, bad housing and perpetual uncertainty of work in the lives of human beings, is a pitiless, ignorant, blind, reckless, cruel mockery of a system."

His pamphlet offered a simple program to correct these evils: a constitutional process of reform. "Alone and apart, some of you Republicans, some Democrats and some Independents, you are divided and powerless. Working together, en masse, planning toward one end, you can send the man you choose up into the legislatures and the national Congress to write laws that will get you better working and living conditions right now."

The radical reforms these men were to write concerned higher wages and fewer hours, aid to the labor unions, government pensions for old and worn-out workers, sickness and accident insurance for workingmen, abolition of child labor, free textbooks for the public schools, and government guarantee that every man has a right to a job.

"If the capitalists will not provide, the Government must," concluded his peroration.

But in the past fifty years, the "Capitalists" did take warning. No one is sure yet whether the capitalistic system is a success and whether it will endure or not. But what success it has achieved, it owes really to its early critics, who in America were mostly Socialists and who came armed for battle with the vision that there was enough for all if some did not have too much.

You and Your Job is a lesson in American Socialism. For the reforms Socialism generated came not from the intellectuals here, as they did in Europe, but from the working classes, as once we were wont to say. The reason unions and legislators were able to gain these advances was because Socialist leaders, since the time of Daniel De Leon, were able to speak to the workingmen in a language easily understood. Americans never had much patience with the logical convolutions of dialectical materialism and the lessons in which history instructs. From the beginning, American Socialists saw that reform was work for politician and poet, and no one fitted this need better than the early, crusading Carl Sandburg.

The strong men keep coming on

In accepting the Albert Einstein Award at the Yeshiva College on April 16, 1956, Carl Sandburg talked of "America's fat-dripping prosperity."

> When the goal of a country is only happiness and comfort there is danger.
> Albert Einstein said as much . . . Why he sounds like an old Swede! Listen: "To make a goal of comfort or happiness has never appealed to me." You see, he wants us to have the elements of struggle in life . . .

All these things in the advertisements—anytime the main goal of life is to get them, so that they override your other motives, there's danger.

Before going to sleep, say to yourself, "I haven't reached my goal yet, whatever it is, and I'm going to be uncomfortable and in a degree unhappy until I do." When you reach it, find another . . .

Yet for all his social criticism, Sandburg has always summed up America with hope and optimism: "The strong men keep coming on."

The Red Special

Socialism never "arrived" in Wisconsin until the 1890s when Victor Berger, an Austrian immigrant, became the paladin of the movement.

Berger saw clearly that Socialism needed more than immigrant workers as adherents. He was one of the first Socialists to see how widespread an appeal the Party had. Not only was the American Socialist not an anarchist or a Communist, but often a simon-pure native Anglo-Saxon who gloried in his Bible Belt background.

Who would have thought that in 1910 Oklahoma had more paid-up Socialists than New York, 800 more to be exact? Who would have thought that 5,842 Oklahomans paid party dues in 1910, or that 41,674 Sooners voted for Eugene V. Debs in 1912, or that they increased their vote in the Congressional elections two years later to 52,963? It surprises people today and it surprised some even then. The home-grown blend of Socialism and Populism appealed mightily to Western and Southern debt-bound tenant farmers. These movements urged them to the polls to cast out politicians who served the monopolies. Berger made progress toward fusion with the native Populists until the election of 1896 made it impossible for Socialists to go along with William Jennings Bryan who committed Democrats and Populists to the conservative issue of free silver.

The following year Berger helped form the Social Democratic

Party, and in 1898 he was instrumental in helping convert Eugene V. Debs to Socialism. For years thereafter the party headquarters remained in Milwaukee with the magnetic Debs as perennial candidate for President (the same role Norman Thomas played in the 1920s and 1930s).

Milwaukee was the scene of the party's greatest success. In 1905 the Socialists elected two assemblymen to the State legislature. In the election of 1908 these Wisconsin Socialists staged the most ambitious of all Socialist publicity efforts. They sent the "Red Special" around the country.

The Red Special was a campaign train that carried Debs into every nook and cranny of the United States. It was made up of a sleeper, observation and dining coach, baggage car, and locomotive. A Red Special band traveled along to help stir the public as the train came into towns. Local speakers went aboard at each stop. The baggage car was filled with Socialist literature, much of which was sold to help the always-weak treasury.

The Socialists had no hope of beating William Howard Taft for President; he was the anointed successor of the popular Teddy Roosevelt, and his Democratic opponent was the forlorn, three-time loser, William Jennings Bryan. But the Socialists counted on this excitement of an election year to get their message across to a wholly new audience.

Eugene Debs spoke from six to eight times a day for sixty-five straight days. Samuel Gompers, President of the American Federation of Labor, who supported the Democrats, charged the Red Special was financed by the Republicans; whereupon Debs replied by printing the names and addresses of some 15,000 working people whose nickels and dimes had paid the train's cost of $35,000.

The Red Special left Chicago, and Debs and Taft spoke on the same night in Evansville, Indiana, where newspapers reported that more people paid to hear Debs than went to hear Taft free. After a tour of the Skyline States and California the Red Special invaded the East. By the time it got to New York, the old Hippodrome was sold out four days in advance.

Carl Sandburg spoke from the Red Special throughout Wisconsin at Oshkosh, Fond du Lac, and Appleton.

(A few years later there was another Red Special. This was the name given by newspapers to the train taking radicals across the country for deportation in the drive against the I.W.W. and aliens, which became known as the "Palmer Raids" after the Attorney General of the United States, A. Mitchell Palmer. On February 11, 1919, this new Red Special arrived at Ellis Island in New York with fifty-four radicals arrested across the country during the winter of 1918 for deportation to Russia on the United States transport *Buford*, nicknamed the "Soviet Ark."

At the height of these raids and deportations, Federal Judge Augustus Hand sustained a writ of *habeas corpus* in nineteen cases which gave the American people their chance for a "second look."

This hysteria had its roots in World War I when nervous America began to call sauerkraut "liberty cabbage," banned the music of Beethoven, and cracked down on "aliens and radicals.")

Although the Red Special of 1908 did not win the Socialists many more votes in the national election, it strengthened them in Wisconsin. In 1910, Emil Seidel was elected Mayor of Milwaukee. He appointed Carl Sandburg his secretary.

(On the day Carl became secretary to Mayor Emil Seidel of Milwaukee, Harvard-graduate Walter Lippmann became secretary to the other Socialist mayor elected that previous November, George R. Lunn of Schenectady. A few years later Mr. Lippmann wrote the Introduction to Carl's booklet, *The Chicago Race Riots*.)

Another Socialist mayor of Milwaukee was the more colorful Dan Hoan whom Carl had known in Chicago when Dan was a short order cook, and, says Sandburg, "Dan could shake a mean pan of fried eggs." About the Socialist mayors of Milwaukee, Carl sent me this note: "Hoan, like Emil Seidel before him, ran the city hall like a man who knows how—American mayors having their efficiency and vision without fool personal greed have been few and far between."

The record of Milwaukee municipal government during this time compares with the best of reform administrations anywhere. Seidel reorganized the Department of Public Works; reduced the cost of asphalt paving from $2.40 to $1.35 a square yard; replaced the chaotic city budget with a scientific one; pushed through an advanced set of public health ordinances, and enjoined the chief of police to stop any interference with the legal activities of strikers.

Berger dominated the Wisconsin party with his views. The conservative *Saturday Evening Post* of those days thus described Berger's party: "Though nominally Socialist (its aims are) really civic and social reform. It is mild and gentle and uplifting and thoroughly housebroken."

In 1912, Berger, "a versatile person with an eye to the main chance," was elected to Congress and won five times in all. From 1910 on, the Socialists were the first party of Milwaukee. For an even longer period they had the solid backing of the city's labor movement.

Outside Milwaukee the Wisconsin Socialists never made great headway until 1918, when they got the votes of many people of German descent who opposed America's entry into World War I. It was the kind of success that helped kill it. When Berger got more than 110,000 votes as Socialist candidate for Senator in 1918, it was the beginning of the end. He had just been expelled from Congress because of a criminal conviction for disloyalty (he was acquitted on appeal), but his support was too patently a *German* protest against the war.

Out of this atmosphere grew the impression of the Socialists as wild-eyed immigrants—a bearded Russian perhaps; a Pole who worked in the coal mines; an Italian anarchist; an argumentative Jew.

Mayor Frank T. Zeidler of Milwaukee took office in 1948 as a Socialist (although the Socialists had little to do with his election), and he was replaced by Democratic Mayor Henry W. Maier in 1956. At the start of a second term in 1952, Mayor Zeidler quietly changed his party affiliation from "Socialist" to "Non-Partisan."

A few years ago Sandburg made a speech in which he said that Milwaukee was "the best governed of all the large cities in America." He later asked Mayor Zeidler which cities the Mayor thought were runners-up in excellence of city management and Zeidler said: "Cleveland or Cincinnati." Carl believes that Milwaukee's excellent municipal management is due to "its Socialist tradition, plus the newspaper, the Milwaukee *Journal.*"

"Please do not step out of my life"

When Bessie Abramovitz, a pieceworker in the Hart Schaffner and Marx clothing factory, led four other girls out of the shop in protest over a wage reduction, most of the men made fun of the walkout. The women had been receiving 4 cents for seaming pants. Their wages had now been cut to 3¾ cents an hour.

But soon the workers in the other Hart Schaffner and Marx shops were impressed and refused to handle any finished product. A sympathy protest. Within two weeks the workers began to straggle out of the shops in ever-increasing numbers. Although there was no central strike board or workers' committee, the strike began to spread spontaneously.

Three weeks after the first women had walked out, the cutters in the shops, who were organized, picked up their tools and also marched out. The strike became epidemic. By October, 8,000 employees of Hart Schaffner and Marx shops were out.

This was the Amalgamated Clothing Workers strike of 1910, the strike destined to help mold the American trade-union movement.

The strike gathered the diffused discontent of the needleworkers of Chicago—Italians, Jews, Greeks, Poles, Turks, Bohemians, Albanians, and Bulgarians—who knew only that they were exploited, that thousands of them received only two to four dollars for a workweek averaging sixty or seventy hours and that thousands of others were perennially unemployed in slack seasons. All of them were foreigners and vaguely distrustful of anyone who tried to rescue them from the Promised Land's perdition. While they did not know what they wanted from the strike, they did know that conditions had to be changed.

All of the clothing centers of the city were picketed. Police squads tried to disband the picket lines with clubs, arrests, and brutality. Because the workers were greenhorns, the city officials, the police, management, and the union officials themselves underestimated their temper. The officials of a New York clothing union tried to arbitrate the strike by making an offer to Hart Schaffner and Marx which precluded union recognition, but the workers chased these men out of the auditorium (their place was taken by a young cutter named Sidney Hillman who had been on the picket lines and who had made a favorable impression on the rank-and-file committees).

The newspapers of Chicago particularly underestimated the mood of the strikers and the purpose of the walkout. They kept berating the strikers for disturbing the economy of Chicago, the second largest clothing market in America, and urged these immigrants back to their workbenches. Embattled and alone, the mass of citizens and public institutions arraigned against them, the workers might have lost impetus, but a small weekly newspaper, the *Chicago Socialist*, began daily publication of the events transpiring in the clothing strike and urged a strike call to all clothing workers in Chicago. Other workers responded.

The strike became grim and desperate when a crowd of 10,000 strikers tried to gain access to the union building to collect strike benefits and were beaten off by the police. For the most part, these workers were recent immigrants, they knew no English and in despair they tore up their vouchers.

The strike lasted into December with more and more attendant violence until on December 3, 1910, a picket named Charles Lazinskas was shot and killed by mounted police.

Ten thousand ragged workers paraded silently through Chicago's streets in the funeral procession. They sang no dirges but they all carried banners asking for their rights.

This demonstration did not win the editorial support of the newspapers, but it made them change their tone. The editors now asked for a quick settlement of the dispute. And it won for the strikers the aid of Clarence Darrow and a young liberal lawyer named Harold Ickes.

Then another worker on the picket line named Frank Nagrekis was shot and killed. Again the workers paraded through Chicago, but this time they were attacked by the police.

The violence awakened the conscience of Joseph Schaffner who decided the situation was out of all control, especially with a worker murdered in front of his plant gate. Like many other manufacturers he had left labor relations to his supervisors. Subsequently, testifying before an industrial relations committee, Mr. Schaffner said, "I was so badly informed of the conditions in my shops that only a few days before the great strike I called the attention of a friend to what seemed to me the highly satisfactory state of my employees. When I found out later the conditions that had prevailed I concluded that the strike should have occurred much sooner."

On January 14, 1911, Hart Schaffner and Marx signed a simple agreement that brought their employees back to work.

In 1915 came the Amalgamated Clothing Workers' fifteen-week strike. Carl wrote a story, long or short, about it every day in the *Day Book*, with sometimes a front-page story. During two weeks Sidney Hillman conducted the strike in bed with flu and Carl came to his bedside nearly every day and gave him the latest reports that he had. (In one way or another he kept in touch with Hillman and his lovely wife, Bessie, and in the 1944 campaign he wrote part of a leaflet widely distributed in Los Angeles. In this leaflet he replied to Hearst's vicious interpretations to the line, "Clear it with Sidney." "Like David Dubinsky," says Carl, "Hillman had integrity and constructive abilities all too rare in the world of organized labor.")

In reporting the strike news for the *Day Book* Carl was a frequent visitor to the office of Clarence Darrow, who was handling the union's legal work. Outside Darrow's private office was the loyal Bessie Abramovitz who had inspired the strike of 1910 and now was a union leader carrying messages back and forth between the leaders of the strike and Darrow. Bessie Abramovitz, who later became Mrs. Sidney Hillman, told me recently that one afternoon Darrow came out of his private office and said to Carl, "Bessie gets very restless sitting on that bench and I would appreciate it very much, Carl, if you brought your guitar to the office sometime so you can sing to her."

And so one day when labor reporter Carl Sandburg had a few moments to spare, Darrow, Bessie, and the office staff sat spellbound as Carl sang "Leave her, Bullies, Leave her":

> Oh the times are bad and the wages low,
> Oh leave her, bullies, leave her. . . .

The strike also cemented a friendship between Carl Sandburg and Clarence Darrow. It lasted all of Darrow's life. When Darrow read Sandburg's *Chicago Poems*, he wrote him a letter saying, "Dear Carl: Please do not step out of my life."

Pie in the sky

One of the songs Carl may have strummed to Bessie Abramovitz was the one written by Joseph Hillstrom, an I.W.W. agitator, now famous as Joe Hill. Hillstrom wrote many songs but his most popular was the one which was a takeoff on the hymn "The Sweet Bye and Bye":

> In the sweet (gimme some meat)
> Bye and bye (gimme some pie)
> You'll get pie in the sky by and by.

In the early days of the century every union meeting closed with it. When workers all over Chicago were singing it, Carl wrote:

> All of this should interest Chicago's neighbor city just over the Illinois-Wisconsin line. We refer to Janesville, where they show sightseers the home of the author of the hymn "In the Sweet Bye and Bye." Post cards may be had in Janesville, so you can mail a picture of the house of the famous hymn writer. This is Janesville's leading cultural tradition, unless we mention a fountain pen which has helped literature no less than life insurance.

Foreign correspondent

In 1918 the Newspaper Enterprise Association asked Carl Sandburg to go to Stockholm and report on the Finnish Revolution, which the October Revolution in Russia had inspired. Carl dispatched a story along with photographs of mass executions of Finnish revolutionaries.

One day, while Carl was sitting on a park bench with pencil and paper in hand, a stranger seated himself beside him and said, "Carl Sandburg, you are from Chicago, is not that so?" When Carl nodded his head, the stranger said, "I am from Chicago, too." The man said his name was Berg, and that he had run a private school of English classes for immigrants in Chicago. Sandburg bade the stranger welcome because he saw an opportunity of acquiring a story of sorts. Berg delivered. He knew a great deal about the Finnish Revolution and even more about the Russian "experiment."

Carl was suspicious. He discovered Berg was a man of multiple names—and identities. Berg was born Gruzenberg and had later adopted the Bolshevik code name of Borodin. Borodin became one of the top Communist philosophers and later went on to China to help communize Mao.

Borodin had been exiled by the Czar and had lived in the United States where he married a Russian student. When he went back to take part in the Russian Revolution, Lenin gave him the mission of smuggling propaganda and money into the United States. Borodin's fame as a revolutionary, however, preceded him and he was unable to get a visa. He decided upon an intermediary. The story of the Sandburg and Borodin relationship has been recounted by Theodore Draper, *The Roots of American Communism.*

Borodin was useful to Sandburg as a source of information, but only because Borodin hoped that Sandburg would be useful to him.

Berg–Gruzenberg–Borodin and Carl had many interesting discussions. The man was anxious to help a foreign correspondent. Sandburg knew the fellow could not possibly tell everything he knew, but he also knew that there were some interesting bits of information that he would have to tell as a come-on, and which Carl could use in his dispatches. These included a partial conversation between Lenin and Radek, who was eventually liquidated (the best information available is that Borodin himself was eventually liquidated).

Before Sandburg returned to the United States, Borodin, just as Carl suspected, approached him with a definite proposition. He asked Carl to carry back revolutionary literature printed in Russia. When Sandburg agreed, Borodin shipped him an entire trunkful of material which Sandburg thought would make a nice gift to the University of Chicago. Borodin also gave Sandburg a check in the amount of $10,000, drawn on a New York bank, which Carl was to deliver to Santari Nuorteva, a Finnish revolutionist active in America. Borodin lastly pressed an additional check for 400 Norwegian kroner on Sandburg for Mrs. Borodin, still living in Chicago.

After receiving these, Sandburg spent some time wondering about his future course of action. It had been easy enough to say yes to Borodin; it was another thing to smuggle sedition into his own country. Carl made up his mind and told the story to the United States Minister in Oslo. In New York, Government agents met Carl and took charge of the Communist literature and the $10,000 check. Sandburg, however, retained the check for 400 kroner which he delivered to Borodin's wife. He also kept several of Lenin's pamphlets entrusted to him (separate from the trunkful of literature turned over to the Government), including the rare *Letter to the American Workingman*, which along with Carl's own papers is now at the University of Illinois.

The last days of Eugene V. Debs

In 1921, President Warren G. Harding commuted the ten-year prison term of Eugene V. Debs. Debs had been convicted in 1918 for violation of the Espionage Act. His espionage, such as it was, consisted of opposing the war effort.

Debs was sixty-six years old, in bad health, and badly needed rest. He entered the Lindlahr Sanitarium in Elmhurst, a suburb of Chicago. Nearby the sanitarium lived the Sandburgs.

Debs recorded the experiences of his first visit from Carl in a letter to David Karsner which Karsner later published as part of the series "Letters from Lindlahr" in the Socialist newspaper, *The New York Call*:

Had a wonderful two hours with Carl Sandburg and his sweet little eleven-year-old daughter (Margaret) this afternoon, and his visit rested, refreshed, and rejuvenated me. We sat in the shade of the great old elms and poured out our souls to each other. I had not seen him for fourteen years. Since then he has scaled the peaks and written his name among the stars. Carl Sandburg is one of the very few really great poets of our day, and the future will know him to the remotest generation. He lives only three blocks from here and I shall have his three little household gods for playmates and that will be the most vital part of my restorative treatment . . . Last night (August 23, 1922) I was with Carl Sandburg and Sinclair Lewis at the Sandburg home till midnight and then that beautiful brace brought me home. It was a wonderful occasion—an event in our lives. Mrs. Sandburg had her mother, and the three dear children did the hospitable services for us and we were in paradise after our own hearts . . . Carl came with his guitar Saturday evening and gave the patients here a most charming entertainment in folklore. It was a complete conquest and they all love him. Lewis will also entertain them . . . Lewis and Sandburg are fit companions, genial, fun-loving, whole-hearted and generous, as well as princes of the pen and masters of the literary art. Lewis and Sandburg as distinctively American novelist and poet, with the cosmic understanding of the universal appeal, have already acquitted themselves with enviable distinction and achieved enduring fame, but they are still in their adolescence and have but laid the foundation of the temple that will bear in fadeless letters their deathless names.

In his book *Wobbly*, Ralph Chaplin, who also served time for opposing the war, says Debs may or may not have forgiven Carl for deserting the Socialists on the war issue in 1917: "He never mentioned the subject. But he continued to insist that Carl and I should understand one another better."

Chaplin says Debs made mention of Carl's defection only once. Chaplin, Debs, and Sandburg were walking through the garden of the Chaplin home, and Top, the Chaplin airedale, a notorious one-family dog, had been chained up for the day. "When Debs and I passed the kennel, there was a welcoming wag of the tail. A moment later, however, as Sandburg followed, Top, growling, leaped at him the full length of the chain.

" 'Carl,' remarked Debs slyly, 'the dog was just looking for your graduation certificate.'

"That was the only reference made to the fact that Sandburg had not been honored with a prison sentence."

Except for that one reference that Carl had supported President Wilson and the war against Germany, Debs never again brought up the matter. Carl himself, in later years, quite seriously gave his position: "I fight against war between wars but once we are in it, I give it everything I have."

Debs, who was to die at Lindlahr in 1926, gave every indication that his last years were made pleasant by his neighbor, Carl Sandburg. He argued with Sandburg about historical facts concerning John Brown and sang along when Carl brought over his guitar and strummed melodies.

Carl never lost his affection for Eugene V. Debs. We can say that Debs has been one of his heroes, along with Clarence Darrow and John P. Altgeld, and they are still his heroes. But Carl has never been doctrinaire (I doubt seriously whether Eugene V. Debs himself was a doctrinaire Socialist), and it was a rather simple matter for Carl to take Franklin D. Roosevelt and Justice William O. Douglas and now Chief Justice Earl Warren in stride. "I am in their stream," he says.

A dark horse

When it was obvious that Franklin D. Roosevelt was going to run for a third term, not only did a log jam of potential Republican candidates start piling up, but many of the shrewder party officials realized they needed a special kind of dark horse to win in 1940. A dark horse adds an extra dimension to the campaign. But he must have three qualities: the ability to garner wide popular appeal, a personal past that is admirable, and, above all, he must be a legitimate surprise to the voters.

The 1940 Republican Convention came up with Wendell Willkie. Against anyone but Roosevelt, Willkie might have won. But Wendell Willkie wasn't the only dark horse considered by Republican Party pros. Indeed not. One man they considered was —Carl Sandburg.

The machination of these politicians has been preserved in a private memoir signed by Carl Sandburg's publisher, Alfred Harcourt, and Harcourt's secretary, Catherine McCarthy.

It started sometime in 1940 when F. P., a high Republican who was a member of a Wall Street brokerage firm (and who impressed Sandburg because he had made two flights abroad by China Clipper), proposed to Carl at New York City's Union Club a "Sandburg for President" movement.

F. P. had a certain simplicity and a completely fresh approach to national politics. He was an intimate friend and a close personal adviser of Kenneth Simpson, Chairman of the New York State Republican Committee.

Sandburg heard him out and demurred: any real vitality on his part, Sandburg said, would require a strength he didn't have. F. P. waved this aside. The physical demands, he said, were not as great as Sandburg assumed. He wanted one guarantee: no effort would be required on Sandburg's part up to the Convention; but should a movement get going, would Sandburg promise to make a fight for it?

On that point, Sandburg told him he would like to hear what old-timers thought about the scheme. Would F. P. sound out Joseph Medill Patterson and William Allen White? F. P. promised.

A week later Sandburg received a letter from Joseph Medill Patterson which said, "If you say I should see F. P. I will." The letter made Sandburg think the proposition untenable and he wrote F. P. congratulating him on his "valor and creative imagination" but disparaging the project. Sandburg said he hoped they could continue friends and promised to help him in any way he could.

F. P. was not discouraged and reported that several leading Republicans were cordial to the idea. Kenneth Simpson, when it was first broached to him, said, "Colossal but impossible. The politicians won't stand for it." Henry Luce replied, "It's a good idea. I'd like to go along with it."

When F. P. explained the plan to Geoffrey Parsons, editor of the *New York Herald Tribune*, Parsons said, "It's lousy." But the idea kept Parsons awake a good part of the night and he called F. P. the next morning to say the possibility of Sandburg's candidacy ought not be thown away without further consideration, "though I am not yet convinced it isn't lousy."

Sometime in January 1940, Sandburg had a telephone call at his Harbert, Michigan, home from Sidney James, head of the *Time Magazine* office in Chicago. James wanted to see Sandburg as soon as possible and if Sandburg couldn't come to Chicago, he would come to see him.

"About what?" asked Sandburg.

"About those fellows that want to take care of your future."

When Carl met James a short time later, James told him he had been at a *Life Magazine* party and that Luce and his general managers thought the possibility of Sandburg's candidacy a newsworthy story. In fact, Geoffrey Parsons, who had just left to report the United Mine Workers Convention, was by this time utterly enthusiastic. Sandburg said simply it was a story he wouldn't like to put his neck out for, no particular good would come of running it.

Carl went to New York and in company with Harcourt met F. P. at the Union Club again. At luncheon, Sandburg told F. P. to forget the idea, they just didn't have a President sitting at the table. To emphasize his point he told the story of the three worms, Papa Worm, Mama Worm, and Boy Worm, who came to a fence with rails so close to the ground it was hard squeezing through. It took the three worms one hour to pass under the fence. When they were safely past, Boy Worm began shouting in glee, "Us four made it. Us four made it!"

Papa Worm said to Mama Worm, "What's the matter with that Boy? You haven't raised him right. What does he mean 'us four'?"

To which Mama Worm replied, "Why, he's all right, he's as nice a Boy Worm as ever was—only he can't count."

Thus, says Sandburg, ends the tale of a little balloon which doesn't even qualify as a trial balloon.

Running for President was one of the few things Sandburg never tried. I have a strong suspicion, however, that Carl went along with this "Presidential candidate" idea so that one day a book such as this would contain a paragraph about it. He might well have been pulling Republican legs. For in 1940 he stumped the country for FDR.

It is quite possible that as Carl sat in the Union Club with Kenneth Simpson and other Republican leaders, his thoughts wandered back to a day in Chicago when the Wobblies (I.W.W.) were on trial before Judge Kenesaw Mountain Landis for "10,000 crimes," including allegations of attempting to sabotage the war effort. The defendants, including W. D. Haywood, the boss of the I.W.W., and Ralph Chaplin, the editor of the Wobbly paper, *Solidarity*, spent many days in the courtroom and, wrote editor Chaplin: "During the tedium we were all reading Carl Sandburg's *Chicago Poems*."

In 1942, however, there was a more serious attempt to urge Carl to run for public office—for Congress against organized labor's bitter enemy, Representative Clare Hoffman, Michigan Republican.

Archibald MacLeish, then in the Administration, suggested to the United Automobile Workers that Sandburg might be induced to run from Michigan's 4th District.

The union boys had pleasant dreams for a few nights, envisioning the white-haired poet, a seasoned platform artist, stumping the District with his guitar and telling the audiences about America and the workingman from his *The People, Yes*.

So that Michigan labor would not be embarrassed by a public turndown, Carl sent word to the UAW leaders that he would not consider the candidacy under any circumstances.

He is one of us

Since 1917, Carl Sandburg has been a political independent and millions of Americans identify him as a symbol of the independent voter. This is not to say Carl isn't an active supporter of the Democratic Party. Indeed he is. As a matter of fact he campaigned vigorously for Franklin D. Roosevelt in each of his four compaigns and for John F. Kennedy in 1960. Sandburg made four speeches for President Franklin D. Roosevelt in the 1936 campaign against the Republican Alfred Landon, always comparing the issues with those America faced in 1860:

> Then as now the occupant of the White House was the issue. Each occupant had conducted a zigzag course with many inconsistencies. One difference was that the leaders of Lincoln's party believed he was vacillating and undecisive and sought to replace him. The great newspapers were against him. But after weeks of military disasters came the victories of Sherman and Sheridan and the tide turned in favor of the President.
>
> The same can be said today. Men tear their hair and run around in circles at the mention of planned economy. But all the vast detail of our production, agricultural and transportation machinery has given us no new means as yet to meet fundamental problems.

He delivered his most effective political speech in 1940 in support of FDR against the Republican candidate Wendell Willkie.

The Democratic National Committee had arranged for a national network radio program from 10 P.M. to 12 midnight the night before election. The Republicans had from 12 midnight to 1 A.M., with Clare Booth Luce and John L. Lewis making speeches that Carl says were hysterical, alliterative, and wickedly bombastic. Sandburg spoke for twenty minutes on this coast-to-coast hook-up and Lloyd Lewis, dramatic critic for the Chicago *Daily News*, later said that Carl's broadcast clinched the votes of two or three million independents across the country. They said the same thing at Democratic National Headquarters.

Early in 1946, Sandburg commented publicly on FDR's successor: "Whatever President Truman does is wrong somewhere among 160,000,000 people. That is 130,000,000 more than Lincoln had to handle."

During the election campaign of 1960, when I made speeches

on behalf of Kennedy to Jewish audiences in California, Carl, who every year turns down five hundred to six hundred invitations, gave generously of his time to follow me around to these political meetings. I played the impresario. I kept Carl in the wings until I finished my speech and announced, "Ladies and gentlemen, I brought you a bonus—Carl Sandburg."

The audience always rose and applauded. On each occasion, Carl told them the same thing, "We are just a couple of North Carolina boys plugging for a young fellow from Boston who will make us a good President."

If, however, you think Carl Sandburg is just a political war horse, take everything I have said and throw it out. He is not. He has a profound understanding of political undercurrents and social and cultural phenomena. When the left-wing Social Democrats enthused about the Russian experiment, Carl accurately prophesied what the Bolsheviks were up to. Like Bertrand Russell who said he lost more friends criticizing the Five-Year Plans than he did by refusing to serve his country in World War I, Sandburg has also sacrificed fellowship for truth. He saw that whatever the Russians might have, none of their plans had a chance in America and he voiced this opinion when it was unpopular to do so. Time and time again he has told me the greatest bigots in the world are the Communists.

After World War II, when the Cold War began, Sandburg refused all petitions, solicitations, and requests for his signature when he was able to recollect an old name or an old face from the American Communist movement. It meant he had to turn his back on some old friends and deny men whose music he admired or whose poetry excited him. But he would have no part of them.

Twice as perfect

Sandburg has an anecdote about the early 1920s when the Ku Klux Klan was having a rebirth. He tells about the fellow who started a restaurant and put the sign out: "One-hundred-per-cent American, nothing less." Across the street another restaurateur put a sign out, "Two-hundred-per-cent American." The first fellow crossed the street and said, "Look here, what are you trying to do, what is the idea putting out that sign, 'two-hundred-per-cent American'?" The second man said, "You're a Kluxer and you hate only Negroes, Jews, and Catholics. Me, I hate the whole Goddamned human race." Sandburg says the second fellow was doubling the ante.

A favorite short story

This is a good time to get back to pleasanter things than Communists and Ku Kluxers.

Along about 2 o'clock in the morning, if Carl happens to be sitting among a few close friends, he will suddenly put his glass down on the floor beside him, pick up the guitar, and sing us a favorite short story:

> Papa loved mama
> Mama loved men
> Mama's in the graveyard
> Papa's in the pen

August Sandburg, the poet's father. (Carl Sandburg Collection, University of Illinois Library)

Sandburg (seated on left) with his Swedish Lutheran confirmation class, 1891. (Carl Sandburg Collection, University of Illinois Library)

Sandburg (standing, far right) with "The Dirty Dozen," a Berien Street youth gang. (Atkins Library, University of North Carolina at Charlotte)

At Lombard College (left) and shortly after leaving the school in 1902. (Carl Sandburg Collection, University of Illinois Library)

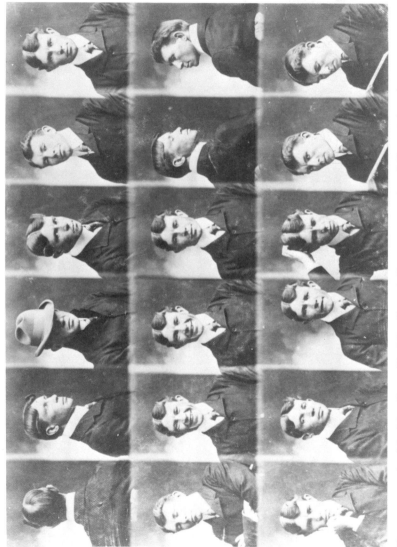

The many moods of Carl Sandburg. (Carl Sandburg Collection, University of Illinois Library)

THE world goes forward by personalities.

A suit of clothes can't talk with you nor shake hands nor touch your heart into new beauty and joy and knowledge. But what touching, tangible, beautiful things have been done by suits of clothes with men inside!

Books are but empty nothings compared with living, pulsing men and women. Life is stranger and greater than anything ever written about it.

CHARLES SANDBURG

LECTURER : ORATOR

Address care of THE LYCEUMITE,
Steinway Hall,
Chicago, Illinois.

From an announcement of the Walt Whitman lecture "An American Vagabond," 1909.

Sandburg was a member of the Socialist Democratic party of Wisconsin, 1908. (Atkins Library, University of North Carolina, Charlotte)

Sandburg with Eugene V. Debs in Elmhurst, Illinois, 1924. (Carl Sandburg Collection, University of Illinois Library)

At the *Day Book*, E. W. Scripps's adless Chicago daily, circa 1913. (Carl Sandburg Collection, University of Illinois Library)

Sandburg with daughters Helga, Margaret, and Janet, and his mother, Clara Anderson Sandburg, circa 1925. (Carl Sandburg Collection, University of Illinois Library)

Connemara, the Sandburg home in Flat Rock, North Carolina. (Photograph by L. Dunlap. Carl Sandburg Collection, University of Illinois Library)

Carl and Paula Sandburg in the company of their goats, at Connemara. (Carl Sandburg Collection, University of Illinois Library)

Sandburg with Edward Steichen (left) and David C. Means of the Library of Congress, at the opening of the Lincoln Sesquicentennial Exhibition, February 12, 1959. (Library of Congress photograph. Atkins Library, University of North Carolina at Charlotte)

PART 5

Street and Prairie

What waiting for a judge can do

He received five dollars for "Fog" and it has earned hundreds of dollars since. Every year Carl receives a check of some kind for its use in an anthology. It is one of his poems set to music, and so there's a check from ASCAP (American Society of Composers, Authors, and Publishers) every once in a while.

"About 'Fog,' " Sandburg says, "I had been sousing myself, soaking myself, in the Japanese poetry of Haikus. One day when I had done my piece for the Chicago *Day Book*, I rambled down to the lake and went over to the courthouse for an interview with a juvenile court judge, I had to wait a half-hour. While waiting, I wrote this 'masterpiece' 'Fog.' So often I meet people who have read 'Fog,' and hundreds of high school teachers ask their children to write on 'Fog,' but what about my eight hundred and forty-six other poems? I meet people regularly that don't know whether I write arithmetics or geographies!"

On the Lower East Side

Carl Sandburg is at home all over America and can call each part of it his, as Hawthorne called New England his and Faulkner the South his.

While he was waiting for his passport in New York on the way to Stockholm for his newspaper syndicate, he spent the days walking among the teeming immigrants on the Lower East Side. Just as the pushcarts on Madison Street in Chicago had interested him so deeply, so he was intrigued by the ghetto of New York, particularly after he had read Jacob Riis's *How the Other Half Lives*. He wrote a poem about Rivington Street, the very heart of the Lower East Side, and as he composed it I wonder now whether we passed each other on that street where I spent the first fifteen years of my life.

149

Home Fires

In a Yiddish eating place on Rivington Street . . . faces . . .
  coffee spots . . . children kicking at the night stars with
  bare toes from bare buttocks.
They know it is September on Rivington Street when the
  red tomaytoes cram the pushcarts.
Here the children snozzle at milk bottles, children who have
  never seen a cow.
Here the stranger wonders how so many people remember
  where they keep home fires.

The uses of poetry

I am no expert. I do not know an alexandrine line in sprung
rhythm from one in vers libre. I forbid myself the right to set up
as a critic of modern poetry since I do not understand it.

But I do not forbid myself the right to quote freely from the
more "unsophisticated classics"—and to defend them, no matter
how agonized modern critics deplore my naïveté.

Though Tennyson, Kipling, and Robert Louis Stevenson are
academically passé, that is not to say they are not read and
enjoyed daily. Nor is it to say their verses don't make music for
hundreds of thousands of people whose notion of poetry is Longfellow, Tennyson, and Kipling.

There was a time in recent years when I felt terribly left out
during a discussion on T. S. Eliot, E. E. Cummings, or Ezra
Pound. I was ashamed to confess my affection for Longfellow,
Tennyson, Kipling, and Robert Burns. After reading many thousands of letters from educated people I decided the time has come
to speak out. In recalling their childhood, people nearly always
include the story about reciting "The Charge of the Light Bri-
gade," "The Ship of State," and similar poems. I wonder whether
this generation of high school boys and girls will ever recall
reciting *The Pisan Cantos*. Is modern poetry recitable at all?

Nor is the old poetry without its meaning.

In the darkest days of World War II, when England stood
alone, beleaguered by the Nazis and fighting for her very life,

President Franklin D. Roosevelt sent Wendell Willkie on an important errand. Roosevelt wanted to tell Winston Churchill that despite America's neutrality, in passion and in fact the United States was behind Britain's cause.

All the President gave Mr. Willkie to present to the English Prime Minister was a piece of paper on which he wrote:

> Thou, too, sail on, O Ship of State!
> Sail on, O Union, strong and great!
> Humanity with all its fears,
> With all the hopes for future years,
> Is hanging breathless on thy fate! . . .

Mr. Churchill read these lines from Longfellow and addressing Parliament replied in kind with the poetry of Arthur Hugh Clough:

> Say not the struggle naught availeth,
>   The labour and the wounds are vain,
> The enemy faints not, nor faileth,
>   And as things have been they remain. . . .
>
> And not by eastern windows only,
>   When daylight comes, comes in the light;
> In front the sun climbs slow, how slowly!
>   But westward, look, the land is bright!

Were I a poet able to choose who would recite my verses and under what conditions, could I ask for more? The two great men who were battling to save Western civilization!

The uses of poetry are not necessarily to improve upon metrical systems and make new convolutions in syntax. The uses of poetry are to hearten the courage of men and make meaningful their struggles. Thus the poetry of Sandburg.

A question from the audience

"How do you write your poetry?" she asked. Carl replied: "With a pencil, with a fountain pen, with a typewriter, but I draw the line at dictating 'em." The woman nodded intelligently.

For a women's club audience Carl gave another version in answer to the inevitable question: "How I got started as a writer? Well, I was living in a big house and felt sort of lonesome one day and I said to myself, 'Maybe if I could be a writer I would be a little less lonesome,' so I went out of the house and found me a lot of verbs. I came back to the house with these verbs and the verbs looked so terribly lonely I knew they needed nouns to connect. So I went out of the house again and came back with a lot of nouns. I had done a few sentences, coupling nouns and verbs and I said, 'I know what it is I need, a few adjectives, not many, but a few.' So I went down the cellar and in a big barrel in a corner I found it was full of adjectives, enough to last a lifetime. Then I went upstairs and began writing and have been writing ever since."

"Dante, Milton, and me"

In the years following the publication of *Chicago Poems* Sandburg used to say publicly, "Here is the difference between Dante, Milton, and me. They wrote about hell and never saw the place. I wrote about Chicago after looking the town over for years and years."

Poet of industrial America

In her preface to the *Selected Poems of Carl Sandburg* which she edited in 1926, Rebecca West wrote: "It is a curious fact that no writer of Anglo-Saxon descent, no representative of the New England tradition, has described the break between Lincoln's America and modern industrialized America so poignantly as Carl Sandburg has."

John Peter Altgeld, Governor of Illinois just before the turn of the century, was the only figure on the national scene in an elective office who realized the Lincoln idea had passed into something else; Oliver Wendell Holmes, Justice of the Supreme Court, probably realized it, if naively; perhaps Willa Cather in

A *Lost Lady* realized it; but Miss West is right. No one realized it *so poignantly* as Carl Sandburg.

The poem "Chicago" is Sandburg's affirmation and accusation of America. The face of America is the city, and it is a face more wicked, more crooked, more brutal, and more sinful; but at the same time a prouder, coarser, stronger, and more cunning face.

Sandburg himself prefers his poem "The Windy City," published six years after "Chicago":

> . . . The hands of men took hold and tugged
> And the breaths of men went into the junk
> And the junk stood up into skyscrapers and asked:
> Who am I? Am I a city?

But both poems make essentially the same point. While the city is a bold enterprise on the part of men, it is also an enterprise which corrupts natural emotions. For some, the corruption is almost total.

Mag

I wish to God I never saw you, Mag.
I wish you never quit your job and came along with me.
I wish we never bought a license and a white dress
For you to get married in the day we ran off to a minister
And told him we would love each other and take care of each
    other.
Always and always long as the sun and the rain lasts any-
    where.
Yes, I'm wishing now you lived somewhere away from here
And I was a bum on the bumpers a thousand miles away
    dead broke.
    I wish the kids had never come
    And rent and coal and clothes to pay for
    And a grocery man calling for cash,
    Every day cash for beans and prunes.
    I wish to God I never saw you, Mag.
    I wish to God the kids had never come.

(Carl read this poem, incidentally, seven or eight years ago on Garry Moore's morning television program. Out of his study of Sandburg poems in college, Moore liked this one so much he insisted Sandburg recite it.)

Love has been perverted and dissipated by the lack of money. This is one of the corruptions issuing from the industrial society where the making of money is paramount. The industrial society —for which Chicago is the symbol—also submerges human values. It introduces a new type of neglect, which we shall conveniently call "exploitation," into the course of daily affairs. The desire for exploitation leads to the denial of human worth, to cruelty, and to meaningless death. Witness:

Anna Imroth

Cross the hands over the breast here—so.
Straighten the legs a little more—so.
And call for the wagon to come and take her home.
Her mother will cry some and so will her sisters and brothers.
But all of the others got down and they were safe and this
    is the only one of the factory girls who wasn't lucky
    in making the jump when the fire broke.
It is the hand of God and the lack of fire escapes.

Let us dispense with the argument whether or not Sandburg is a propagandist in his poetry. He is. So, for that matter, are Leonardo da Vinci, Mark Twain, and Dante propagandists. So, too, is T. S. Eliot a propagandist for the Anglo-Catholic Church. The issue about propaganda is not whether a man is or isn't propagandizing, but what he propagandizes for and what he propagandizes against. Neither the poet who propagandizes "In sua volutad, nostra pace" nor the poet who propagandizes against factory girls jumping six floors to the pavement can be said to be without his own truth.

The industrial society is inequitable. It makes millionaires out of the few but for others it offers no rewards. Sandburg's prostitute wails:

        I got nothin' to show for it.
        Some man got it all,
        Every night's hustlin' I ever did.

Another poem recounts the relief a family feels when a sick child dies and they realize they have no more doctor bills.

These are precisely the criticisms Karl Marx and Friedrich Engels leveled against the capitalistic system when they argued it had destroyed the normal family relationship. We know, however, both Marx and Engels had emotional problems above and beyond the iniquities produced by capitalism. Marx was a terrible father and a dead beat. Engels was so busy lending money to Marx he himself never found time to take his sweetheart out of the factory in which she worked; when she died of fatigue and tuberculosis Engels could only hold her hand and cry. This is not the kind of leftist Sandburg is: not doctrinaire and careless, but flexible and inclusive.

For all his poetry is polemical, it is even more symbolic. It was Sandburg who first introduced the symbols of industrial society: skyscrapers, steel, exploitation, and—mobility.

In one of his poems everybody wonders where Chick Lorimer went, a pretty girl who packed her bags and left for Chicago and never came back. And of the boys who ran barefoot in the leaves throwing clubs at walnut trees in the yellow and gold of autumn, he says:

I remember their cries when the nuts were ripe,
And some are in machine shops; some are in the navy;
And some are not on payrolls anywhere.
Their mothers are through waiting for them to come home.

Since he was the first poet to capture the poignancy of intense mobility he is also one of the first to see the significance of the motorcar:

It's a lean car . . . a long-legged dog of a car . . . a gray-ghost
eagle car.
The feet of it eat the dirt of a road . . . the wings of it eat
the hills.
Danny the driver dreams of it when he sees women in red
skirts and red sox in his sleep.
It is in Danny's life and runs in the blood of him . . . a lean
gray-ghost car.

and one of the first poets to capture in verse new class distinctions:

> I thought of killing myself because I am only a bricklayer and
> you a woman who loves the man who runs a drug store.

Yet Sandburg welcomes the industrial society and forgives it. It brings to men a new source of pride and a new feeling of accomplishment. He points to all the achievements men have gained: "the perpendicular alphabets" of the skyscrapers and "the changing silver triangles of stars and streets." Sandburg's fame came not because he sang of the American past but of another America beginning. He wrote poetry which captured the constant change permeating America:

> *Armour Avenue* was the name of this street and door signs on
> empty houses read "The Silver Dollar," "Swede Annie"
> and the Christian names of madams such as "Myrtle" and
> "Jenny."
> Scrap iron, rags and bottles fill the front rooms hither and
> yon and signs in Yiddish say Abe Kaplan & Co. are running
> junk shops in whore houses of former times.
> The segregated district, the Tenderloin, is here no more; the
> red-lights are gone; the ring of shovels handling scrap iron
> replaces the banging of pianos and the bawling songs of
> pimps.

The past is gone, irretrievably vanished; the day is always new. Nor is it a joyless society.

Let us listen to Sandburg again:

"The ice handler who spends a dollar or so every Saturday night on a two-hundred-pound woman who washes dishes in the Hotel Morrison also remembers when the union was organized he broke the noses of two scabs and loosened the bolts so two wheels came off six different wagons one morning."

And "Jack, the railroad man, may die in a poor house, sitting on a bench in the sun, telling reminiscences to other old men whose women are dead and children scattered. But there will be joy on his face when he dies as there was joy in his face when he lived: 'He was a swarthy swaggering son-of-a-gun.'"

"After drinking musty ale with the millionaire manufacturer who spoke of a beautiful daughter and listening to a speech at the advertising association on the trade resources of South America," Sandburg, in "Fellow Citizen," visits a man with his jaw wrapped for a bad toothache: "He is a maker of accordions and guitars and not only makes them from start to finish, but plays them after he makes them . . . anyway he is the only Chicago citizen I was jealous of that day."

Art is one of the redeeming features of industrial society. Most of Sandburg's work is a definition of new values.

His poetry has different moods and textures. His diction is at one time slangy and onomatopoeic, at others reportorial and conversational, as still others hortatory and imperative. All of it abounds in images of vivid color. He calls a traffic cop a spot of blue, and:

> Five white houses on the half strip of land . . .
> Five white dice rolled from a tube.

If he is adept at the use of irony as in: "The children play the alley is heaven," so is he a master of the poetic conceit: "Night gathers itself into a ball of dark yarn."

But, at bottom, his poetry is always about the same thing: it is about men—American men.

The men vary in age and occupation, in goals and skills—but no matter; Sandburg always sees their essential individuality. He sees, metaphorically, men in everything:

> A bar of steel—it is only
> Smoke at the heart of it, smoke and the blood
>   of a man . . .

The book *Good Morning, America* was a more thoughtful, more tranquil work than those produced before. While the socialism of the *Chicago Poems* had diminished and the sadness of *Cornhuskers* was almost invisible, the poetry was still about men who shared hardships and learned from them, men who came of age, men who learned how to live with suffering.

One of the best summations of his poetry was written by Sandburg himself in *When Death Came April Twelve, 1945,* which recites tributes due Franklin D. Roosevelt:

> and they will go on remembering
> and they is you and you and me and me. . . .
> And the whitening bones of men at sea bottoms
> or huddled and mouldering men at Aachen,
>   they may be murmuring,
>   "Now he is one of us,". . .

Not even his personal dedication and admiration of Roosevelt was enough to blur from Sandburg's lines his unremitting belief that one great man is a combination of many men who suffer and bleed—and win.

He stayed behind

While many other writers went to Europe, Carl Sandburg stayed behind to write about America. After the publication of his long poem, *The People, Yes,* and the last four volumes of his *Lincoln,* he could sit back. He had done his share. There was nothing he really had to do now except pick up his honorary doctorates. But not Carl Sandburg.

When World War I broke out, he broke with the Socialists in order to support Woodrow Wilson. At the beginning of World War II, he began writing a political column for the Chicago *Times* Syndicate, although three years before he had turned down an offer from Hearst for $30,000 a year for a column. But now he said he was enlisting to fight the America Firsters at home and the Fascist dictators abroad.

Among voices and faces

It is perhaps unfortunate for many who read Sandburg's poetry that they do not hear his voice. Sandburg reads his poetry best of all living poets. His voice adds something integral. It is his voice that gives his poetry its tactile, physical qualities. It is a vigorous and dramatic voice.

The critics who have tried to dismiss Sandburg in recent years forget this. For that reason they cannot account for his ever deepening and growing popularity. Whatever Sandburg's prosody and rhythms may be, to hear him read is to be actually and totally involved in the experience of poetry.

Gay Wilson Allen, in *The South Atlantic Quarterly* (Summer 1960), said, "God made Sandburg a writer, and by his own efforts he has become a poet." There is something ruggedly honest in this evaluation. (When Carl reads comments like this, he adjusts his eyeshade angrily, clamps his jaw, and says querulously aloud, "Is that so?")

A Sandburg poem is substantial and all of a piece. Single quotable lines are rare since one line always suggests and tugs at the next. When someone once asked him his favorite poem, Sandburg answered, "It is a long poem, runs through a whole book titled *The People, Yes.*"

The People, Yes was published in 1936, in the midst of the Great Depression and initial opinion had it that the book was a sociological and political declaration.

More correctly it has been described as a series of psalms which sing the American experience: hardship, humor, fortitude, and—speech. Described briefly it is a book not only about the American people but about the way American people talk and the things they say and their reasons for saying them. It is affirmative, optimistic; in some places tender, in others tough. It is not as politically biased as early reviewers might have us believe, although it would be unwise to say Sandburg is without sympathies.

There is this exception to *The People, Yes*—Sandburg's commitment to "the people" was not a political commitment but a spiritual commitment. When Sandburg praises, glorifies, and hymns the day laborer, the railroad fireman, the hobo, he is no different than Mark Twain recalling the Mississippi river pilots and the adventurous Huck Finn.

The People, Yes consists of 107 poems consecutively arranged. It is history told by poetic particular, soliloquy, and dramatic incident, exactly the kind of book Ezra Pound has been trying

to write these long years in *The Cantos*. But where *The Cantos*
interrupt their lyricism to digress about "kikes," introduce count-
less Chinese ideograms, and meander into the fiscal policies of
Martin Van Buren, *The People, Yes* does not dissipate attention
or purpose. Without fear of contradiction, one can say *The
People, Yes* is apolitical.

When Sandburg writes about George Eastman, the Kodak
king, it is not about the giant factories his camera industry has
spawned nor about exploitation of the workers:

> . . . Mr. Eastman stepped into a bathroom,
> took his reliable fountain pen and scribbled on a
> sheet of paper:
> "My work is finished. Why wait?"
> He had a guess deep in his heart that if he lived
> he might change his will; he could name cases; as
> the will now stood it was a keen dispersal for
> science, music, research, and with a changing mind
> he might change his will.

More directly, this is a poem about attitudes men have toward
money and the good and evil it can do.

The book is a poetic definition of elemental forces: love, death,
life, but especially—work. The personnae talk constantly about
work and forward practical considerations of what makes a man
a good or bad worker.

> "A long, tall man won't always make a good fireman,"
> said the Santa Fe engineer to a couple of other rails
> deadheading back. "Out of a dozen wants to be firemen
> you can pick 'em. Take one of these weakly fellers
> he'll do his best but he's all gone time you get
> nine miles. Take a short, stout fellow, low down
> so he can get at his coal, and he'll beat one of
> those tall fellers has to stoop. But if a tall feller's
> got long arms he can do wonders. I knowed one
> engineer used to say he had a fireman he never saw him
> throw a shovel of coal on the fire—his arms was
> so long he just reached and laid the coal on!"

Now, to be sure, Sandburg's book is not without its political and sociological implications:

> "Why," said the Denver Irish policeman as he
> arrested a Pawnee Indian I.W.W. soapboxer,
> "why don't you go back where you came from?"

But these implications are invariably a background for his humor.

I am perhaps an unconscious victim of modern critical techniques in that I must employ ostensive definitions; if modern poetic criticism has a weakness, it is in its inability to elaborate upon humor.

Sandburg's humor is probably one of the reasons why he is read and reread and probably one of the reasons why with each generation he gains a new audience. His humor is first of all couched in actual, not rhetorical or stylistic, language: "Wedlock is padlock," and his use of direct speech gives his humor greater immediacy; also he never writes self-conscious jokes:

> They were ninety years old and of their seventeen
> children had just buried the first born son who
> died seventy-two years of age.
> "I told you," said the old man as he and his hillborn
> wife sat on the cabin steps in the evening sunset,
> "I told you long ago we would never raise that boy."

The People, Yes is more than a joke bag. It is a tour de force of Sandburg's facility not only with the English language but with the way people use it and what they mean by it.

Sandburg's diction runs from the argot of the streets to the brogue of an Irish cop to the twang of a Midwest farmer to the solemn dignity of a Lincoln eulogy.

Everyone who speaks is one of Sandburg's people. He is not militant about any of them, as many writers in the 1930s were—and indeed still are today. There are politically good and bad people in Sandburg; there are selfish and unselfish people; visionary and narrow-minded people; haves and have-nots. He sees them not through a political or social screen but through a poetic and humorous screen.

His belief in the people is based on the hope they will have a real and accurate idea of their own interests.

> "The people," said a farmer's wife in a Minnesota
>   country store while her husband was buying a
>   new post-hole digger,
> "The people," she went on, "will stick around a
>   long time.
> "The people run the works, only they don't know it
>   yet—you wait and see."

The people, yes—not because the people are humanity and need pity, but because the people make law and persevere and "run the works."

Debts and love letters

In *The American Language*, H. L. Mencken quotes Carl Sandburg on slang. "Slang is language that takes off its coat, spits on its hands, and goes to work." Perhaps of all the definitions Carl Sandburg has forwarded, this is the one of his most quoted.

Sandburg tells a funny story about this. He says he was speaking to a woman's club in Moline, Illinois, many years ago and after he was through a young, aggressive newspaperwoman came up for an interview.

"Would you say, Mr. Sandburg," she asked, "that slang is language that takes off its coat, spits on its hands, and goes to work?"

"Yes," Carl said.

Thus she quoted him. Sandburg says if he knew who she was, he would send her a book and a love letter.

Yrs gratefully received . . .

In 1912 Harriet Monroe of Chicago started a little magazine she called *Poetry* which she published at 543 Cass Street. The first issue of September 23, 1912, included verse by Ezra Pound and

Arthur Davison Ficke; the third issue introduced Rabindranath Tagore to American readers. Vachel Lindsay's "General William Booth Enters Heaven" was first published in *Poetry*, and in 1914 "Chicago" by Carl Sandburg was printed. In the same March volume appeared "Love Songs" by Sarah Teasdale; "Poems" by Frances Shaw; "Eros Turannos" by Edwin Arlington Robinson; and "The Seabird to the Wave" by Padraic Colum.

In the same year, William Butler Yeats, Robert Frost, D. H. Lawrence, Edgar Lee Masters, Amy Lowell, Hart Crane, Glenway Westcott, were proudly presented in *Poetry*.

Alfred Harcourt, an editor at the publishing house of Henry Holt and Company, read *Chicago* and was deeply stirred. On one of his business trips to the Midwest he tried to find Carl Sandburg. Mr. Harcourt, however, did see Alice Corbin, Harriet Monroe's assistant, and asked her to "steer Carl my way when he has enough poems for a book."

In his essay, "Forty Years of Friendship" (*Journal of the Illinois State Historical Society*, Winter, 1952), Mr. Harcourt relates that in the fall of 1915 Miss Corbin brought into his office in New York a manuscript from Carl entitled *Chicago Poems*.

"I saw at once that it was of first importance and quality. There was something of a skirmish to get it past the inhibitions and traditions of the Holt office, for its middle western atmosphere, its subject matter and strength, seemed to them rather raw for their imprint, but Henry Holt himself agreed to let me try it."

Rarely does a book of poems receive the attention, the respect, and the enthusiasm that greeted Carl Sandburg's *Chicago Poems* under the Holt imprint.

"For some years after that," Mr. Harcourt writes, "my association with Carl was largely by correspondence, and what correspondence! Every letter he wrote, even of humdrum details, seemed to sing. He had a regular job on the Chicago *Daily News* so he couldn't get to New York, and when, in 1919, I started my own firm, Harcourt, Brace and Company, I was too busy to get to Chicago. I did drop in on him once in Elmhurst, I think it was in 1921. I found Eugene V. Debs there, just freed from a federal penitentiary, where he had been serving a sentence for trying to keep the United States out of the First World War." A career, a reputation, and a contribution were under way.

The first review in the metropolitan press was in *The New York Times* on June 11, 1916:

"*Chicago Poems* is one of the most original books this age has produced."—Amy Lowell

Followed by an article in the *Poetry Review* (July, 1916), concluding with this sentence:

"Carl Sandburg has shaped poetry that is like a statue by Rodin."

Until 1914, Sandburg received little for his poems. "Billy Sunday" brought him attention but not money. After Max Eastman had printed it in *The Masses*, it was reprinted in the New York (Socialist) *Call* and subsequently seized by the police in New Haven, and forbidden distribution and sale. Sandburg says this is the only instance of a work of his coming under a police or censor ban. Sixteen years after the publication of "Billy Sunday" as "To a Contemporary Bunkshooter," Sandburg asked a professor at New York University to send a copy of the poem to Billy Sunday asking the Evangelist what he thought of it.

Billy Sunday asked: "Who is this Sandburg? Isn't he a Red? He sounds to me like a Red."

Sandburg's first real money came from *Poetry* magazine. It was $100 for a group of poems of which the lead was "Chicago." For this poem he won the Helen Haire Levinson Prize of $200. Salmon O. Levinson, a millionaire attorney, and Mrs. Levinson later invited Harriet Monroe and Sandburg to a dinner. It was an enjoyable evening for Sandburg and introduced him to artichokes and the ritual by which fingers take off leaves and dip them in a butter sauce. The two-hundred-dollar prize paid the hospital bill for the arrival of Janet Sandburg.

"The Windy City," which Sandburg considers a better portrait of Chicago, brought him $50. He can't recollect when and where the long poem, "Slabs of the Sunburnt West" was published or how much he received.

Mencken paid him $50 for "Many Hats," a symphonic treatment of the Grand Canyon of Arizona, and since the poem fitted the *Mercury*, Sandburg considered himself well rewarded.

Like firemen and teachers, poets are notoriously ill-paid. So when Sandburg received $1,000 for "Good Morning, America," which occupied two elegantly illustrated pages in *The Woman's Home Companion*, he was on his way to becoming one of the two American poets able to support himself by verses alone.

In 1943, *The Saturday Evening Post* paid him $1,000 for his poem "The Long Shadow of Lincoln" and furnished a Norman Rockwell illustration for it.

He walked into the *Fortune* magazine office of his old friend Archibald MacLeish, who was in consultation with publisher Henry R. Luce, and in the course of their talk both agreed *Fortune* ought to have a Sandburg poem. He sent them "Moonlight and Maggots," got a check for $500, and brags, "I was the first poet to break into *Fortune*."

On the Fourth of July, 1926, Carl got a telegram from Arthur T. Vance of *The Pictorial Review* asking for a Christmas poem. "I said to myself, to write a Christmas poem on the Fourth of July is a challenge. I will tackle it." He wrote "Special Starlight": and from year to year this poem appears in journals and on Christmas cards and has earned as much money as "Fog."

"Mr. Longfellow and His Boy (An old-fashioned recitation to be read aloud)" ran in *Collier's* June 14, 1941, the check, $1,000. At President Roosevelt's request, Sandburg wrote this poem in a large script on heavy rag paper, which is now among the Roosevelt papers at Hyde Park.

To such publications as the New York *Call, The Milwaukee Leader, The Masses, The Little Review, The New Leader, The Nation*, and others, Sandburg has donated at least thirty poems, "free, gratis, not a nickel, and pleased to have my pieces published." He also gave nine poems to Alfred Kreymborg's whimsical magazine, *Others*.

At the Great Neck, Long Island, High School recently, Carl read a poem from the IBM magazine, *Think*, entitled "Micrometric Mirrors." After the program a man came to Sandburg saying, "I'm a professor of psychology and I have a book coming out this fall. I'm wondering if you could let me have this poem for the book."

Sandburg said, "I'm sorry I can't let you have it, but I salute you for certifying I am a psychologist."

I include this information not because I think it is important, or because Carl does, but because people do. Americans carry a heavy neurosis in their worry about how much writers make. No matter how much or how little, it is my contention people feel poets and novelists and scriptwriters are overpaid. On the other hand, baseball players, who ought to play for nothing, are a source of great concern. If the New York Yankees tried to cut Mickey Mantle's salary, from where I sit I know five people who would have apoplexy in pity for the Commerce, Oklahoma, athlete.

There are textile salesmen who would not consider taking a $1,000 order. There are "industrialists" in my city alone who could buy and sell Carl and me, with John Steinbeck thrown in for good measure, many times over.

There is this difference between the poet and the successful commercial man or ballplayer. The salesman, the Madison Avenue account executive, the metropolitan stockbroker will purchase Samsonite luggage for their field trips. Not Carl. He still carries the same old fraying carpetbag on his trips, cuts all his cigars in half, and wears neckties he bought in 1921.

"Yew gotta do it"

Ezra Pound was the foreign agent or correspondent of Harriet Monroe's little magazine, *Poetry*. In 1916 Pound wrote to Professor Felix Schelling of the University of Pennsylvania suggesting the English faculty institute a "Fellowship given for creative ability regardless of whether the man had any university degree whatsoever." Pound named Carl Sandburg as a candidate.

Pound wrote: "I have in mind a couple of youngish men whose work will stay imperfect through lack of culture. Sandburg is a lumberjack who has taught himself all that he knows. He is on the way toward simplicity. His energy may for all one knows waste itself at an imperfect and imperfectible argot."

Professor Schelling replied with the epitaph for the American university system: "The university is not here for the exceptional man."

Between Pound and Sandburg there grew a wealth of friendship. Both were working poets and shared similar aims and difficulties. They admired each other and admired each other's work. Carl wrote one of the most cogent and appreciative analyses of Pound's poetic purposes ever to appear in America. The essay was published in *Poetry* in the February 1916 issue and I reproduce a few paragraphs here for those who might still wonder about the mistaken charge that Carl is the poet most untouched by learning and understanding.

> If I were to name one individual who, in the English language, by means of his own examples of creative art in poetry, has done most of living men to incite new impulses in poetry, the chances are I would name Ezra Pound.
>
> When Nicodemus wanted to know more about the real Jesus of Nazareth, he had the justice to make a night call and ask Jesus some questions.
>
> Let some of those thrusting spears and ink pots at Ezra Pound try to be fair enough to read him.
>
> In the early regulations of the University of Paris, this oath was required of professors: "I swear to read and to finish reading, within the time set by the statutes, the books and parts of books assigned for my lectures." Some like form should be insisted on for reviewers and commentators who in this push-button and dumb-waiter age rush into type with two-minute judgments on twenty-year accomplishments.
>
> Drawing a style of writing from hitherto obscure Romance literature and the troubadours, from the Chinese and the Egyptian, from modern science, Nietzsche and syndicalism, the technique of Pound baffles any accurate analysis in a single paper. His own statements of his theories do not get at the gist of the matter, and he passes his warmest inspira-

tions to others through poems in the actual instead of
theoretic.

There are those who play safe and sane in poetry, as in
mechanics and politics. To each realm its own gay madmen.
Some win their public while they live. Others must mould
a very small public while alive, and be content with a larger
one after death. Still others need no public at all, and in
the role of by-standers they get more enjoyment and knowledge of life than as performers.

Poetry is a sort of inspired mathematics, which gives us
equations, not for abstract figures, triangles, spheres and the
like, but equations for the human emotions. If one has a
mind which inclines to magic rather than science, one will
prefer to speak of these equations as spells or incantations;
it sounds more arcane, mysterious, recondite.

I like the pages of Ezra Pound. He stains darkly and touches
softly. The flair of great loneliness is there. He is worth
having.

On August 21, 1917, Ezra Pound wrote to Miss Monroe, "I'm
sorry Sandburg don't like 'Three Cantos' . . . I discount Sandburg's objection, by the fact that he would probably dislike anything with foreign quotations in it . . . Still one can't stop merely
because some people haven't read Latin . . . Don't for God's sake
say this to Sandburg. A decent system would give him time to loaf
in a library."

In April 1958, Sandburg joined a group of poets in a plea for
the release of Ezra Pound from St. Elizabeth's Hospital for the
Mentally Disturbed in Washington, D. C.

The plea urged the Government to dismiss the treason indict-
ment that had been pending against Pound since 1945.

Robert Frost headed the committee and his statement in-
cluded comments on behalf of Pound by John Dos Passos, Van
Wyck Brooks, Marianne Moore, Ernest Hemingway, T. S. Eliot,
W. H. Auden, and Archibald MacLeish.

At the time of Pound's commitment to the mental institution,
Sandburg was publicly quoted, "It won't hurt Ezra to do a little
time. I hope to visit him at St. Elizabeth's and I will tell him

that I will read Ezra Pound as long as I live. I sent this message to him by a friend who called on me and had a postal card signed Ez a few days later saying, 'If there is any visitin to be done yew gotta do it.' "

Haircuts

"Who was the poor fish," Sandburg asks, "who originated the saying, 'There is more truth than poetry in that'? Was the poor fish trying to sideswipe Shakespeare, Shelley, Keats, Browning, Li-po, or who, or what? No scientist or any practical man struggling to tell the plain, unvarnished truth ever said as much about a tree in 10,000 words as Robert Frost says in ten lines about a tree."

There was a time when Sandburg and Robert Frost were inseparable, but there is a coolness between them now; a coolness which dates from 1933 when Mr. Frost showed less than enthusiasm for Carl's support of Roosevelt and the New Deal. "The People, Yes," said Mr. Frost. "Sandburg is wrong, I say; 'The People, Yes, and No.' " At another time Frost said, "'The 'helpless'?—that's Sandburg's department, not mine." But Carl has never disowned his praise. Indeed, I suspect he would insist it has more application than ever.

Whether Frost has learned from Sandburg or not, I cannot say, but Sandburg credits Frost in *The American Songbag* (1927) with having taught him a breezy, lusty sailor ditty, "Blow the Man Down," which Frost learned in San Francisco. (Curiously enough, Frost was born in California.) In *Good Morning, America*, Sandburg has these lines in his poem "New Hampshire Again":

> I remember a stately child telling
> me her father gets letters
> addressed "Robert Frost, New
> Hampshire."
> I remember an old Irish saying,
> "His face is like a fiddle and
> every one who sees him must
> love him."

The stately child is Lesley Frost, a headmistress at a Washington, D. C., girls' school for whom Sandburg has always had a great affection.

At times Mr. Frost too has been generous. Graciously he sent a copy of his letter that went to the Blackstone Hotel in Chicago wishing Carl a happy seventy-fifth birthday:

> Dear Carl:
>
> Congratulations old man—congratulations *old* man. Seventy five years is quite an achievement though nothing of course compared with what you have done for us in prose and verse. I was glad to be reminded of your birthday. You've been creeping up on me. At three you were half my age. Now you are better than twelve thirteenths. A little more and I shall have you for a contemporary. And proud of it. Keep grandly on.

The Chicago poet and the New England poet have teased each other across the years. Both are cagey about their "coolness" but it is inescapable, of course.

Frost loves to tell the story about Carl's hair. Frost was preparing steaks for his guest Sandburg one time. Carl was an hour late for dinner, with the result the steaks were irreparably burned. When another guest asked Frost why Sandburg was late, Frost replied, "He was upstairs, fixing his hair."

"Trying to get it out of his eyes?"

"No," said Frost, "trying to get it in his eyes. He *likes* it that way."

Frost has told this story to dozens of audiences and it has reappeared in reprints, digests, and a dozen newspaper interviews, whenever the name of Sandburg crops up.

Last March 9 when I was invited along with a score of other newspapermen to attend the opening of the Sheraton Tel-Aviv Hotel in Israel, I flew in the El Al airplane beside this eminent poet. Mr. Frost was on his way to give a ten-day series of lectures on American culture and civilization at the Hebrew University in Jerusalem. He was making, as he said, "a beeline for where the human race has come from for the last two thousand years."

While we were zipping across the Atlantic in the jet, Mr. Frost dozed off and a lock of white hair came down over his forehead.

When he awoke, I said, "Mr. Frost, your hair looks a little like Carl Sandburg's right now."

Mr. Frost's annoyance was of such proportions that his reply not only furnished a column for Art Buchwald, the *Herald Tribune* Paris correspondent, but was included in the News Notes of *Poetry Magazine*.

"Dare he say I have the same kind of hair as Carl?" said Mr. Frost to Mr. Buchwald. "My hair's my own, and I don't copy anyone else's haircut. I've been cutting my own hair now for twenty years. Haven't been to a barber since then. Got sick and tired of those fellows. I didn't mind them talking to me. I guess every barber's supposed to do that, but I did mind them always telling me my hair was falling out. So I started cutting my own hair. As you grow older, you don't care about those things. Of course, Carl's a very careful fellow. I'm sure he goes to the barber."

Donated by Mr. Ernest Hemingway

Why hasn't Carl Sandburg won the Nobel prize?

So many of his admirers have asked this question of the committee members in Stockholm for the last twenty-five years that that might be one of the reasons why he has not been selected.

Or maybe the Swedes are leaning backward in considering the award for a fellow Swede.

Carl does, however, have the Nobel prize by proxy, donated by one of the Nobel prize winners—Ernest Hemingway. When Mr. Hemingway won the prize in 1954, he told the first reporters who interviewed him that there was another writer more worthy than he. He said that writer was Carl Sandburg.

Later that year, Carl attended the National Book Awards and chatted with Harvey Breit, then one of the editors of *The New York Times Book Review*. Mr. Breit reports that Carl took a cigar out, sliced it in half with the accuracy and confidence and professionalism of a butcher cutting away the tail of a steak, put one half in his pocket, and smoked the other half. They talked for a while and reminisced about past meetings and reminisced about the Nobel prize and the fact that Hemingway who had just been awarded the prize had singled out Carl as someone who should have won the Nobel prize. And Sandburg's answer to Breit's question about how he felt about the singling out went like this:

"Harvey Breit, I want to tell you that sometime thirty years from now when the Breit boys are sitting around, one boy will say, 'Did Carl Sandburg ever win the Nobel prize?' and one Breit boy will say, 'Ernest Hemingway gave it to him in 1954.'"

Carl loved Ernest Hemingway with a very deep love. "I liked it," he says, "whenever I heard anyone say that Hemingway was indestructible. When he was referred to as an expatriate I liked his simple comment, 'I took a hand in every war that my country has been in.'"

Good guys and bad guys

Criticism is part of the game. If you don't like mean things said about you, you have to give up writing poetry, as Carl puts it, and become a jovial plumber. Carl is all for criticism—of a certain kind. When his *Chicago Poems* were published, he told me someone at a party remarked, "That *Chicago Poems*, that book, that writer—he ought to be shot!"

"Now that's what I call criticism," Carl says.

Sandburg is more baffling to himself than he is to his critics. A hostile review full of scorn and derision actually pleases him. I've heard him say, "I call myself a fool far more often than the critics do. I have always been elusive to myself, and have actually written poems asking why I'm so doggone elusive."

Sandburg has had his share of criticism. He has been the subject of monographs, critiques, books, articles, and newspaper accounts. There have been good guys and bad guys writing about him. The good guys, Carl considers, are the ones who understood; the bad guys the ones who did not.

One of the first of the good guys was Lincoln Steffens who wrote: "Now this bloke that God made to express Him and His works in Chicago is no better and no worse than Chicago. He went nosing around that city for many years seeing the sights, and hearing the sounds and the sayings, and sensing the meanings to man and God of all that transpired there . . .

"And Carl Sandburg reported all that he knew, as he learned to know it day by day without a judgment, without a tear, without a laugh; he reported daily his daily news on the Chicago *Daily News* . . . and now behold, Carl Sandburg's stuff turns out to be poetry, Carl Sandburg proves to be a poet. Chicago is found good. God can rest."

Almost immediately after *Chicago Poems* was published Carl became the battleground for a literary war. The classicists, or more precisely, the academically trained critics, focused their attacks on free verse on him. For the curious thing about good poets—Shakespeare and Marlowe are respective examples—is that they tend not to go to school, and if they go to school, it is the wrong, unfashionable school. Thus the early critics on Sandburg: they said he was the poet most untouched by classical beginnings.

Harry Hansen, Carl's close friend and colleague on the Chicago *Daily News,* came to his rescue. Hansen published *Midwest Portraits* and began one of his chapters with the heading: "Carl Sandburg, Poet of the Streets and of the Prairie."

Hansen wrote:

> But with Carl writing in free verse was not so much an acquired habit as a yielding to "a natural bent." He is not derivative even though he is often spoken of as the most successful follower of Whitman; he read Whitman early in his career but there is little of him in his poetry. He is familiar with the imagist, vorticist, and other schools, but it is doubtful whether he ever made an intensive study of them; his poetry is an example of a man writing himself down, and not attempting to pour his thoughts into a standardized mold . . .
>
> This brings us to the two moods that are ever recurrent

in Sandburg: the social and the lyrical; the note of protest, of indignation, of grief at the oppressive conditions under which the humbler brethren of this earth live, and the note of exultation that has as its basis love of life, love of laughter, love of beautiful, fantastic and colorful pictures in nature . . .

His poems of the streets, his emphatic pounding with hard words, have become so characteristic of him that many persons know no other side of him; when they think of Sandburg they picture the Sandburg of the "Hog Butcher of the World" forgetting that in him live fantasy and whimsicality, lyricism and lyrical beauty.

Carl was working on the Chicago *Daily News* as motion-picture editor when Bruce Weirick, Professor of English at the University of Illinois, published *From Whitman to Sandburg in American Poetry* in 1928. Harry Hansen took it to Carl: "There, you big slob! See who they are ranking *you* with."

In his essay "Poetical Circuit Rider" in the special Sandburg issue of the *Journal of the Illinois State Historical Society*, Weirick writes about meeting Carl in Chicago a year later.

"I found (Sandburg) large, vigorous, reddish haired, and completely surrounded by all the Chicago papers, all editions, and enormously excited over the accounts of a shooting fray.

" 'Wonderful,' said Carl. 'The old West has nothing on Chicago!' "

Mr. Weirick added significantly, "The Valentine Day Massacre was yet to come; but by then Carl's gusto was deep in *The War Years*, hunting bigger and better game.

"About midnight we took off down darkest Madison Street for Carl's 'owl train' for Elmhurst. The neighborhood was dark and pretty gruesome. I asked Carl if he thought it was wise to walk it alone as he usually did. 'Not a bit of danger. Been doing it for years, and never been held up.' I remember I was in an ice cream suit, blue bow tie, and Panama hat, and looking quite robbable. And then I looked at Carl, unpressed, sloppy, rolling along like a workman just off the line, and huge, and a bit formidable, and I guessed why he was so safe. But I took a cab back from the station to my hotel."

Admittedly, the good guys tend to be friends—and most of Carl's friends become cronies. This, however, is not to deny their objectivity. It is also true that there have been more good guys than bad guys.

There have been, however, enough bad guys.

There is a whole posse of bad guys Carl has been feuding with for years known as the "New Critics." The New Criticism is not so new at that. It was formed by a group of scholars teaching at Vanderbilt University right after World War I, among whom were John Crowe Ransom and Allen Tate and they were joined later by one of their students, Robert Penn Warren. Briefly, the New Criticism is an empirical discipline for evaluating and judging poetry. It manages its empiricism by a concentration on the poem itself and excludes from consideration irrelevant attribution, such as the date of composition, historical milieu, author's intention, and public meaning. Each poem, argue the New Critics, has an "ontological" existence (ontology being a word derived from the Greek participle for "being"), which is to say each poem has an independent existence apart from its author, society, etc. The New Critics have formulated a nomenclature and a scheme of values. Professor Ransom formulated the New Criticism as a pedagogical endeavor—a way of teaching poetry to a class—in this his discipline is completely successful. The New Critics have sent from the colleges where they taught a body of literate readers able to understand, comprehend, and love poetry. They have also encouraged poets and now the New Criticism numbers among its disciples such poets as Richard Wilbur, William Meredith, Robert Penn Warren, James Wright—not Allen Ginsberg, however, or Carl Sandburg.

The New Critics have been hard on Carl. They find no formal aspect to his poetry, no tight organization of techniques, no innovations in style and language. Despite this, it is my guess that though they are wrong in dismissing Carl, they have nothing to be ashamed of.

If they have been hard on Carl, so has he been hard on them.

Down in Ohio, there's a college called Kenyon where a new movement started that designates itself "the New Criti-

cism." It comes in cellophane and has not known the touch
of human hands.

Certain sacrosanct things that belong in this country and
in the lives of its people don't belong in poems, says the
New Criticism. A poem should not deal with *action* and
not with acting and should have nothing to do with leading
men toward acting. It must concern itself with *being*.

Now Walt Whitman was perhaps the head spirit of an
opposite viewpoint. He took the word democracy and threw
it around like a juggler does a fireball and wrestled it until
it came to have something of the elements found in men's
hearts and in the *Gettysburg Address* that made people
understand the implications—that whenever men have freedom there have been men who fought for it and died for it.

But even freedom itself is a theme that in the general
run of obscurantists is not looked upon with favor. I helped
found and worked for years and did everything I could for
the success of a magazine in Chicago, *Poetry*, founded by
Harriet Monroe, and I feel melancholy about turning through
its pages to see how seldom occupied it is with the theme
Harriet Monroe included.

I think of the "New Criticism" and I think about my
friend, Bill Nye, not a famous music critic but a fellow who
ran a newspaper in Laramie, Wyoming, called the *Boom-
erang*. He wrote a sentence you can post up high in connection with modern poetry and some of the music today:
"You know they say this music of this fellow Wagner is
better than it sounds."

The issue is joined. The New Critics do not believe in a con-
textual approach to the study of literature. They feel a poem
should be apolitical, and Sandburg has always been the politician.

I cannot help but sympathize with Carl, and this not necessarily because he is my friend.

Scientists could study the independent existence of a plum
pudding for one thousand years before they discovered it had
been steamed in a towel.

If the New Critics would ignore, say, Stephen Vincent Benét,

Sandburg would not. During World War II when radio stations, at the urging of the Government, wanted an anti-Axis free-American piece, time and again they came to Benét and Benét always delivered, asking no pay for his services. Carl says Benét was keenly aware it would not do to wait, revise, wait longer, revise yet more. The dawn, Carl says, does not come twice to wake a man.

For Carl, the bête noir of the bad guys is Mr. Edmund Wilson who wrote, "Carl Sandburg wouldn't know an abstraction if he met one on the street"; to which Carl replied, "According to Edmund Wilson my trouble is that when I want to write about smoke and steel, I write about smoke and steel and not something else."

Edmund Wilson got under Carl's skin when he wrote an article about Sandburg which appeared in the November 20, 1920, issue of *Vanity Fair* magazine. He called it "The Anarchists of Taste" and Ivan Oppfer contributed a caricature of Carl to illustrate the piece. It is a likely caricature.

However sterile one may consider a great deal of the New Poetry, the New Music and the New Art, it seems to me that most of the criticism of them is superficial and based on a fallacy. It is assumed that the modern artist deliberately makes art ignoble and anarchic . . . The vers librists, the advanced composers and the futurist painters are supposed to have conspired in a plot to blow up the temple of the Muses.

Now there is probably a certain amount of truth in this point of view—that is, it is true that the New Art represents a reaction against Victorian floridness and inanity, just as political radicalism is the inevitable result of Victorian laissez-faire.

Take the case of the Chicagoan, Carl Sandburg. If he had been born in France, for example, his mind would have been pervaded by harmony as soon as he could see and hear; he would have learned it unconsciously and easily from the softness and measure of the landscape, from the fine proportions of the buildings, from the incomparable elegance and grace of the language which he would speak.

But Carl Sandburg, born in Chicago (sic), is a very different matter. There is nothing in Chicago to encourage a sensitive lover of life. There is no suggestion of harmony in anything about him: the language which he hears spoken is the harsh *patois* of the city; the streets through which he walks are drab and unspeakably ugly, dark gulches with barren walls built of department stores and offices. Instead of the swift little rivers of France, lined with grey-green poplars, he sees only the dull sprawling Lake, lined with sooty railroad tracks.

There is no ecstasy of beauty here, no calm and high reflection: his emotions simply cannot find expression in the forms of Milton and Shelley. If he tried to write an ode to a skyscraper or a sonnet to a locomotive, he would immediately become ridiculous . . . But the poetic feeling of our time, cramped, untrained and starving, has found a proper vehicle of expression in what is called "free verse." This form is lifted a little above prose, but is never "harmonious numbers." It is bare, prosaic, sordid, or of a sterile preciosity but it is undoubtedly the best that can be done under the circumstances. It fits exactly Mr. Sandburg's Jewish peddler selling fish in the streets of Chicago . . . It has, in short, been the vehicle of some of the best as well as some of the worst of our poetry. When Mr. Sandburg deserts the street-cars and fish-carts, for Love, and Fire, and Beauty, he is not so satisfactory. One is bored by the dryness of his emotions and the poverty of his vocabulary. He cannot rise among these noble abstractions with a free sweep of wings. He can walk the streets with sympathy, but he cannot fly among the clouds.

It is not poor Mr. Sandburg who is the enemy of Virgil, nor even Mr. Leo Ornstein who is warring against Bach. These men only found themselves in love with life at a time when life was loved but little: they were filled with joy by the shapes of things as they saw them bright in the sun.

No, it is not the artists who are responsible for blackening the face of Apollo; it is the commercialism of the time which has blackened the face of the world. It is not the poets whom you should denounce: it was not they who first broke the rules—the rules of harmony and order and measure and taste. These things began to decline simultaneously with the progress of the industrial revolution—with the rise of the bourgeois and the tradesman, who put a tradesman's valuation on everything that the human mind could imagine or the human hand construct.

It is they and not the artists who were the true anarchists of taste!—the shopkeeper and the manufacturer who moulded the world to their likeness and to whose bourgeois ideals you yourselves, professors and critics, have proved among the promptest apologists and the fiercest supporters!

To my mind, the weakness of Mr. Wilson's argument is that Carl's poetry has endured. Wilson is really trying to say Carl's poetry is reporting and its value topicality. We have forty years of hindsight on Mr. Wilson and one cannot blame him if his prophecies do not always come to realization. As time passed, Sandburg's poetry came to have a wider and wider interest rather than a lessening popularity.

Carl says he hates Edmund Wilson like he hates William Zeckendorf: "Away back in *Vanity Fair* he thought he had something in calling me an 'anarchist of taste.' The first time I saw a picture of his face I said, 'Why, that's the Arrow Collar man. He is handsome is as handsome does.' And I would never have thought that a man so peculiarly and classically handsome could go on from year to year having such troubles and miseries he has had with women."

Carl reserves his real anger for those critics who attack writers and artists Carl considers "in the American stream." Some years ago when the critic Alfred Kazin wrote a front-page piece for *The New York Times Book Review* denigrating the reputation of John Steinbeck, Carl wanted to challenge him to a duel. In the next few weeks, every time the name John Steinbeck came up between Carl and me, Sandburg stopped and took time out. He would change his happy expression to a dour, hard one and in that slow drawl he uses for contempt, he would repeat, "Al-fred

Kay-zinn," then quickly, "What the hell does he know about Steinbeck," followed by an explosive "Hah!" with head thrown back and mouth wide open.

Carl has not only survived all criticism, he has actually thrived on it. If you think a critic annoying, Carl will say, "I remember lying on the green grass of Grant Park one summer afternoon and hearing Vachel Lindsay laugh and expostulate, 'It is a wonderful thing to be a poet and not a jackass.' "

One of our natural resources

"You must have an idea that I have been worried about critics," grumped Carl as he read this portion of the manuscript: "Hell, I never paid the slightest attention to the critics, not even to that Diana Trilling, is that her name, who wrote in 1949 that my *Remembrance Rock* was not worth reviewing. Hah, not worth reviewing, and that *Nation* . . . with those few silly lines about my *Sandburg Range*; do you know how many poems I gave to *The Nation* across the years; but I'm not the least bit concerned about the critics, never pay the slightest attention to them . . ." and off came the eyeshade, the head thrown back, and that delightfully loud—Hah!

"But Carl," I said, "there's nothing to worry about, you are like Albert Einstein today, untouchable; you are one of America's natural resources like the Grand Canyon, only more important. There's nothing to worry about, Carl, let me go along, in my own little way . . . Hah."

Carl Sandburg and his contemporaries

Like anything else, poetry, alas! is subject to the whims and vagaries of fashion. Compare any two of the several different editions of Palgrave's *Golden Treasury* and you will find that whereas one age preferred Tennyson and Wordsworth another prefers Dryden and Yeats.

If time treats the poet harshly and benignly, so, too, does it treat poetry's critics. Dr. Samuel Johnson's pronouncement about the metaphysical poets was that "contemplative piety, or the intercourse between God and the human soul, cannot be poetical." This led him to dismiss the efforts of John Donne, George Herbert, and Richard Crashaw. He complained they had "no regard to that uniformity of sentiment which enables us to conceive and excite the pains and pleasures of other minds."

With a little more hindsight, Lytton Strachey remarked of Johnson some centuries later that his aesthetic judgments always had some good quality about them, except one: they were never right.

The poets, the critics of poetry, and the students have it today that indeed the highest poetic expression is the dialogue between God and soul.

A grain of salt, therefore, with any criticism which dismissed the preceding generation of poets, especially that criticism which has attempted to dismiss the poetry of Carl Sandburg and the poetry of some of his contemporaries.

The day will come, perhaps, when the scholarly journals and the professional quarterlies will be filled with exegeses and explications of the poetry of Carl Sandburg, Vachel Lindsay, Edgar Lee Masters, Amy Lowell, and Stephen Vincent Benét. But to be fair, it is inaccurate to say they have been eclipsed or surpassed.

These poets were one with Mark Twain in trying to utilize the American diction and establish the American experience. By American experience, I mean a certain unique identity, one disparate from European origins and models.

By and large, this is not the aim of the *modern* American poets. They are not unpatriotic, but their poetic concerns are entirely different. It took the interest of the French *symbolistes* to awaken once again an American interest in the poetry of Edgar Allan Poe and this is an entirely different way to arrive at an understanding of poetic forms and techniques than Sandburg, Lindsay, Masters, Lowell, or Benét found.

Vachel Lindsay was down and out in Atlanta and Newark when the Salvation Army gave him food and lodging. Out of this experience came his famous poem "General Booth Enters Heaven." T. S. Eliot, while not reduced to this grim poverty, was a bank clerk, but from his experience came *The Wasteland.*

Lindsay, who was an artist as well as a poet, became in his time not a pre-eminent critic but probably the most popular of all performing lecturers. He was as well an evangelical moralist and unashamedly wrote propaganda poems. "Abraham Lincoln Walks at Midnight" was a forthright plea for world peace:

> He cannot rest until a spirit dawn
> Shall come;—the shining hope of Europe free:
> The league of sober folk, the Workers' Earth
> Bringing long peace to Cornland, Alp and Sea.

Edgar Lee Masters was also intent on using the vehicle of America as a poetic subject. The first copyrights on the *Spoon River Anthology* were taken out in 1914 and 1915. Essentially, although it is an anachronism, the *Spoon River Anthology* was a sort of *Winesburg* set to poetry. Each of the residents had a separate voice and their subjects included such peculiar American virtues as local option pro or contra Prohibition to solve the alcohol problem.

There was a time when all the poets found America an uncharted continent, a continent which inspired love unlimited. Stephen Vincent Benét, who also began publishing in 1916, never tired of it:

> I have fallen in love with American names
> The sharp names that never get fat,
> The snakeskin titles of mining-claims
> The plumed war-bonnet of Medicine Hat
> Tucson and Deadwood and Lost Mule Flat.

And Amy Lowell, who founded the American Imagist School (which Ezra Pound, annoyed that she had usurped his nomenclature, called the "Amygists"), found her best poetic voice in praise of New England:

> Heart leaves of lilac all over New England
> Roots of lilac under the soil of New England,
> Lilac in me because I am New England,
> Because my roots are in it,

Because my leaves are of it,
Because my flowers are for it,
Because it is my country
And I speak to it of itself.

Not all of these poets were of equal quality nor was their discipline always consistent. Their command of rhyme and meter was often a childish command and their erudition was as often a self-conscious erudition. Their quality of mind and their sophistication at times seem rudimentary. But what their poetry captured, and what *modern* poetry does not, is that American naïveté, that combination of innocence and hope that made a playpen out of this jungle in less than 150 years.

It was because they struck an absolutely responsive chord that their poetry had wide circulation and their audiences numbered thousands.

People filled the concert halls to hear those poets; factory workers and coal miners carried their books. These people did make poetry a universal joy where today it has become a specialized industry, an industry of specialists who write for each other, and then they review each other to make things even all around.

The college graduate who can name four young poets is teaching in a university, and magazines of poetry and volumes of verse are by and large subsidized publications. Before you call me naive, I would have you recall the Roman epigrammatist Martial who wrote: "He writes not whose poetry nobody reads."

Carl Sandburg on the death of Ernest Hemingway

"Hemingway throws a long shadow over the pages of American literary history. I prize a letter from him where his hand wrote, 'Three muskrats swim west on the Desplaines River.' After quoting this line from one of my poems, he told of a long canoe trip down that river which flowed between his Oak Park home and my Maywood, Illinois home.

"Over the phone from my North Carolina home to his place near Havana, Cuba, he said, 'I am lonely. Miss Mary is on a train from New York to Minneapolis for a visit with her mother. I'm sort of helpless without her.' I was on the Chicago *Daily News* when Mary Welsh came from Bimidji, Minnesota to be our Assistant Society Editor. Plenty of men have said, 'My wife is perfect,' but no other man has ever surpassed Hemingway in telling why his mate for life was perfect. Deeper than any sea grotto is the grief of 'Miss Mary,' who possessed Ernest because of rare and deep mutual bonds."

PART 6

The Babe, Big Bill, and
the Pre-eminent Hearst

"Is art on the bum in Manitowoc?"

I have carefully refrained from calling this book "a biography of Carl Sandburg" because I do not have footnotes and the usual dozen pages of fine print in the back.

Quite frankly I did not go near the Sandburg Collections at either the Library of Congress or Knox College in Galesburg; nor did I visit the Sandburg Room in the Library of the University of Illinois where Carl has all his Lincoln papers.

Furthermore, at the last minute I decided not to touch the Sandburg correspondence, the copies of hundreds and hundreds of letters he has written across the years. I saw at once that Carl's correspondence will some day make a separate book—a book that could tell us much of the literary and political history of the first fifty years of the twentieth century.

But even without these vast sources, the material I have accumulated on my own reaches to the ceiling, and I could write another book on Carl right now without moving out of my chair.

In my Introduction I said that Carl is the only literary figure of this century to have distinguished himself in five fields: poetry, history, biography, fiction, and music; and I did not even mention—journalism.

Believe me, Carl's output as a reporter, a feature writer, and an editor would have been enough achievement for any good newspaperman. And after studying this mountain of journalistic material, I have no superlatives left when I consider also the one-thousand-and-more poems, the six volumes of Lincoln, the eleven-hundred-page novel, the thousands of letters, the *Rootabaga* tales for children, the *Songbag*, the speeches, the dedications, the forewords and introductions; the deep involvement in politics and ideologies, and the care with which Carl has nourished and preserved his friendships, and all of it is quite fantastic and almost unbelievable.

It is not easy to keep up with Carl's vast output as a newspaperman. In addition to the regular jobs on Wisconsin and Illinois papers, Carl filled in for editors and reporters whenever they needed a helping hand. For example, here's a note from Jim Howe, editor of the Milwaukee *Daily News*, August 2, 1910: "C.S. write the editorials for me while I am on vacation." A month later Carl made his first Labor Day speech, Eau Claire, Wisconsin:

"Years ago we asked for old age pensions that would enable played-out and done for workers to live with rest and comfort in their last days. But the years went by, we were laughed at as agitators, and it is today as it always was—old age is a time to be feared.

"Years ago we asked for a minimum wage to apply among all workers, a wage that would keep all workers above the poverty line, above the level of degradation. But the years went by, we were ridiculed as impractical, and today millions of wage earners get pay so miserably low that they cannot live decently, cleanly, rightly.

"This is what the System has done for us and to us. And we are tired of it. We are ready for *change*. We are done with our old ways. We are striking out along new lines."

A year before he had filled in for Chester Wright, Labor Editor of the *Daily Tribune*, Manitowoc, Wisconsin. Mr. Wright, an old friend, was busy in the courts defending himself in a libel suit and Sandburg took over for him as editor. In passing, it is worth remembering that Carl had a great advantage over other "Labor" and "Socialist" writers of the day. He spoke of "minimum wages" and "old-age pensions," it is true, but he also wrote of art and poetry, and his editorials were full of anecdotes and humor. For example, he conducted a symposium in the *Daily Tribune*: "Is art on the bum in Manitowoc?" A few days later he published a poem in the editorial column and asked his readers for comment: "What do you think of this poem? Do you like it? What do you make of it? Let me know."

Carl worked also on the Milwaukee *Sentinel*, general assignments from the city editor, Bill Evjue, later owner and editor of the Madison, Wisconsin, *Capital Times*, famous as one of the most independent free-shooting dailies in America. The staff included

Dan Hoan, who later was elected Mayor of Milwaukee on the Socialist ticket; Chester Wright, who later became secretary to Samuel Gompers, President of the American Federation of Labor; and Martin Quigley, later publisher and editor of motion-picture magazines.

Sandburg also did a stint on the Milwaukee *Journal* as City Hall reporter. He was on this job when Emil Seidel, first Socialist mayor of an American city, asked him to become his secretary. But the Social Democrats needed Carl and asked him to leave the mayor's office to work on promotion of a daily newspaper which would honestly report the party running the city and the county governments. A magazine article of his, "Where Is My Wandering Girl Tonight?" was reprinted widely from the *Delineator*. It reported the use of a new and big municipal auditorium for dances and sports where young people had been kept off the streets through the introduction of carefully planned social programs.

A year later the opportunity Carl and Paula were waiting for finally came to them—Chicago. There was a strike of pressmen on the Chicago dailies, all except the (Socialist) Chicago *World*, and they sent for Carl. Paula has told me that for some years both she and Carl had looked forward to the day when they would move on to Chicago. This was 1912. "Chicago and Carl," said Paula Sandburg, "were made for each other."

Five rules for boys

"If some kid ball players asked you for five rules, five big points to watch—what would you tell them?" Carl Sandburg, reporter and columnist for the Chicago *Daily News*, asked Babe Ruth in St. Petersburg, Florida, on March 24, 1929.

"The Babe gave these:

(1) Cut out smoking and drinking.
(2) Get enough sleep.
(3) Get the right things to eat.

"The Babe wouldn't think of two more and was willing to let it go at these three. But he came down heavy on the first point, saying: 'A boy can take to drinking and harm himself so he'll never get over it.'

"The inquiry was made: 'If some boys asked you what books to read, what would you tell them?'

" 'I never get that. They don't ask me that question. They ask me how to play ball.'

" 'If you were to name two or three books that you like a lot, what would they be?'

" 'I don't know. I like books with excitement, dramatic murders . . .'

" 'You have met President Coolidge, haven't you?'

" 'Oh, yes.'

" 'If some boys asked you for a model of a man to follow through life would you tell them Coolidge is pretty good?'

" 'Well, I always liked President Harding.'

" 'If some boys asked you which one of all the Presidents of the United States was the best model for boys to follow is there any one you would tell them?'

" 'President Wilson was always a great friend of mine . . .'

"The past doesn't interest the Babe. He is concentrated on the present hours. There is no ancestor worship about him. His face lighted with a sudden glee when he was asked:

" 'Is there any one character in history you are especially interested in, such as Lincoln, Washington, Napoleon?'

" 'I've never seen any of them,' he replied.

" 'Some people say brunettes have always been more dangerous women than blondes. How do you look at it?'

" 'That's a question. You can't tell. It's the personality that counts.'

" 'What's your favorite flower?'

"With a quick laugh, 'I don't care about flowers.'

" 'What's your favorite horse?'

" 'Oh, I quit that, I quit playing the ponies long ago . . .'

"And I thanked Babe Ruth, the business man, for giving me so much of his time. And I told him I hoped as a ball player his legs and eyes won't give out for many years . . ."

He also wanted to see Philadelphia before he died

Carl wrote of a newspaperman who, having killed his sweetheart and convicted of murder, was doomed to the gallows. The condemned man ate a hearty breakfast of ham and eggs and was led up the steps to where the halter was suspended above him. As the hangman was adjusting the hemp around the reporter's neck, the tragic victim remarked, "No noose is good news."

The Day Book

In the years before his *Chicago Poems* was published, Carl had a variety of newspaper jobs. One of them was on the adless Chicago tabloid, the *Day Book*.

In 1912, there was a lockout of the pressmen's union and no daily paper was published in Chicago. The Chicago *Daily Socialist* (changing its name to Chicago *Daily World*), took advantage of this situation by putting a paper on the stands every morning. Circulation boomed to 600,000 and the *World* hired Sandburg and brought him to Chicago as a feature-writer. When the strike was settled, the dailies almost immediately recovered their circulation and the *World* slowly died of newsprint costs and no advertising. Carl joined the more solvent *Day Book* as a reporter at $27.50 a week.

The *Day Book* was the brainchild of E. W. Scripps, who called himself a "damned old crank" but who was one of the giants of American journalism.

It was shortly after his supposed retirement, in 1911, that Scripps got Negley D. Cochran, one of his editors who later became his biographer, to set up the *Day Book* as an adless tabloid with two short columns to the page.

Scripps wanted to prove that American newspapers could get along without advertising. Moreover, the old man—fearless himself—thought that in the future some of his editors might prove amenable to advertisers' pressure. Scripps' instructions to Cochran were:

FIRST: The paper shall receive no income except from the sale of newspapers.

SECOND: It shall always be the organ, the mouth-piece and the friend of the wage-earners who get small wages and of that class who are not working for wages but still maintain themselves by daily labor of the humblest sort. Our paper is to be the poor man's advocate whether the poor man be right or wrong.

Arbitrarily Scripps limited the paper's expenses to $2,500 a month, except for newsprint. Not surprisingly, the paper lost money, but the deficit was whittled down by circulation growth. By 1916 the average monthly deficit had been more than halved, down to some $1,200, and by the time the *Day Book* suspended publication in 1917, it was making a slight profit.

World War I brought Scripps out of retirement and made him order Cochran to Washington. Both men were convinced they had proved their point, that the adless paper would have continued to flourish.

Scripps stayed behind the scenes of the *Day Book*, never revealing himself as publisher. He insisted on such details as large 12-point type which was easy to read and even insisted upon a tone of vulgarity to help identify the paper with the masses. Routine news was boiled down, so that the *Day Book* could play up stories the other Chicago papers wouldn't print. Instead of killing the story about the death of several people in the elevator of a State Street store, the *Day Book* publicized everything, names, addresses, funeral directors, grief of the family—everything.

Once Scripps gave an editor a raise for publishing a routine item that E. W. Scripps was fined ten dollars for driving his horses recklessly while intoxicated.

Carl Sandburg and his colleagues rejoiced in reporting a host of happenings the regular newspapers wouldn't touch. One of these was the recurrent wars between newspaper sluggers who fought and even murdered in the struggle for newsstand and street-corner sales.

Alderman Michael Kenna, known as "Hinky Dink," came to the rescue of Scripps and the *Day Book* when the paper was thrown off the stands. He took the matter up with Mayor Carter Harrison who promptly ordered the police to see to it that the *Day Book* was not molested.

The great muckraker Lincoln Steffens wrote of Scripps to sculptor Jo Davidson: "You must do a great thing with Scripps. There is no other like him: energy, vision, courage, wisdom. He thinks his own thoughts absolutely. He sees straight. He sees the line he is on and his thinking sticks to that. I regard Scripps as one of the two or three great men of my day."

Ten thousand separate and distinct crimes

On September 5, 1917, agents from the United States Department of Justice swarmed down upon every I.W.W. branch office and hangout. All of the Wobbly leaders and editors of the I.W.W. press were arrested. Among them was Big Bill Haywood. The men were locked up in the Cook County Jail, charged with "Ten thousand crimes of sabotage aimed at hindering the war effort."

On October 2, 1917, Haywood's first interview was printed in the Chicago *Daily News*. Carl Sandburg was the reporter.

> Through a steel cage door of the Cook County Jail, Big Bill Haywood today spoke the defiance of the Industrial Workers of the World to its enemies and captors.
>
> Bill didn't pound on the door, shake the iron clamps nor ask for pity nor make any kind of a play as a hero. He peered through the square holes of the steel slats and talked in the even voice of a poker player who may or may not hold the winning hand. It was the voice of a man who sleeps well, digests what he eats, and requires neither sedatives to soothe him nor stimulants to stir him up.
>
> The man accused of participation in 10,000 separate and distinct crimes lifted a face checkered by the steel lattice work and said with a slow smile:

"Hello, I'm glad to see you. Do you know when they are going to bring the rest of the boys here? It would be home-like for all of us to be together. . . . Ten thousand crimes! If they can make the American people or any fair minded jury believe that, I don't see how they'll do it. . . . It is true we called strikes, but they were not aimed at stopping the war . . . The I.W.W. has been fighting and will keep on fighting for higher wages to pay for a higher cost of living. Eggs a while ago were two for a nickel. Now they are a nickel apiece. A porkchop costs double what it used to. It takes a week's pay for a lumberjack to buy a wool shirt."

The checkered face in the steel slats and electric light kept a perfect calm. Where LaFollette is explosive or Mayor Thompson overplausible and grievous, Haywood takes it easy. He discusses the 10,000 crimes with the massive leisure of Hippo Vaughn pitching a shut-out.

Prophecy

"When a gag doesn't go over," Will Rogers told Sandburg, "I concentrate on my rope tricks." Wrote Carl in the Chicago *Daily News* on April 11, 1928, "Television eventually will help Will. He will use his rope then."

"Get us right, we'll dig coal"

In the fall of 1917, the coal miners in Illinois came out of the pits on strike. They were accused immediately of sabotaging the war effort. But miners have always engaged in a war with the operators—sometimes a shooting war. To this day, the casual visitor may see machine guns on some of the street corners of coal towns in Harlan County.

Sandburg did not believe the miners were saboteurs. He went down to the mine towns in Illinois and interviewed miners and wrote a story for the Chicago *Daily News*—"The Miners' Side."

Said James M. Davis, coal digger of the Peabody Company, "We're not on strike. We have just quit work that's all, Anybody could tell it was coming. The men all expected a raise of 10¢ a ton." Davis is a college man, has taught public school and digs coal, he says, because there is a higher income in it for him than in school teaching.

"A miner's pay is all luck," says Davis. "It depends on how the vein runs. My tonnage the last ten days of May paid me $50 clear. For all of June I made $44. For the first half of August I made $49.74." This uncertainty of pay and the natural hazards of underground work give the miner a temperament all his own. He's different!

"Everything go high, the beef, the shoes, everything," says Sam Viola, top man for the Wilcox Coal Co. "I get $3.50 a day. I have a wife and 2 kids in Italy. I no can do. I want the more mon."

"Let 'em conscript us," said M. Montgomery, digger for the Citizens Coal Co. "We'd rather work for the government than the operators."

Fred Cooper, digger at the Old Citizens Company, an Englishman, said, "We are fighting the operators, not the government. The operators are trying to use us. It is the operators who are unpatriotic. We are ready to go to work."

Nathan Lee, a Negro, digger for the New Jones and Adams Co. shook with feeling, it was almost a sob as he said, "We'll dig coal for the government. We want to win the war. We paid officers to fix up our grievances, but they haven't done it. Something's wrong. We thought we were going to get 10¢ more a ton this pay day. The committee said come out and we came out. But you get us right, please, we'll dig coal for the government."

Obit

When Mr. Scripps closed down the *Day Book*, Sandburg took a job with the American Federation of Labor and went to Omaha and St. Louis for labor stories and strike news which were used by the labor press.

In 1917, Carl joined the staff of William Randolph Hearst's Chicago *American* as an editorial writer at one hundred dollars a week, the highest pay he had ever received. I asked Carl to tell me about his experience as a Hearst writer and he gave me the following out of his personal journal which he wrote the day after Hearst's death.

Mr. Hearst died of a Tuesday, ten minutes to ten, Pacific time, of a Tuesday morning.

This was William Randolph Hearst, who was the world's most preeminent Hearst, the one and only Hearst and there was no other Hearst before him.

Having died at ten minutes to ten of a Tuesday morning he was still dead at ten minutes to eleven, at ten minutes to twelve and so on through the night and the next day and the day after that he was still dead at ten minutes to every hour.

Yet why should I be a Hearst hater? He acted warm toward me and wanted to be my friend in the main way he could be a friend. In October of 1927 he sent telegrams to his Chicago *Examiner* managing editor, Rank by name, to get in touch with me and sign me for a column or half a column a day, six days a week, to run in all the Hearst papers. I had dinner twice with Rank at the Palmer House. He would go as high as $30,000 a year and I could write whatever I pleased. I told Rank that after thinking it over, I would thank Mr. Hearst for being so thoughtful of me but I had other work in view, work that would take all of my time, having in mind *Abraham Lincoln: The War Years*.

And again how could I be a Hearst hater? I get off a train at St. Cloud, Minnesota, to take a bus to a Catholic school for girls to give a program, reading a Sunday *New York Times* on the bus, to find that Paul Mallon writes to Mr. Hearst asking if Mr. Hearst himself was writing the one- and two-column editorials so often then running in the Hearst papers, Mr. Hearst replying that during the day he is occupied with executive matters of circulations, policy, newsprint, but night comes and with it thoughts come to a man and he puts them on paper, Mr. Hearst saying that he was well aware that what he writes for tomorrow's paper is dead the day after, adding to this effect, "Of course, if I could write books like Mark Sullivan or Carl Sandburg, I would write books."

I talk with Fremont Older, editor of *The San Francisco Call*, a Hearst paper, and at my murmuring misgivings of Hearst, Older said that one year when there had been concerted and savage attacks on Hearst as pro-German and anti-American, Hearst wired him to say, "It looks like I'm the loneliest man in the world but we'll go straight ahead on the same policies we have been following." Older spoke his impression, "For sheer guts I've never in my life seen anything like it."

I remember Lloyd Lewis saying the Chicago *Examiner* offered him $30,000 a year to leave the Chicago *Daily News* and become their managing editor, Lloyd saying he went on to New York for a conference with Bill Curley, a high Hearst executive, Lloyd then going to Alfred Harcourt and laying the matter before him and Harcourt asking, "Did you ever know a man who didn't disintegrate on going to work for Hearst?" And Lloyd told me, "I had to turn down the offer though I would have liked the money."

At Harvard I was shown the statue of its founder, John Harvard, a bronze figure in knickerbockers, low shoes, good legs, a torso, head and garb of dignity, John Harvard seated in a fine bronze chair. They told me thousands of loyal old Harvard men came for the unveiling of this unique memorial—and when the canvas was drawn aside and the distinctive sculpture revealed there in plain sight, before the applause died down they saw beneath the enshrined figure of John Harvard, under the chair wherein he sat, a large antique thundermug, an oldtime pisspot—placed there, it was said, by the maliciously mischievous William Randolph Hearst who was thereupon dismissed from the university with reproaches, excoriations, and maledictions.

I remember how after the *Day Book* folded in 1917, Alderman Charles E. Merriam told me that Bill Curley, then head man of Hearst's Chicago *American*, had been trying to get him, Merriam, to write editorials for the *American* and he, Merriam, had told Curley he couldn't do better than to get Sandburg and I was put on the *American* payroll at $100 a week, the nicest money I had ever pulled down on any job in my life. I did some dandy editorials, better than Art Brisbane was doing. I look at my scrapbook of those editorials and can say, without bragging, that they could stand among the best of the time: I had learned my craft. One day Bill Curley said Mr. Hearst would like an editorial giving a good hand to Ed Hurley, the washing machine magnate who headed the National Shipping Board in that war summer of 1917. I accommodated Mr. Hearst and Mr. Curley. There came other requests from Mr. Hearst and I accommodated and Mr. Curley said my work was "very satisfactory." I could have gone on and up into the big money paid to good "Hearstlings." Three weeks went by and I began to feel some kind of a deterioration, something happening to the deeper roots of my personality, a thing hard to define yet definitely there. I didn't like to part with Bill Curley; we had got along fine. I had to tell him I was going back to the Chicago *Daily News* and my old chief Henry Justin Smith—at $50 a week. The stars I was under said I wasn't fated for a Hearst career.

I look back at the Hearst life and career and wonder what to make of it. He was man, mountebank, and monster. Certainly not at all times was he all three. Definitely he could be picturesquely human or again the innovator of outrageously silly monkeyshines or again he could be a ruthless falsifier and manipulator comparable to the carnivorous animal who slashes and kills for the joy of dramatic violence, without the pressure of physical hunger. He began with dramatizing himself as a Man of the People. He ran for mayor of New York City and he ran for governor of New York State and found he couldn't make the people want him. He slowly changed from radical policies almost revolutionary. He became a faithful servant of the interests he had once denounced and ridiculed to the point of over-vilification. He became America's foremost Grand Duke, his San Simeon palace and grounds not being "swank" but royal and aristocratic in strictly Old World meanings. No longer did he mix with street and hall crowds in the shouting and tumult of political campaigns, with huge photographs of himself amid cheering throngs as when he organized the Independent Party, nominated himself for President and after vast outcry and screaming headlines and editorials managing to get something like 100,000 votes for himself for President. Now he would manage the American rabble from the silence of his San Simeon rooms. His thirty newspapers would arrive to be spread on a room floor as he moved among them and scanned their front pages and then sent telegrams and made phone calls with commands and suggestions to his executives and editors in thirty cities. He favored "the American way of life," the free enterprise competitive system. And yet where was the element of struggle and fair competition to be seen in his life? James Gordon Bennett started his New York *Herald*, as he wrote, "in a cellar, one man against the world." Scripps, Pulitzer, Greeley, Medill, they began with little or nothing and fought their way up in a competition where they had no such unlimited millions as Hearst had for the payment of any and all losses and deficits. It was a saying, "When Willie Hearst isn't doing so good with any of his papers, he goes to his mother, Phoebe Hearst, and she goes to the endless profits of the Homestake mines in South Dakota, and gives Willie whatever millions he needs." He was born a Grand Duke, for a change tried being a Man of the People, then went back to being a Grand Duke, summoning his henchmen and servitors to San Simeon and telling them what to do about the American rabble. And as one obituary writer had it, "What can you do with a man who stands himself at a church altar and wraps the American flag about him?"

Mr. Hearst died in the month of August, 1951, of a Tuesday morning, ten minutes to ten, Pacific time.

This was William Randolph Hearst, the world's most pre-eminent and important Hearst, the one and only Hearst, a man, a mountebank, and a monster, America's foremost and indubitable Grand Duke, in whose personal presence men spoke not of that dark and democratic stranger who comes to any and all men, whatever their possessions and powers, saying, "Come with me now—it is your time."

Business was not his dish

While in Milwaukee Carl had written two articles about industrial relations. A Workmen's Compensation law had been passed in Wisconsin and Carl's pieces, "Muzzling the Machines" and "Training Workers to be Careful," were in line with new ideas.

He took these articles to the magazine *System*, the largest business magazine of the day, and the editors hired him at a salary of thirty-five dollars a week.

In one of the issues, *System* had Carl on the front cover.

Fifty-five years later one of the several writers on *System*, Carroll D. Murphy, gave out a statement for a radio biography of Carl. In this statement Murphy wished to reveal himself as a valued counselor to Carl, giving valuable advice:

"I had Carl along about 1913 as I remember. He was one of many young editors I put on and I usually paid them somewhere around $100 to $125 a month.

"I sent Carl out on an assignment to interview some of the leaders in the 'safety movement' and he came back with a short story which I planned to use in factory magazines. It was a typical story by Carl. It brought tears to my eyes. He had written it beautifully. He was sorry for this working man who had broken the rules and stuck his hand into a clipping machine and lost some fingers, but the story, as Carl wrote it, made you 'hot under the collar' against management as if it were their fault, as if the men above him were not sorry but maybe a little pleased that this poor guy had gotten what was coming to him for his carelessness.

"In going over this story with Carl, I tried to have him modify it so that it would fit into the magazine and adhere to our editorial policy. I said, 'Carl, listen, you always take a crack at the businessman in your stories. You are always on the working man's side. Now the businessman is our bread and butter and he is not a fellow who delights in seeing his people suffer and lose fingers. He is a decent guy just like you and me. He is trying to make his place safe and he is sorry when anybody gets hurt and we have to keep him happy. We have to remember that he is our bread and butter, and our job is to help him with these new and safer methods.'

"I don't remember how Carl took all of that, but he was a little stubborn and the chances are that he tossed his Abraham Lincoln-like cowlick and stuck out his stubborn Swedish lips and gave me some little wisecrack. I had this problem all the time with him. One day I said, 'Now look here, Carl, you write beautifully; some day you are going to be a great writer; but you don't like to write our factual unexciting stuff. You like to write literature in which there is feeling and sentiment and for your own good, I think you just ought to pull out of here and find a place where you can write the kind of thing you like to write'—and he did."

Apparently for Mr. Murphy nothing has happened in these fifty-five years—for Mr. Murphy. As a matter of fact Carl not only earned the esteem of his employers, Daniel Vincent Casey, editor of *System*, and F. M. Feiker, editor of *Factory*, but an officer of Inland Steel Company urged Sandburg to join the firm as Safety Engineer.

From *System* Carl went back to the *Day Book*. On the *Day Book* there were no favorites. News prejudicial to business was news all the same. "The *Day Book*," said Cochran, "prints the news, names and all." Sandburg had a lot of fun at the *Day Book* at twenty-five dollars a week.

When sandwiches at Thompson's Restaurant went up from five cents to ten cents, Paula and Carl discussed the matter and found that the twenty-five dollars would not stretch far enough and so Carl asked Mr. Cochran for a raise and he finished his stint on the *Day Book* at twenty-seven fifty.

"Give us this day our daily opinion"

I would like to paraphrase from Ben Hecht's autobiography, *Child of the Century*, in which he describes his first meeting with Carl Sandburg.

"It was a dull rainy day of 1914 in the press room of the Chicago County Building when Carl was presented to his working colleagues of the various newspapers, or I should say, presented himself because the man who brought him in fell asleep before he got around to the formalities and introductions.

"None of us paid much attention to Sandburg but our rummy game was interrupted by the awakening Jack Malloy who suddenly announced we were to hear some of our guest's poetry. I had seen one previous poem by Sandburg in the little pocket *Day Book* on which he was then working and poetry was no novelty in our press room, but to this day, I remember Sandburg's voice, the finest I ever heard, reading and talking, and in Sandburg's voice lived all his poetry.

"He started reluctantly pulling from his pocket some notes he said would be called 'Chicago' when he was finished. He read:

> Hog Butcher for the World,
> Tool Maker, Stacker of Wheat,
> Player with Railroads and the Nation's Freight Handler;
> City of the Big Shoulders:

"It was a voice that made sounds fresh and clothed the simplest of sentences with mystery. The next day I talked to my boss on the Chicago *Daily News*, the Managing Editor, Henry Justin Smith. I told him there was a reporter he ought to hire named Carl Sandburg. 'This is a man who can write poetry like Whitman,' I told Smith. Smith loved our paper with an interest that ignored circulation figures and editorial policies. He saw the paper as a daily novel written by a school of 'Balzacs,' but we were missing a poet. He put Sandburg on the city staff and told the city editor to give Carl assignments worthy of his talents."

Some of his fellow poets and even some reviewers deplored

Sandburg's association with newspaper work, fearing the work would dissipate his talents. Sandburg, however, understood the newspaper was primarily his great research laboratory and that he belonged there; moreover, the critics did not know his position on the Chicago *Daily News* possessed advantages few poets have been able to gain in their formative period.

Carl Sandburg was at home on the Chicago *Daily News* for several reasons. He had sold the paper on the streets of Galesburg and read day after day the signed columns of "Sharps and Flats" by Eugene Field and "Fables in Slang" by George Ade. He admired the scrupulous way the publisher, Victor Lawson, kept editorial opinion on the editorial page. In the Chicago *Record*, a morning paper that Lawson published, Sandburg read the "Home University" series which Lawson intended to be educational material for those who couldn't go to grade or high school. He strolled into Lawson's office one day to tell the publisher that he prized this "Home University" series and counted it definitely a bright spot in what might be called his education. Sandburg's deep-woven fellowship with Henry Justin Smith, the *News* editor, might be compared with his fellowship with George Stevens which brought him out to Hollywood.

(Because of his *Daily News* stories the Newspaper Enterprise Association (NEA) eventually sent him to Stockholm, upping his $50.00 a week to $75.00 and expenses.)

Harry Hansen, Literary Editor of the Chicago *Daily News* from 1920 to 1926 and Sandburg's fellow reporter, writes (*Journal of the Illinois State Historical Society*, Winter, 1952):

"Only Smith could have held the loyalty of so many men and women who have achieved distinction in literature and journalism. They included Ben Hecht, Vincent Starrett, Robert J. Casey, John Gunther, Paul Scott Mowrer, William Hedges, Howard Blakeslee, Junius Wood, Sterling North, Keith Preston, Henry Blackman Sell, Rose Caylor, Lloyd Lewis, Howard Vincent O'Brien, Gene Morgan, Henry Luce, and a number of others."

Carl had a knowledge of labor activities and most of his copy dealt with that. At that time labor news was not an important item. It didn't sell papers, nor did the doings of labor leaders move mountains. Carl was not limited to labor, however; he had other assignments, but solving murder cases was not among them.

In 1919 W. K. Hollander, the motion-picture editor, took a vacation for several weeks and Carl replaced him. Soon thereafter Hollander left the Chicago *Daily News* and Carl became the motion-picture editor of the newspaper. Carl would go to the Loop on Sunday afternoon and by midnight Monday have seen five or six motion pictures and have his pieces written, together with a special feature story for the motion-picture trade for the following Saturday. For the first time in his life Carl had four or five days free and during this time he composed *Smoke and Steel, Slabs of the Sunburnt West, Rootabaga Stories, Abraham Lincoln: The Prairie Years, Good Morning, America, The American Songbag, Steichen the Photographer,* and *Potato Face.*

Carl did not care too much for the movies, but this assignment pleased him because it gave him a chance to sit in a dark place and compose poems.

He also had the opportunity of writing an editorial occasionally and turning it in as the spirit moved him.

Sandburg loved journalism. He told Smith, "They call newspaper work a trade, or a profession, more often it is an art . . . Besides writing, there is staging the effect. Dramatists do that; so do newspapermen. Dramatists set a stage; newspapermen, dealing with the great event, give a setting of type a proper bally-hoo . . . The novelist has his control—character; the painter has his—beauty. The newspaperman has his control—news. What is news? It is what interests everybody. How do we know it interests everybody? Why we simply know . . ."

Carl was always deeply grateful to Smith for giving him the desk which had been occupied by the poet Eugene Field whose work Carl loved.

Smith himself wrote a delightful book, *Deadlines,* and one of his chapters, "The Poet," pays tribute to Carl:

> It is certain that our days would be gloomier were it not for the leisurely, genial, enigmatic being who moves about among the shades. To find him at one's elbow, quite unexpectedly furnishes a moment of novelty and of warmth. To hear him boom: "Some first page today—man, that's

journalism!" is almost as forceful praise as a note from the Owner. Besides this, it does us good to gather around his desk and hear him talk. There is nearly always—at least, during The Poet's variable "office hours," a knot of young reporters listening to his wisdom. And it sometimes makes the Old Man nervous when he comes in and finds work at a standstill. But the Old Man knows he is chiefly to blame, so he smiles secretly and goes away.

The Old Man is wont to boast: "I've managed to keep that man on my staff for five years without a break."

A rightful boast. It is no joke to keep a poet anywhere.

Most of the writers and reporters Smith gathered were Socialists, although their socialism was more academic than barricadic. Albert Parry, a fellow reporter, recalled in his book, *Garrets and Pretenders, A History of Bohemianism in America*, that in 1913 when Sandburg for the *Day Book* and Ben Hecht for the *Daily News* were sent from Chicago to neighboring Wheaton to report a hanging, they debated not the right or wrong of capital punishment, but the right or wrong of free verse while waiting inside the gallows stockade in front of their telegraph instruments. Harry Spencer, the doomed, mounted the platform with the noose around his neck. He was told that he could pronounce his last words, and he said: "The Lord is my Shepherd, I shall not want." Sandburg was delighted; he pinched Ben's leg under the telegraph table, whispering, "Listen! what better authority do you want? Pure vers libre and in the Bible!"

As well as Socialists, the *Daily News* boasted a Bohemian population, chief of whom was Ben Hecht, who with his Chicago *American* buddy Charles MacArthur provided action, scandal, and amours.

Carl was not privy to their pranks, nor amours, but he was far from a sissy. His colleagues for a long time called him "John Guts" and with the title went not only respect but a deep affection.

Sandburg was already writing about Lincoln. He spoke of his Lincoln poems with great modesty and often mentioned a discovery he had made—what Lincoln said and did on a specific occasion—and he was beginning to go to the offices of Oliver R. Barrett, whose Lincoln manuscripts were the largest private collection in the country. A close friendship followed and their fellowship lasted up to the time of Barrett's death. Sandburg wrote a book, *Lincoln Collector*, which still holds an honored place among his works and contains reproductions of manuscripts and photographs, some of which do not appear anywhere else.

His friendship with Harry Hansen has lasted through the years. Mr. Hansen's book, *Midwest Portraits*, begins with his chapter "Carl Sandburg, Poet of the Streets and of the Prairie," an idea which I borrowed from Mr. Hansen for the title of the preceding section of this book, because it expresses so perfectly the idea of Carl Sandburg.

In those days Carl was always clipping newspaper items of historical interest about Lincoln. To this day he is forever collecting stray items that interest him. In letters he often includes a clipping or two from a newspaper. (He reads Ralph McGill's front-page column in the Atlanta *Constitution* every day. IIe clips the columns and keeps bundles of them for reading a second time. He says, "McGill is reporter, spokesman, foreteller, and current historian. He connects today's news with what will probably happen tomorrow. When I hear that President Kennedy reads McGill every day I feel better about tomorrow.")

While Ben Hecht and Charles MacArthur and the others were off roughhousing, Carl was walking into the twilight on the outskirts of Chicago thinking about Lincoln.

One day, Hecht and MacArthur hired an actor from one of the boardinghouses in Chicago and dressed him as Lincoln—beard, shawl, and tall hat. He looked more like Abraham Lincoln than Raymond Massey. Hecht and MacArthur hid the actor in the bushes at the base of the hill Carl climbed every night. As Carl reached the hill, "Lincoln" came forward, nonchalantly passed, tipping his high stovepipe, and saying, "Good evening, Mr. Sandburg."

Ben Hecht says Carl never said, "That was a pretty good trick you fellows played on me last night."

"Maybe he thought it was Lincoln," says Hecht; "he just never said anything."

When I asked Carl about this, he said, "That story has been floating around for years and it never happened. If I had seen Lincoln's shade from the grave or from the Actors Studio, I would have greeted him with a bit of humor."

Carl continued, "It reminds me of the time Ben Hecht and Charles MacArthur sent a telegram to Mary Garden the same night this opera star was opening in *Carmen*, 'We would like to meet you after the performance at Schlogl's to discuss the future of art in Chicago and America. If you agree to meet us, please come out in the third act with a rose between your teeth!' "

When Ben Hecht sent in bloody preliminary details about a hanging, Henry Justin Smith sent word saying: "Please omit gruesome details of the hanging. Remember ours is a family newspaper."

Ben Hecht replied, "Will make hanging cheerful as possible."

These reporters, Bohemian and intellectual, frequented several clubs: The Fabian Club, the Cheesebox, the Cliff Dwellers, the Mary Garden Forum, Schlogl's Restaurant, and the Dill Pickle. While Sandburg and Starrett spent most of their evenings at the Dill Pickle, Ben Hecht, Bodenheim, Burton Rascoe, and Gene Markey, all of them in the money, frequented Schlogl's whose tables were of polished wood, the legs of which creaked under the weight of excellent and exotic foods.

Sinclair Lewis stopped in at both Schlogl's and the Dill Pickle whenever he came to Chicago and often his main purpose was to deride the groups in each for their futile aestheticism.

Of all the clubs, the Dill Pickle was the center for Chicago's Bohemia. It was the hang-out of poets and other assorted conversationalists.

The Dill Pickle, according to Albert Parry, was Chicago's first successful attempt at a Latin Quarter. It was organized by Jack Jones, who had been an active I.W.W. man when an unrequited love for a lady Socialist embittered him and he decided to pass the remainder of his days in the "peace" of Bohemia.

Under the rules of the Dill Pickle the theme of a debate was announced only after the debate started. One of the debates

Hecht arranged was: "Resolved: That People Who Attend Literary Debates Are Imbeciles."

On certain nights of the week the Dill Pickle was turned over to the playwrights. Now and then a group of hobos would come in and be greeted by the poets and the writers, and now and then a Wobbly would get up and deliver an impassioned speech.

Henry Justin Smith describes first hearing Carl recite poetry at Le Petite Gourmet, operated by the widow of William Vaughn Moody, author of *The Girl of the Golden West*.

"It is a voice familiar enough, yet charged with a new element. It is a deep voice, deliberate, casual, rich with earth-tones, it comes as though some organist were idly exploring the pedals. . . . The figure before us, with its luxuriant bangs of hair, with the military shoulders and the careless drab clothes, is familiar, yet it is now remote, inexplicable. Well, there is something we have overlooked. We have seen him write but we have never heard him read. We have thumbed over his poems, and asked him questions about them, and he has showed them to us and we have given him encouraging grins. But . . . boys, we never fathomed him at all."

Sandburg says he may yet write at length about the time that H. L. Mencken termed Chicago "the literary capital of the United States." "Quite possibly no other newspaper in the United States ever had at one brief period of time such an array of authors as came daily to the ramshackle building at Madison and Wells Streets where the blessed and patient Victor Lawson owned and published what we termed 'the world's greatest afternoon newspaper,' the Chicago *Daily News*. There was a news editor, Henry Justin Smith, who wrote good books and was known among newspapermen as a loveable character and nearly a saint. At times he could actually bawl a man out and the man knew definitely that he was forgiven for whatever happened. Lloyd Lewis, dramatic critic, wrote *Myths After Lincoln* and *Sherman, Fighting Prophet*, one of the great American biographies. The versatile and colorful Ben Hecht, whom Harry Hansen called 'Pagliacci of the fire escapes,' was baffling even to himself. One morning Ben strolled over to my typewriter and yawned and I said, 'I can tell you were up late writing last night.

What were you writing?' And Ben said, 'Poems.' 'About what?' and answered Ben, 'As usual—about the night—the night.'

"Paul Leach, who covered politics and wrote a biography of Charles Gates Dawes, strode to my desk one morning and just stood looking at me. I said, 'How are you, Paul?' And Paul drawled and droned, 'O-o-old Carl Sandburg. O-o-old Carl Sandburg.' I said, 'How old?' Paul groaned again, 'Older than the oldest pyramids in Egypt. Older than the oldest pagodas in China.' "

The Chicago race riots

On the last Sunday of July, 1919, a colored boy at a Chicago beach swam over an imaginary segregation line. He was immediately stoned by some white boys who knocked him from a raft into the water where he drowned. Colored people rushed to the policeman and asked him to arrest the stone throwers. The policeman refused. As the body of the drowned boy was brought to shore more rocks were thrown on both sides. The policeman held to his refusal to make an arrest. Fighting broke out on the beach, then spread to all borders of the "black belt." A full-scale race riot was on.

The riot, of course, furnished an excuse for every delinquent, antisocial thug, and criminal. Teen-age bands of both white and colored roamed the streets. Workingmen of both races stayed home to form vigilante committees. At the end of three days, twenty Negroes and fourteen white men were dead, and a large number of Negro houses had been burned.

Three weeks before the riots began, the Chicago *Daily News* had assigned Carl Sandburg to do a series of articles on the booming Negro population of Chicago. His articles had been running two weeks and were near inspiring some sort of concerted community action when the stone throwers took over.

"Then," writes Sandburg, "as usual nearly everybody was more interested in the war than how it got loose."

In the winter of 1919 Harcourt, Brace and Howe published Carl's articles in a little paperback book called *The Chicago*

Race Riots and prefaced it with an introduction by Walter Lippmann. On the inside cover of the book Carl lent me he had
written this note: "On rereading this I find that ten years after
I have not learned much that is new about the race question.
C.S. 1929."

This little paperback had everything in seventy-one pages that
Gunnar Myrdal discussed in one thousand pages in *An American
Dilemma*. To be sure, *The Chicago Race Riots* is not documented,
nor do its statistics, such as they are, offer a wide numerical
picture of the situation. But the question remains with us—and
in this paperback Sandburg has not only defined the question,
How shall we grant equality to the colored minority?, but answered it. It is a journalistic answer, its arrangement hit-or-miss,
as Sandburg himself confessed, but it is a dramatic and evocative
answer and—a right answer.

Grim as they were, the Chicago race riots were a break with
the past. The riots were not justified by claims of race supremacy
or by fears of Negro sexuality, nor was the nation indifferent. It
is no oversimplification to say the Chicago race riots stated the
problem we still labor to resolve. It is to Sandburg's everlasting
credit that he understood this in advance of the riots and that
he was able to publish this—the greatest news story of the century—the black man's demand for equality.

Three new conditions were attendant in the 1919 riots, Sandburg said. "The Black Belt population of fifty thousand in
Chicago was more than doubled during World War I. No new
houses or tenements were built. Under pressure of war industry
the district, already notoriously overcrowded and swarming with
slums, was compelled to have and hold in its human dwelling
apparatus more than twice as many people as it held before the
war."

He goes on to say that a large number of returning colored
soldiers had settled in Chicago. Added to them were thousands
of new colored residents imported to the city to service the in-
dustries of wartime Chicago. On top of this, into Chicago poured
streams of Negroes from Texas, Virginia, Alabama, Mississippi,
fleeing after each lynching.

Another condition that made the Chicago riots essentially

different was that the Negroes of Chicago had political strength. A city administration refused to draw a color line and lose that strength, and a mayor governed whose opponents failed to defeat him by calling him "nigger lover."

The last and most significant development of the Chicago race riots, in Sandburg's words: "Thousands of white men and thousands of colored men stuck together during the riots, and through the public statements of white and colored officials of the Stockyards Labor Council asked the public to witness that they were shaking hands as 'brothers' and could not be counted on for any share of the mob shouts and ravages. This is the first time that in any similar crisis in an American community a large body of mixed nationalities and races—Poles, Negroes, Lithuanians, Italians, Irishmen, Germans, Slovaks, Russians, Mexicans, Yankees, Englishmen, Scotsmen—proclaimed that they were all organized and opposed violence to 'white' union men and 'colored' union men."

Sandburg described the death of Jim Crow. He prophesied that as the Negro drives for equality, there will be fewer lynchings and more riots.

In the Chicago of 1919, the Negro had allies—union brotherhoods, political power, and whites who would pledge with him a hatred of violence.

The Chicago race riots, surmises Sandburg, were provoked not because a large mass of the illiterate, semiliterate, and unskilled workers were "moving in" but rather because the Negro had become more literate, more skilled, more desirous of his fair share.

The stimulus which triggered the riots was the sudden instability of realty values. When a colored family moved into what was previously an all-white block, realty values dropped. They trebled again as soon as the block became completely colored and landlords jacked up rents.

"White citizens," Sandburg was told by Charles S. Duke, a Negro, a Harvard graduate, former lieutenant of Company G, Eighth Illinois Infantry, and a civil engineer in the bridge division of the city department of public works, "must be educated out of all hysteria over actual or prospective arrival of colored neighbors. All colored citizens do not make bad neighbors, although in some cases they will not make good ones. It is of the greatest importance, however, both to white and colored people, that the real estate dealers should cease to make a business of commercializing racial antagonisms."

The race riots came when unemployment was at a high. The war had ended and the thousands of war workers who had streamed into Chicago were without jobs.

Yet despite this unemployment, Sandburg speculated there was a growing realization that, with immigration stopped, the only great source from which industry could develop a new labor bloc was from the mass of twelve million Negro workers. He quotes Dr. George Edwin Haynes, a colored man who took a Master's degree at Yale and Ph.D. at Columbia, and a director of Negro economics in the Department of Labor:

"The manufacturer is getting more and more to realize that when the pressure comes, as it came during the war, if he can get the labor, he doesn't see any color mark on the bank check or the draft that he gets in payment for his goods. Most of this thing that we call a race question is down at rock bottom a labor question."

While lawlessness did reign in Chicago, the war that was fought was not all the blacks against all the whites. Sandburg quotes A. K. Foote, a colored man who was a hog killer and secretary of Local 651 of the Amalgamated Meat Cutters and Butcher Workmen of North America: "If you ask me what I think about race prejudice and whether it's getting better, I'll tell you the one place in this town where I feel safest is over at the yards with my union button on."

Equality through unionism, however, is still an ideal. But throughout the South, the caste system has been maintained precisely because of the fear of unionism.

The Chicago Race Riots concludes with an interview with Mr. Julius Rosenwald, who was the president of Sears, Roebuck Company and had set up a foundation which had established more than three hundred Rosenwald rural schools in Southern States, three hundred more partially established schools, and four hundred projected ones. Mr. Rosenwald described some of the intelligent Negroes he had met and helped and told Sandburg, "The most expensive thing we can do is not to educate the Negro."

Which led Sandburg to his last chapter, "For Federal Action." "The race question is national and federal. No city or state can solve it alone. There must be cooperation between states. And there must be federal handling of it."

In 1919, Sandburg recognized that the race question was not a local problem but a national question. It needed Federal attention and Federal aid. But it was a long time until Federal action was forthcoming—but come it did—in 1954 when the Supreme Court ruled school segregation unconstitutional.

I remember talking about the ruling with Carl right after the decision. He wondered then why the Negroes had not made their stand in respect to the public facilities like hospitals and nursing homes. But we agreed the society was a school-oriented society and Carl Sandburg guessed if a boy went to school with a colored fellow he wouldn't mind so much the colored fellow joining the same union.

Sandburg is a whole man and his concern with the Negroes' drive for equality and justice has affected every part of him, politically and artistically. That he saw the race riots and understood them must have influenced his desire to write a biography about Lincoln.

The problem of racial equality has never been far from Sandburg's mind. It appears in all his writings.

In his column, Chicago *Daily News* on February 10, 1928, Sandburg was reviewing "The Tragic Era" (Garfield to Harding), by Claude Bowers. He ended his review as follows: "Our 'tragic era' is yet to come—race relations. When the Negro in a northern city buys a house and lot from one white man and is bombed out of his home by another white man, which has happened in our own tragic era, we feel that Mr. Bowers might have given us a few pages on the ins and outs of what is meant by white supremacy."

Again in 1943, he wrote about this ever-growing danger in his syndicated newspaper column, later published in *Home Front Memo*:

The slums get their revenge, always somehow or other their retribution can be figured in any community, whether the slums are Negro rat-holes such as those presented in *Native Son* by the Negro novelist Richard Wright, or slums of Polish white folk over the Northwest Side of Chicago, with an unforgettable and reeking house of vice, as reported in the novel *Never Come Morning* by the Scandinavian Nelson Algren.

No slum is separate from its community. Thousands of mean and sinister secrets stretch out in definite bonds from the slum to the outside world.

Why should some of us find it deeply moving that an eminent spokesman, Bishop Bernard J. Sheil, founder-director of the Catholic Youth Organization, spoke last week his fear and anxiety as to the "Christian ghettos" of the Negro race and of how "in the case of these twelve million Americans . . . a disproportionate number have translated a deep inner frustration into an external attitude that is completely antisocial"?

The bishop sees danger signals. Working with Catholic youth of all sorts and conditions, it has come clear to him that again because of hate and discrimination handed the Negro there may be grapes of wrath trampled in a vintage not so good to look at. "These people are no longer satisfied with weasel words and insincere promises. Their demands are most reasonable. The opportunity to progress, to better themselves economically, to share in the industrial, social, political, and cultural life of America—these are the things that the American Negro seeks—and he can no longer be denied them. If the Negro is worthy to die with the white man, then he is worthy to live with him on terms of honest, objective equality."

Carl talked about Little Rock, Arkansas, to the Graduate Faculty of the New School in New York City on April 6, 1959: "Mr. Faubus of Arkansas wouldn't know what Lincoln was talking about . . . but Mr. Faubus does not know that fearful four-year blood-bath of the 1860's had one curious result. Before that war in the sixties, the Department of State in treaties with foreign nations wrote, "The united States *are*.' But after that war it was written, 'The United States *is*.'

"The war was fought over a *verb*."

As well as political, this concern has always been dramatic and, at times, deeply symbolical for Carl. He has given the Negro a prominent part in his poetry. When Bette Davis and Gary Merrill (and later Leif Erikson) appeared in *The World of Carl Sandburg*, which was adapted and directed by Norman Corwin, in whatever city they played, Miss Davis always received a standing ovation when she recited "Elizabeth Umpsteadt," Sandburg's poem about the colored whore.

It is a poem about beauty corrupted by the caste system.

> . . . I am gone from among the two-legged moving figures
> on top the earth now, and nobody will say my
> heart is someway wrong when I assert I was the
> most beautiful nigger girl in northern Indiana,
> and men wanted my beauty, white men and black
> men—and I learned what they wanted and I traded
> on it, I schemed and haggled to get all I could
> for it—and so I am one nigger girl who today
> has a grand funeral with all the servitors paid
> in spot cash . . .
> They lay me in a grave today, and I leave behind one
> child fathered by a white man lawyer, thousands
> of dollars in the bank, eight houses I owned as
> property in the same way my mother was owned as
> property by white men in Tennessee, and the
> mystery of whether or not Ray Lamphere told me
> he was going to burn down the Gunness house and
> change the living bodies of Mrs. Gunness and the
> three children to ashes—all these I leave behind
> me—I, who was the most beautiful nigger girl in
> northern Indiana.

Before finishing my discussion of Carl's amazing insights into the race issue, I would like to quote the closing sentences in the Introduction written by Walter Lippmann on August 26, 1919:

We shall have to work out with the Negro a relationship which gives him complete access to all the machinery of our common civilization, and yet allows him to live so that no Negro need dream of a white heaven and of bleached angels. Pride of race will come to the Negro when a dark skin is no longer associated with poverty, ignorance, misery, terror and insult. When this pride arises every white man in America will be the happier for it. He will be able then, as he is not now, to enjoy the finest quality of civilized living —the fellowship of different men.

Throwing with everything he had

The War Years were done. Sandburg heaved a sigh of relief: "What if I hadn't lived to finish it!"

No one expected him to do anything more than to sit back and relax, perhaps even bask. The four volumes had been as profound an interior struggle as any man dare undertake.

But the Chicago *Times* asked him to write about the war in Europe. Sandburg said no. The *Times* persevered. It was too important. Sandburg said yes.

It was rumored an important Washington official helped Carl make up his mind. He told Carl the country needed someone to study quietly the quick changes which the Capital was too close to to analyze.

Carl wired the Chicago *Times.* "No contract. Just a letter."

The *Times* asked for one article a week, five hundred to a thousand words. Sandburg went to work, conscientiously as always, and soon the *Times* was syndicating his column in newspapers all over the country. Some of his pieces were read over the radio program, *The Treasury Hour.* One of these was called "The Man With the Broken Fingers." It was about a Norwegian captured by the Gestapo. The Norwegian refused to talk. The Gestapo tortured him by breaking his fingers one by one, and then his arms, but "no names came."

A credulous reader in Boston wrote and asked if these were the actual facts.

Sandburg replied that he had attended a mass meeting of Swedes and Norwegians in Minnehaha Park, Minneapolis. He had listened to a speech delivered by a Norwegian flyer from Camp Little Norway in Toronto, Canada, who told the story. He had interviewed the flyer, obtained names and dates, and written this story "cruelly repressive, befouling of human dignity."

In 1943, these pieces were collected in a book entitled *Home Front Memo*. Commenting on it, the *New York Herald Tribune* said: "This book, *Home Front Memo*, is proof that America's chief poet is not too proud of his reputation to risk it in controversy, not so careful of his artistic independence as to stay in an ivory tower when his beloved democracy is endangered."

A column in *Home Front Memo*, dated August 24, 1941, is addressed to Colonel Charles A. Lindbergh. It was the week after Colonel Lindbergh had delivered a speech for the America First Committee, an organization of considerable influence before the Japanese attack on Pearl Harbor. Colonel Lindbergh and the America Firsters pleaded for neutrality and Carl's article is entitled "Sure We're Neutral—Who For?":

> If you favor the republican form of government and the democratic system which is the basis of American political life, why have you managed in 17 speeches to carefully, scrupulously, evade and avoid any slightest word of disapproval of Hitler, of the Nazi movement, and the Nazi plans which aim at conquest of democratic countries?
>
> Does your silence about Nazi Germany mean that you are trying carefully and scrupulously to maintain yourself as an honest neutral?
>
> Are you aware that when your mouth opens and you tell an audience of millions of listeners, including army and navy units, that we have a government of "hypocrisy and subterfuge," you are saying the same thing Hitler and the Nazis say about our democratic system?

Another column was an open letter to Norman Thomas, who spoke from many America First platforms:

Bruddah Thomas and Our Jitters

I listened the other night to Bruddah Norman Thomas. His subject was our national hysteria. About this and that, in connection with the well-known war, he finds as people we are far too hysterical. I could tell by the way he spoke of hysteria that it is not a good thing to have and he is in favor of our having less of it. . . .

On the other hand, however, he wished to convey the impression that the appeasers are cool, calm, collected, serene, well-poised, considerate, reasonable, moderate, urbane, amiable—and if you know how to listen to them, your case of the jitters will pick up and improve right away and after a while you will be a convalescent and you may even be completely cured.

As I listened on and on to the verbal cadenzas of Bruddah Thomas, I found he was grinding and gnashing some of his syllables . . . I wished for Herb Graffis, for Lloyd Lewis, for Bugs Baer, for William Saroyan, to tell me whether you can cure the jitters with the jitters, or whether it does any good to hiccup in the face of someone who has the hiccups.

Likewise in the case of the Montana Senator, Wheeler by name. He meets hysteria over the country, sees it, hears it, smells it. So he combats hysteria . . . by telling with his open mouth to the country that we have a President of the United States who wants a war that will "plow under" every fourth boy of draft age.

And the distinguished aviator, the fair-haired boy whose record of thirty-three hours crossing the Atlantic has been cut to seven-and-a-half hours by flying bombers from Newfoundland to Britain, how is he on our hysteria? Like his colleagues, he says it is bad. He would allay and tone down our hysteria. And how? By telling us that England had the war lost when she declared it and when the Nazis come to take us we will wait until we can see the whites of their eyes and then shoot.

Yes, Carl Sandburg, more than any other literary man of the twentieth century, was totally involved in the affairs of his time, and he threw with everything he had.

PART 7

In Prose You Say
What You Mean

The American fairy tales

"The children asked questions, and I answered them," says Carl Sandburg, describing how he wrote the *Rootabaga Stories*, published at the end of 1922 by Harcourt, Brace, illustrated by Maude and Miska Petersham, and advertised as "Fanciful Stories for Children."

Ease of arrangement, spirit of play, simplicity—this is what Sandburg has undertaken in the *Rootabaga Stories*.

Children find great amusement in listening to someone toy with the alphabet; the people who live in Rootabaga Country are all essentially alphabetic curiosities. There is Blixie Bimber who finds a gold buckskin whincher (a good luck charm) and promptly falls in love with a series of "X's"—Silas Baxby, Fritz Axenbax, and James Sixbixdix.

Henry Hagglyhoagly wins Susan Slackentwist by serenading her on a bitterly cold winter night accompanying himself on the guitar with his mittens on. Eeta Peeca Pie, Googler and Gaggler, Dippy the Wisp, and Meeney Miney are all residents of Rootabaga Country. They are different forms of alliteration, sound, and euphony.

While each of the adventures in *Rootabaga Stories* is short, Sandburg relates each with infinite patience. The book has no elliptical sentences. Every word is included and often repeated: "The ticket agent was sitting at the window selling railroad tickets the same as always," is redundant, but it is also unsophisticated.

I do not mean to imply the book is composed solely of nonsense syllables. To the contrary, Mrs. Spider in "Molasses and Secret Ambitions" washes clothes wearing a frying pan on her head.

> "Why do you wear that frying pan on your head?" they asked her.

"In this country all ladies wear the frying pan on their head when they want a new hat."

"But what if you want a hat when you are frying with the frying pan?" asked Eeta Peeca Pie.

"That never happens to any respectable lady in this country."

"Don't you never have no new style hat?" asked Meeney Miney.

"No, but we always have new style frying pans every spring and fall."

Throughout these stories Sandburg employs an artless poetry (I believe it is some of his best): "Sometimes on that kind of a January night the stars look like numbers, look like the arithmetic writing of a girl going to school and just beginning arithmetic." All of the poetry, moreover, uses for its materials what can be included in a child's experience.

Rootabaga Country is an American country. It has a railroad, ragpickers, policemen, ball teams, tall grass. It is mapped out. If it existed, you could get to it and find your way around. Geographic reality is what makes the *Rootabaga Stories* the first genuinely American fairy tales.

The stories are fairy tales because the population of Rootabaga Country does not know about social distinction (although they differ one from the other); and because they do not have money (although the Potato Bug Millionaire collects fleems). The stories are American in diction, in foolishness, in fancy, and American in *place*.

Thus, Rootabaga Country is also more than a fairy tale. Rootabaga Country is Carl Sandburg's Main Street, his Yoknapatawpha County, his Gibbsville, Pennsylvania.

American writers have the compulsion to create their own city or place, house by house, street by street, year by year, word by word. The truths they find differ from author to author and from area to area. But calling Rootabaga Country Sandburg's Main Street is more than a historical or literary convenience.

Rootabaga Country (like Galesburg, Illinois, itself) is a good place to live because of the people who inhabit it. Sandburg never fell for the temptation to seize upon this aspect—life in the small town—and use it for ridicule, and do with it what so many other of our writers have done to point out the dullness and the narrowness of the lives and interests of the people. Sinclair Lewis set the fashion with *Main Street*, Sherwood Anderson in *Winesburg, Ohio*, Phil Stong in *Village Tale*, and James Gould Cozzens in *The Last Adam*. All have dealt with the sinister side of small-town life, the dirty stories around the stove of the general store, the love affairs in haystacks, the sadism, and the abnormalities.

Sandburg understood in the strict sense none of this is true. There are such phases of life, of course, even in Galesburg, Illinois, but they are phases. To dwell on them distorts the picture.

Sinclair Lewis's Main Street and Carl Sandburg's Rootabaga Country are more or less contemporary places. *Main Street* was published in 1920, the *Rootabaga Stories* in 1922. (*Rootabaga Pigeons* was published a year later.)

Main Street by Carl's friend, Sinclair Lewis, was a clinical study of the dismal mediocrity in a small northwestern Minnesota town. What made the book important was not so much Lewis's castigation of the American small-town businessman, his lack of manners and his shameful rejection of culture—all of which were true—but rather that Lewis constructed Gopher Prairie. The town was geographically and poetically real—Lewis saw the buttercups bloom in the wagon ruts, and the pools of mud turn to slippery, black lozenges in the winter. Gopher Prairie became more than a town and more than a symptomatic idea—it became a condition of life, a condition of life at a precise time in American history.

Sandburg did not seek the same truths in his Rootabaga Country. He is not clinical, not trying to re-create mediocrity but creating joyousness. All the same Rootabaga Country is a condition prompted by the same causes that led to Main Street.

Rootabaga Country and Main Street are places in an America caught abandoning the old agrarian values with no substitutes for the responsibilities of a new, emerging urban way of life. As a consequence, much of life is irresolved. The citizens of Gopher Prairie "had lost the power of play as well as the power of impersonal thought." One of Lewis's more sympathetic residents speculates: "I wonder if the small town isn't, with some lovely exceptions, a social appendix? Some day these dull market towns may be as obsolete as monasteries."

It is exactly the power of play and the power of impersonal thought that the citizens of Rootabaga Country will not give up. They had lived in a house, perhaps in Gopher Prairie, "where everything is the same as it always was," and they have begun to ask each other "Who's who? How much? and What's the answer?" Rootabaga Country is an escape from a condition.

It would be foolish to attempt further correlation between these two books. Perhaps I have already tried too hard to force the same reflections out of diverse books with diverse effects written out of diverse reactions. But the process of literature and history does have multiple reflections. Sandburg and Lewis are mirroring the same image at different angles. It is the image of a changing America lacking a plan for the future.

Because the change has been accomplished, because the market town and the farming community are vanishing, the *Rootabaga Stories* have all the attributes of a fairy tale. They are about a place the old folks do not remember, and only children can guess at, about a country without money in which children name themselves.

Nothing modern is alien to him

The Family of Man created by Edward Steichen for the Museum of Modern Art was perhaps the greatest photographic exhibition of all time and a very fine book. It consisted of five hundred and three pictures from sixty-eight countries. Carl Sandburg wrote the Prologue which opened the photographic exhibition and was published in this book.

By a roundabout method, he possibly lent Steichen the title. Years back, Sandburg says, he told Steichen how five or six times in his letters and speeches Lincoln used the expression "the family of man," meaning by the phrase humanity as a whole over the earth. Steichen's *Family of Man* was a literal attempt to show how the needs of men the world over are basically the same elemental needs.

"As you read the book over the years," says Sandburg in his Prologue, "you can catch yourself saying . . . 'I am not a stranger here, I am not a stranger.'"

Carl's feeling about the book and his Prologue is a deeply poetic feeling. He has great respect for the exhibition and profound admiration for his brother-in-law, Steichen.

I have insisted that Sandburg is one of the first great poets of the New America filled with factories and cities. It is not surprising then that Sandburg should have a good understanding and work at developing the techniques for dealing with analyses and criticism of photography.

I mean no disrespect to the poets who were contemporary with him but Edward Arlington Robinson wrote poems about the Round Table; Robert Frost about a New England long gone; and Edgar Lee Masters and Vachel Lindsay about a frontier rapidly disappearing.

Sandburg's insight into photography long antedated his Prologue to *The Family of Man*. Sandburg was the first American to write a biography of a photographer: *Steichen, the Photographer*, published in 1929. In it Sandburg told the story of his wife's brother who was a lithographic draftsman, artist, photographer, and painter for the Paris salon, Army officer in charge of aerial photography, all of which Steichen renounced to give his whole affection to art's first principle, life itself. Sandburg described how Steichen, alone in a cottage at Rue Voulangis, Paris, spent a year photographing a white cup and saucer against a black background, making one thousand exposures, experimenting in control of light on the object and on the negative. With his medium in complete control Steichen returned to New York to make photographs of those who could pay.

The book *Steichen, the Photographer* contained forty-eight examples of his work. In his Foreword Sandburg asked that he be allowed "prejudices in writing about one of the family." The book was well received though Sandburg's narrative was severely criticized. In truth, it probably was too breezy. But I think we will have to accord credit where it is due. This was a poet, after all, for the first time trying to synchronize the language of poetry with the language of photography. That no other poets have been successful in this, and that *The Family of Man* was an achievement, is a reflection of Sandburg's vision.

Jacques Barzun and the bulrushes

"Edward Steichen's photographic exhibition, *The Family of Man*, has been seen by more than five million people over the earth and its book sales have gone more than two million copies. This exhibition affirms the unity of mankind more simply and more eloquently than any other pictorial or literary production of the past or present."

Thus Carl Sandburg on *The Family of Man*.

Jacques Barzun in his book, *The House of Intellect*, does not agree. He writes: "The book opens with a rather tendentious female nude, prone amid the ferns of a forest glade. This is followed by episodes of kissing and caresses in public places. Next, in the middle of a black page, is a small square transom through which one sees a shoulder, face, and hand belonging to a couple making love. The vignette is printed horizontally so that there shall be no mistaking the subject. The theme of copulation is frequently repeated, notably as a restorative after the half-dozen pages devoted to schoolwork."

Mr. Barzun's complaint is that the book does not represent intellect and the achievements of Mind. Selection, however, is the right of the artist, as is purpose. Mr. Steichen's purpose was to establish by photography the kinship all peoples of the earth share.

The Hindu still uses a wooden plow; a tractor is lost on him. Not only does this great technological invention remain a mystery to the Hindu but it establishes no kinship for him with other peoples. The Australian bushman does not understand law nor the concept of parliamentary government. To show him by picture that other men govern themselves and accord each other certain rights would not only not enlighten him, but it would not even confuse him. What both the Hindu and the bushman understand is prayer.

Every society doesn't know monogamy, commerce, or even agriculture. But every society does know war, love, and some sort of God. The basic story of mankind is a man and a woman. This is the story Steichen was trying to tell. And Professor Barzun neglects to count the photographs of men praying and in reverence.

As for the sight of young people caressing in public places, one ought to consult the young lovers. Would one rather let them caress and simply make no note of it? But to urge this last suggestion will only give license to the realty developers to rip up all the parks since no one will believe the young need a place to stroll hand in hand.

This book will stick

From the first, most American critics embraced Carl Sandburg with respect and affection.

Henry L. Mencken, on the "New Poetry Movement" in *Prejudices*, discussed Joyce Kilmer (childish gush), Amy Lowell (balderdash), Charles Hanson Towne (McGuffey's Sixth Reader stuff and more balderdash), and Carl Sandburg "who gets memorable effects by astonishingly austere means, as in his famous *Chicago* rhapsody and his *In the Cool Tombs*. And always he is thoroughly individual, a true original, his own man."

Certainly this was exuberant praise from Mencken, who often repeated the medium of poetry was no more than "a device to get off some gassy and high-sounding nothings."

In hundreds of reviews the critics greeted Sandburg with a special salutation. But there came the day when Carl said, "The critics ain't doing so good," as he read the comments on his only novel, the 1,067-page *Remembrance Rock*.

The New Yorker found the novel "passing dull," and *The New York Times* reviewer, Perry Miller, wrote, "at this point in his career Sandburg has lent himself to . . . maudlin devices." *Time* said, "It was the sort of novel a distinguished Supreme Court Justice might write," which wasn't so great an insult, and the *Saturday Review*, "his portrayals of each of the (several) periods of American life are somehow static."

After reading each adverse review Carl took off the green eyeshade, reared his head back, and murmured, "Yeah?"

There were some enthusiasts. Virginia Kirkus of the Bookshop Service, whose reviews are respected by booksellers and librarians, liked the book, and Lewis Gannett called it a sermon.

Fanny Butcher, book editor of the Chicago *Tribune* wrote: "To supremacy as poet, historian, biographer, teller of tales to young America, Carl Sandburg at the age of 70 adds supremacy as a novelist with *Remembrance Rock*. It is the sum of everything that Carl Sandburg has written, learned, done." And Herb Graffis in the Chicago *Sun-Times:* "Some day when my grandson gets old enough and quiets down so he'll sit and listen, there are parts of *Remembrance Rock* . . . that I want to read to him. He'll get the big idea, Sandburg has made ghosts live to give him the close-up on how American liberty was conceived, fought for, and won. The kid'll understand it clearly, the way Carl reports this story."

When Irita Van Doren introduced Sandburg at the Book and Author Luncheon in New York on January 18, 1949, she said that while he called the book a novel, it actually transcended definition. It was an evocation of the meaning of America. "This American story with all its rich variation is told in folk song and proverb, in strong, slow-moving narrative, in emotionally enthralling climaxes, and always with Carl Sandburg's unparalleled ear for the latent music of his country. An accomplishment worthy to stand beside his great biography of Lincoln, *Remembrance Rock* is Carl Sandburg's fullest, ripest tribute to the American people whom he loves."

Sandburg explains his novel: "The questions rise and weave and never end. How did this America we live in, the U.S.A., come to be what it is now? When and where did it begin and how go on? What is this elusive intangible, this mysterious variable that in moments seems to be a constant—what is this ever shifting and hazardous thing often called The American Dream?"

The writing, with revisions and corrections, he says, took five years, and the book ran to 673,000 words. It was termed by reviewers a novel, a saga, a sermon in antique, a dramatic poem, a testament, an epic, an opera, a symphony, a chronicle, a history, a huge muddled and meaningless compendium, a cinematic epos of Hollywood baroque, a timeless masterpiece, an agonizing account of purification through ordeal, a Chaucerian collection of travelers' tales, "a panorama of folks and deeds carrying farther the themes and fabrics of the long tumultuous poem *The People, Yes.*"

Valdemar Vetlugin, the executive at Metro-Goldwyn-Mayer who purchased *Remembrance Rock* and had been the editor at *Redbook* magazine which serialized five articles out of Sandburg's *Abraham Lincoln: The War Years,* read each section as soon as it was finished.

These sections are Book I, an independent novel about the Pilgrim period; Book II, also an independent novel about the American Revolution, and Book III, a novel about the Civil War period. On reading the Epilogue which ends the book, he intoned, in his Russian accent, "Maybe eet ees a nawvel. Maybe eet ees a long dramatic pome. Maybe eet ees a new fawrm. Eef *Pilgrim's Prawgress* is a nawvel, then thees ees a nawvel."

Remembrance Rock resembles the novels people hoped for in the years before World War I. This is not to say *Remembrance Rock* is old fashioned. Indeed not. *Remembrance* Rock is simply dissimilar, the sort of novel most critics have forgotten how to read. *Remembrance Rock* is in the tradition of the "Great American Novel."

Until the 1920s literary efforts as well as criticism found best expression in the daily papers. It was journalistic. The Great American Novel was in the hands of newspapermen. Precisely what it would be about, people weren't sure. It was a big country and people expected a big novel with representative heroes.

This anticipation was not misguided. Dickens and Butler and

Joyce had expressed the English character. There is also the Great French Novel—either Stendhal's *The Red and the Black* or Proust's *Remembrance of Things Past*. *The Magic Mountain* by Thomas Mann is the Great German Novel. But neither England nor France nor Germany is the great novel-writing nation of the modern world.

The great novel writers are the Russians. And while the Americans do not imitate the Russian novels, the writers of both countries have similar concerns.

The American or the Russian has a country so vast no novel can encompass all of it. The American and Russian writers have concentrated upon a hero trapped by a rearranging and fast-closing social structure which has a direct effect upon his personality.

With the French Revolution and Napoleon's conquests, Russia began to take on Western ways. Industry and colleges and the professions blossomed and a wealthy, erudite aristocracy developed. This sudden growth produced a disaffected class of people. We can say this disaffected class found expression in Russian novels as "the superfluous man."

Turgenev was the first to exploit this disaffection of personality. He coined the word "nihilism" and made his young hero of *Fathers and Sons*, Yevgeny Bazarov, a nihilist. Bazarov knew the new society, part anarchist, part conservative, part radical, had no real place for him. Because he didn't fit, Bazarov condemned all values.

In Dostoevski's novel, *The Possessed*, the superfluous man is Stepanovich. His education and learning have refined his sensibilities too well to let him be happy among the lower classes, but he has neither the money nor the background to call himself an aristocrat. The superfluous man came to a full cycle in Dostoevski's hero of *Crime and Punishment*, Raskolnikov. Raskolnikov, the brilliant graduate student who murders a sleazy pawnbroker because he considers himself a superior person, is the superfluous man turned dangerous.

The conflict between the pioneer and the commercial millionaire in America led not to the creation of a superfluous man and revolution but to the American high school and "the ignoble hero." American writers about 1920 began to describe a similar conflict, but they made their hero ignoble, his motive a base motive, to show how the innocence of the American pioneer had been spotted and destroyed by the business society. Jay Gatsby, the hero of F. Scott Fitzgerald's novel, *The Great Gatsby,* is an ignoble hero. He has courage, he is still innocent, but his past is shadowy and dark and disguised. Sinclair Lewis looked at the ignoble American from another direction in *Babbitt.* Babbitt has lost the courage of the pioneer, his innocence has long been dissipated, and his impulses are all cautionary.

The ignoble hero is a mainstay of the American novel. He is man corrupted by mercantilism. William Faulkner's Yoknapatawpha County is filled with Southerners despoiled by the growing commerce of Jefferson City. John O'Hara certainly, from Julian English to Alfred Eaton, writes about the ignoble hero.

The ignoble hero calls attention to the Achilles' heel of America as the superfluous man summed up the Achilles' heel of Russia. The Achilles' heel in America—according to our novelists —is that heroism and virtue are often incapacitated by commercial greed and selfishness.

This concern with lost innocence put a different emphasis on our literature. No one any more expected the Great American Novel. Perhaps it is due to the influence of Freud, and perhaps to the muckrakers of the eighteen nineties, and the writers of social protest in the thirties; but we have stopped thinking of the Great American Novel because we do not have the heroes we need for its pages. Or we didn't until Sandburg created them in *Remembrance Rock.*

A sermon on patriotism

Remembrance Rock was published in 1948. *Tales of the South Pacific* won the Pulitzer Prize that year. Both books were written out of a profound emotion toward World War II. The attitudes of Sandburg's *Remembrance Rock* are a curious combination of historical and poetic attitudes and, while not disjointed, are separated from the time and place in which they were written. *Remembrance Rock* is also, by linguistic convenience, a historical romance. It is far less dated than either *Gone With the Wind* or *Anthony Adverse*. It is far less dated, for that matter, than *Tales of the South Pacific* because it has more integrity and discovers a higher purpose.

It is the story of the settling of America from the time the Puritans left on the *Mayflower* and landed on Plymouth Rock, to the tradesmen who made the American Revolution in Boston, to the Midwest farmers, abolitionists, and secessionists, who waged the long battle up to the Civil War and the bloody battles during it, to the pilots and infantrymen who fought World War II.

The book is divided into four narratives, each peopled with its own personae. While each of the narratives presents the possibilities of what America may be, historical accuracy is always preserved. The book is as sprawling and as formless as America itself—the land it celebrates.

The Remembrance Rock of the title is a large boulder in the garden of former Supreme Court Justice Orville Brand Windom. Under this rock the Justice had placed a handful of dust from Plymouth; a colonial snuffbox filled with earth from Valley Forge; a small box from Cemetery Ridge at Gettysburg; and another with a handful of dust from the Argonne.

The novel opens in wartime Washington, D. C., on the day Justice Windom makes a radio address to the nation. In the course of this address he asks, "When we say a patriot is one who loves his country, what kind of love is it we mean? . . . You have heard that the shroud has no pockets and the dead to whatever place they go carry nothing with them—you have heard that and you know its meaning is plain. Whatever cash or collateral a man may have, whatever bonds, securities, deeds and titles to land, real estate, buildings, leases and patents, whatever of jewels, medals, decorations, keepsakes or costly apparel, he leaves them all behind and goes out of the world naked and bare as he came. You have heard also the dead hold in their clenched hands only that which they have given away. In this we begin to approach the meaning of a patriot. . . . The dead hold in their clenched hands only that which they have given away. When men forget what is at the heart of that sentiment—and it is terribly sentimental—they are in danger of power being taken over by swine, or beasts of prey or men hollow with echoes and vanities."

This is the statement of the book's purpose. Sandburg isn't talking about America as a culture—I doubt that he ever has— but about America as a nation, the sum of its trials and tribulations, its victories, all measured by the love of patriots.

How does the patriot find this truth?

By avoiding the stumbling blocks to truth while he searches. The Four Stumbling Blocks to Truth are those proposed by Roger Bacon, the English philosopher of the thirteenth century, and set forth by him as "The Four Causes of Error." They are:

1. The influence of fragile or unworthy authority.
2. Custom.
3. The imperfection of undisciplined senses.
4. Concealment of ignorance by ostentation of seeming wisdom.

In Sandburg's novel these four phrases are engraved on a medallion by an English artist in 1607. The medallion is a present to an English Puritan who takes it to the New World. The same medallion reappears in every section of the novel. While Sandburg does not maintain a consistent scheme, each of the four narratives attempts to portray the patriot's struggle to overcome one of these stumbling blocks.

In King James's England, the religious dissidents oppose the influence of fragile or unworthy authority; in Puritan New England, the dissidents, preparing to push off into the Connecticut wilderness with Roger Williams, shake their heads in despair when the Plymouth Colony flogs a woman for "a child born out of wedlock." "Time will help you conquer them," says one of them to the bleeding woman. "Time works for you. They did it because of a living custom. And the living custom will die."

The pendant reappears around the neck of a Confederate captain's wife; and it is an heirloom discovered by the grandson of

Justice Windom home on leave recuperating from his war wounds.

The four narratives have no transitional passages. Each is isolated. But in each, a single relationship between a young girl, an older man, and the young girl's fiancé or husband is repeated.

This relationship is obviously identified by the similarity in initials—the same throughout for these principals. The book is about not only sacrifice and valor but the progress of belief from the initial hope of the Mayflower Pilgrims to the confidence of World War II infantry captains and Air Corps flyers. The three partners in this relationship are able to maintain a continuing dialogue which forms an ever-widening pattern. It is a dialogue uninterrupted by historical changes, a dialogue which proceeds from the past to the future.

Sandburg has always been an accurate historian, but he holds history as a deeply personal fact. His history is closely allied to, and often verges into, the personal and sensitive. History and a personal reaction to history are one and the same. Specific dates in Sandburg are never described as momentous or as the beginning or end of an era. His dates are simply days when it is hot or cold; the completion of the Erie Canal is not an occasion for a description of how this Midwest has been opened, but an occasion for two sweethearts to marry.

The older man and the younger girl represent history at bottom and top, the past and the future. The young men who come back from Okinawa, or who follow Roger Williams, or who die at Valley Forge, who hold secrets "locked in the patriot's breast," are representatives of the present.

These three are not torn by motives between good and evil, but only struggle to realize the extent which sacrifice, belief, and patriotism demand.

Important are Sandburg's women. They exist and find expression independent of sex. It is these heroines who come to possess the medallion with the "Four Stumbling Blocks to Truth" imprinted upon it. Each, in possessing it, has learned the extent of a patriot's sacrifice. Sandburg's heroines are the ones haunted by the vision of America. His women are the dreamers. Most of them feel themselves if not makers and movers of history, a part of its process.

Remembrance Rock may not be the Great American Novel. It is certainly one of the attempts at the Great American Novel. It took for its subject belief in America, and by doing this, ran the risk of depending upon the image of Sandburg rather than upon its considerable literary merits to gain its audience. As fiction, it ran counter to post-World War II writing. It did not have the cynicism we associate with the usual war-inspired novel. It did not rage against authority, nor express hatred of discipline.

Belief is harder to portray than cynicism, and affirmation more difficult to sound than disillusion. *Remembrance Rock* undeniably had a refreshing vigor in its concentration upon narrative and its ambitious four-part form.

Remembrance Rock makes one remember *Intolerance*, D. W. Griffith's great experiment in film technique. *Intolerance*, too, had a story which encompassed four different narratives. Many have called it the greatest movie ever made. Movie techniques have improved, but after *Intolerance* few new techniques, besides sound, have been introduced. By the same criterion, *Remembrance Rock* is one of the great American novels, just in terms of its sheer ambition. No one is as ambitious as Americans are. In its ambition alone—trying to put America down on paper—*Remembrance Rock* is an accomplishment.

Wide horizons

And Carl Sandburg has indeed put America on paper. Lewis Gannett, a Connecticut farmer not averse to flashing poetry in his prose, reviewing *The Sandburg Range*, wrote:

"You can't imagine Walt Whitman settling down to the toil involved in a six-volume biography. You can't conceive Emerson writing a novel, or Hemingway telling stories for children. But in the prairie heart land of America where Sandburg grew up, which is still his home country, the horizon stretched far in every direction."

Norman Corwin on a desert island

Norman Corwin and I both agree that Carl Sandburg's greatest work is *The People, Yes*. Corwin produced this American epic on the radio some years ago and says that on a desert island he would want *The People, Yes* along with his Bible and Shakespeare. The book is the heart of Norman's successful production, *The World of Carl Sandburg*, which starred Miss Bette Davis. It played one month in Los Angeles and toured seventy-seven other cities, "including Little Rock," says Carl.

PART 8

Strange Friend and
Friendly Stranger

"Oh, Lord, if Thou wilt permit me to finish this task, then Thou mayest have me"

I asked Carl Sandburg how he got started on his monumental biography of Abraham Lincoln: the six volumes of *The Prairie Years* and *The War Years*. Carl sent me a note:

"While I was writing the *Rootabaga Stories* for children I got to thinking about the many biographies I had read in grade school. It came over me that there was not in the school libraries nor in the public libraries a book about Abraham Lincoln. I had read *The Life of Julius Caesar for Young People* and *The Life of Alexander the Great for Young People* and a title began running in my head, *The Life of Abraham Lincoln for Young People*. Some twenty years earlier I had read all of the Ida Tarbell articles in *McClure's* Magazine, followed by Herndon's life on Lincoln, and the Nicolay and Hay *Life of Lincoln* as serialized in the *Century* Magazine, and their collected *Letters and Speeches of Lincoln*. As I sat up to my typewriter I had in mind the young people who had listened to me in the *Rootabaga Stories*, and I kept them somewhat in mind in the early chapters of the finished book, *Abraham Lincoln: The Prairie Years*. The early chapters in volume one were later published as a juvenile book, *Abe Lincoln Grows Up*. One night as I was writing a movie review at the Chicago *Daily News* my friend, Sherwood Anderson, dropped in and we had a little talk, and I told him I had two titles for the book I was on: *The Prairie Lincoln* and *Abraham Lincoln: The Prairie Years*. Sherwood favored the title *The Prairie Lincoln*. As time went by I tried several people on the two titles, Lloyd Lewis joining me in favor of *Abraham Lincoln: The Prairie Years*.

"In the preface to this book, I name my adventures amid research materials and I wasn't sure what I had left after covering the life of Lincoln in Kentucky, Indiana, two years in Washington as Congressman, then back to Illinois. When in 344,000 words

I finally had him elected President and on his way to Washington, I believed I had him finished for the prairie years. I began to concentrate on the *American Songbag* which was published the next year, 1927. I found myself in any spare hours doing researches on *Lincoln and the War Years* early. In 1928 I made my decision, without telling it to anyone, that I would take my chances on doing the war years. I had begun writing it and had something over eleven hundred typed sheets when Alfred Harcourt, the publisher, came to our Lake Michigan home on a tall dune across the lake from Chicago. As he looked over parts of the manuscript he felt certain that a number of personality sketches were too long. I said, 'His cabinet members he would have to live with, and some of them were stubborn men. He had to think nearly every day about Horace Greeley, Joseph Medill, Jefferson Davis, and a score of others.' I went farther on this and Harcourt's face lighted up. When he got back to New York he sent me a short note of approval and below his signature to the letter there was a fluent, handwritten postscript: 'Jesus! What a book!' It was a fascinating work, and there were days I was at the typewriter sixteen and eighteen hours. Sometimes I was so dog tired I knew the only thing to do was to break away from the typewriter, the source materials, and notes. There were times there were shots of pain through my head that had me saying, 'Could that be a forerunner of a brain hemorrhage?' A queer little prayer came to me, 'Oh, Lord, if Thou wilt permit me to finish this task, then Thou mayest have me.' When in 1939 I had the finished manuscript of 3,400 typed sheets in New York, I was somewhat pleased because I had bargained with the Lord that when the book was finished He would strike me dead, and that would be okay.

"In late July of 1939 Harcourt told me he had given the order that day to the printers, Quinn & Boden, that they should print 15,000 copies of the volume one of this four-volume book. I saluted Harcourt and told him, 'That's about the nicest and boldest play across the boards that I have ever seen.' The six-volume set of the *Prairie Years* and the *War Years* was $28.00, to begin with, and in the passing years, because of higher costs of labor and paper, the price went to $36.00, then to $48.00, then to $54.00, for one six-volume book. I got letters. 'Who's got $48.00?' 'Who's got $54.00 for a book?' 'Was Lincoln a Capitalist or one of the common people?' So I made a decision. I would cut the million and a half words in the six volumes, and see what I could get by way of a distillation of the essentials of the story. I said to myself over again, 'This is not a digest, not a resume, not a condensation; this is to be a distillation.' Through the six volumes I bracketed sentences or paragraphs to be copied. When these were copied, the result was a manuscript of 700,000 words. I attacked this manuscript with vicious and unconscionable pencils, and went on bracketing sentences to be copied, saying at times, 'I am America's foremost bracketeer.'

"The result was a manuscript of 430,000 words. When my good friend Robert Sherwood reviewed the book, he came near cursing me for the omission of certain passages and sentences. There was one advantage. In this one-volume book published in 1954 is stated in the preface:

> Since the writing of the *Prairie Years* in the early 1920's there have been some 30 years of fiercely intensive research on the life of Lincoln before he became President. In no 30-year period since the death of Lincoln has so rigorous and thorough an examination been given to facts and myths of the life of Lincoln. . . . Now 28 years after publication of the two-volume *Prairie Years* and nearly 15 years after publication of the four-volume *War Years*, I have tried to compress the essential story of Lincoln as a Man and President into one volume."

Sandburg's Lincoln materials

Great books are not written on sudden inspiration. The execution may be impulsive, but the conception, rarely. Sandburg's *Lincoln* was a lifetime work, and the execution was as deliberate as Sandburg's continually evolving conception.

There are paragraphs and poems composed in his college days, editorials written as a newspaperman, and by the time of the

Chicago Poems his dedication had become an obsession, a *raison d'être.*

Sandburg assembled his materials for the six-volume *Lincoln* from people, books, and places.

But the materials also came from the reverence of the American small town for Lincoln. This reverence created an undeviating purpose in Carl Sandburg. He thought about Lincoln and how he would write about the Great Emancipator all of his life.

There were the Lincoln speeches and writings—over one million words in all, and the biographies by men who had known Lincoln—men like Congressman Isaac Arnold—and the three-volume work of William Herndon. Sandburg also went over every word of the Lincoln biography by Nicolay and Hay, Lincoln's wartime secretaries, as well as the diaries of Cabinet members. There was every sort of peripheral material from the unpublished manuscript of Evanston, Illinois, real estate man Nels M. Hokanson's *Swedish Immigrants in Lincoln's Time* to the recollections of Dorothy Lamon Teillard, daughter of the man who introduced Lincoln at Gettysburg. Sandburg visited every library that had Lincoln material, every photographer's studio, every home where Lincoln had lived. His acknowledgments to his six-volume study are perhaps the best catalogue of Lincolniana ever assembled.

There was this constant grappling with materials that went on from boyhood. As far back as 1908 there are editorials that the boy grown to manhood, and now a newspaperman, tried to fit into his scheme—the interpretation of an American myth, the American frontier history.

His Foreword to *The Prairie Years* contains twenty-one pages of acknowledgments and sources. Like the subject he had chosen, Sandburg ranged the breadth and width of the spiritual continent of America. He pays thanks to all his sources, from his brother Martin to Presidents Herbert Hoover and Franklin D. Roosevelt, who granted him unusual courtesies for his White House "Lincoln" visits.

Sidewalk squatter

The search for the Lincoln material began as a boy back in Galesburg. Later Carl's newspaper work gave him an excellent opportunity to talk about Lincoln with many important people who came to Chicago. As a reporter out on the street he also had the time to rummage through bookstores, rare-book and secondhand book shops, and libraries.

Vincent Starrett remembers Carl's gaunt frame bent over the ten-cent bin of the Clark Street Book Store. The bin contained old bound magazines—*Harper's, Century, Atlantic*, etc.—with a lot of Civil War stuff. There were also twenty-five-cent volumes. The trough was a bit low so Carl used to sit himself cross-legged on the sidewalk while he hunted through the old magazine pages for reminiscences of his hero. When he found one he would rip out the relevant pages and take them inside, but of course he always paid for the whole book. There must be many people still living who remember the poet, sitting on the sidewalk in Clark Street, looking through these old magazines, looking for Lincoln material for the great book he was going to write.

Sandburg could not have stayed with his Lincoln so long unless he had acquired a deep affection and reverence for his work. You can feel that he had a "fellowship" with Lincoln. "His versatility amazed me," says Carl:

> Lincoln?
> He was a mystery in smoke and flags
> saying yes to the smoke, yes to the flags,
> yes to the paradoxes of democracy,
> yes to the hopes of government . . .

Choosing a title and finding a farm

When Carl had finished the first two volumes of his *Lincoln*, he brought a manuscript of some eleven hundred typewritten pages to Alfred Harcourt.

To the Harcourt editors Carl said, "Sherwood Anderson tells me he would prefer *The Prairie Lincoln*. But the more I think about it, the more I am sure *Abraham Lincoln: The Prairie Years* is better." Van Wyck Brooks, a special adviser for the publishing house at the time, concurred. And so it was.

Before the two volumes were published, Harcourt had convinced the editors of *The Pictorial Review* that they ought to serialize it and had sold the rights for $30,000. It was one of the joyous moments in Harcourt's life when he could wire this news to Carl who was lecturing that day at Baylor College in Texas.

Carl wrote back:

> Dear Alfred: This is the first time I've understood something about the emotions of holding the lucky number in a lottery. Professor Armstrong of Baylor College at Waco wired your telegram to me at Commerce saying, "I have received the following telegram. Does it mean anything to you?" I replied, "Thank you for sending a telegram with news equivalent to falling heir to a farm."

Some legend and surmise

In *The Prairie Years*, Sandburg could not resist retelling the story of Abraham Lincoln and Ann Rutledge.

James Rutledge, Ann's father, had owned a tavern in New Salem, Illinois, and later a farm in Sandy Ridge, and Sandburg just wanted to see Lincoln riding back and forth to call on the girl. Sandburg has been a man in love all of his life and as he grew close to Lincoln, he was sure that Lincoln was a man in love too.

The Ann Rutledge story in *The Prairie Years* occupies only four pages and seems thoroughly documented.

Ann Rutledge was Lincoln's betrothed but she died before their marriage. Lincoln is supposed to have been grief-stricken for several months before he recovered from the shock of her death.

But the correspondence with which Sandburg documented the story was shortly thereafter revealed as inaccurate.

In the October, November, and December issues of 1928, the
Atlantic Monthly published a series of articles dealing with this
inauthenticity. The experts were Worthington C. Ford, editor of
the Massachusetts Historical Society; Paul Angle, executive secretary of the Lincoln Centennial Association of Springfield, Illinois; and Oliver R. Barrett of Chicago (Sandburg's close friend
and in whose Lincoln collection the biographer found much valuable material). These men proved there were discrepancies between the Lincoln papers and the letters, between the actual
events and the characters.

Sandburg accepted their findings. He explained in a letter to
The New York Times, in December 1928, that heretofore he had
believed the papers which related to the Ann Rutledge love affair were genuine:

> I have never taken part in any controversy touching on
> the life of Lincoln. While I like a good fight and believe
> it is sometimes necessary to fight in order to have peace, I do
> not set up as a handwriting expert and particularly as one
> who should dare challenge a man of the training and ex-
> perience of Oliver R. Barrett of Chicago.
>
> The series of letters and diary entries in the original are
> impressive. I was deeply moved while working at them. They
> called up a story and a background, associations and impli-
> cations.
>
> To the extent that the documents are a hoax and no im-
> portant contribution, they will be so proclaimed and foot-
> noted. If there had earlier been the kind of interest that
> there now is in Lincoln, there would be less of legend and
> surmise.

He had made a mistake, Carl said, and he would make no
bones about it. One other defense was offered. It came from
Bruce Weirick who was a professor of English at the University
of Illinois and the author of *From Whitman to Sandburg in
American Poetry*. In the *Journal of the Illinois State Historical
Society*, Winter, 1952 issue, he wrote apropos of personal recollections of Sandburg: "He professes himself chagrined that he
ever 'fell for' the Ann Rutledge legend, and thinks now that he

should have known it was out of character. Yet still, though in a different way, so were those letters offering to marry the florid Mary Owens, and *they*, though unquestionably authentic, seem just as much 'out of character.' "

The Lincoln penny

It was a stroke of genius, Sandburg says, that prompted our Government to put the face of Abraham Lincoln on the penny. Carl wrote an editorial in the Milwaukee *Daily News* to celebrate the minting of the Lincoln penny in 1909 in observance of the Centennial of Lincoln's birth (when you could still get an ice-cream cone with one).

> The penny is strictly the coin of the common people. At Palm Beach, Newport, and Saratoga you will find nothing for sale for one cent. No ice cream cones at a penny a piece there.
>
> "Keep the change," says the rich man. "How many pennies do I get back?" asks the poor man.
>
> Only the children of the poor know the joy of getting a penny for running around the corner to the grocery.
>
> The penny is the bargain counter coin. Only the common people walk out of their way to get something for nine cents reduced from ten cents. The penny is the coin used by those who are not sure of tomorrow, those who know that if they are going to have a dollar next week they must watch the pennies this week.
>
> Follow the travels of a penny and you find it stops at many cottages and few mansions.
>
> The common, homely face of Honest Abe looks good on the penny, the coin of the common folk from whom he came and to whom he belongs.

One of his best poems is about the Lincoln penny. It is in his *Chicago Poems* and is called "In a Back Alley."

Remembrance for a great man is this.
The newsies are pitching pennies.
And on the copper disk is the man's face.
Dead lover of boys, what do you ask for now?

The Republicans quote

During a discussion on the Farm Bill in February 1938, Republican Congressman Wolcott of Michigan rose to read an excerpt from Carl Sandburg's biography of Lincoln.

He quoted Lincoln as calling President Polk a "bewildered, confused and miserably perplexed man," and implied the words also described President Franklin D. Roosevelt.

Although Mr. Wolcott's voice was scarcely audible in the galleries, Representative Rayburn, Democratic leader, heard. Pushing his way to the Republican side, he shouted: "I'll answer that!"

The Texan said that he had served under five Presidents but had never heard "a member of this House carry partisanship to such a point of personal criticism." He said he himself had criticized, but never admitted or would admit "that there has been a dishonest man or a fool in the White House."

Representative Green of Florida also went to the President's defense. He said Mr. Wolcott had accused the American people of having "blundered!" in their re-election of President Roosevelt.

The Lincoln denunciation of President James K. Polk from the Sandburg volumes as read by Representative Wolcott reads:

The President is in no wise satisfied with his own positions. First he takes up one and in attempting to argue us into it he argues himself out of it, then seizes another and goes through the same process, and then, confused at being able to think of nothing new, he snatches up the old again.

His mind, taxed beyond its power, is running hither and thither like some tortured creature on a burning surface, finding no position on which it can settle down and be at ease.

He knows not where he is. He is a bewildered, confused and miserably perplexed man. God grant he may be able to show there is *not* something about his conscience more painful than all his mental perplexity.

Tall teller of true tales

Every great historian can be said to have added something to the study of history. This something is often intangible but emerges as a quality from the particular historian's art.

Herodotus, for instance, made history out of gossip.

Thucydides was the first historian to put words of his own invention into the mouths of actual historical figures.

Hegel invented the dialectic.

Gibbon used Christ to destroy Rome. And Sandburg is probably the first historian to heap up incident, anecdote, and casual remark to make an objective, reportorial chronicle of daily events to explain all the motives and fill out the whole of an administration's history and make human the central character in his *Lincoln.*

It would be unfair to say that Sandburg is the first great American historian. Indeed, many preceded him and his work is based in large part upon their accomplishments.

But I think it is fair to say that Carl was the first American historian who made use of the native American talent for telling tall tales, for laughing, and for appreciating the vernacular. A historian's work can be judged by his disciples.

No history of an American hero will ever be written without recourse to the same sort of materials and the conclusions Sandburg first manipulated.

Cracker-box writer

When Sandburg settled in the Harbert, Michigan, home he took no lecture or singing dates between April and October of every year. Over the spring, summer, and early fall months he wrote *The War Years,* assisted by two copyists and his wife, Paula.

Sandburg worked in the attic which was furnished with a stove, a cot, a few shelves (which rapidly overflowed), and a typewriter. The typewriter was supported by a cracker box and Sandburg liked to tell people that if Grant and the Union generals could run their war from a cracker box he could, too.

The attic and a room on the second floor became known as the Lincoln rooms. As soon as books overflowed (and in the first year Sandburg went through more than a thousand source books), they were removed to the barn on the property. Two copyists worked downstairs on the glassed-in sun porch, and Paula Sandburg and the daughters helped with the files.

But during the winter months when he did make his concert tours, he achieved two purposes: one, he added to his earnings; and, two, he invented a novel way of accumulating Lincoln research.

There is a part of American literature and history that has been written as heard from the courthouse steps, and Sandburg's *Lincoln* was an elaboration on this system. Wherever he went across the Continent, and he traversed it several times, he delved into the files of old newspapers, followed up the success stories of vintage politicians who were for or against Lincoln, and had the old-timers tell their stories.

His concert tours gave him a chance to interview people whose parents or uncles or family friends had known Lincoln, and he also had access to a thousand libraries with stacks of books that heretofore had held only local interest. More importantly, his travels brought him in contact time and again with the private Lincoln collectors. It was truly an American method, as American as Johnny Appleseed's journey, and it brought forth as great an orchard.

The War Years is not only a biography of Abraham Lincoln, but a history of his administration and of the Civil War as well. (Some years later when James B. Conant, then the President of Harvard University, awarded Sandburg the degree of Doctor of Letters, he wrote: "*Carl Sandburg*, poet and reporter seeking the rhythm of America, lately the Washington correspondent of the Lincoln Administration . . .")

Arthur Schlesinger's volumes on the New Deal and Franklin

D. Roosevelt owe something to Sandburg, if not in method, research, and writing, at least in invention. Schlesinger, like Sandburg before him, did not choose the objective way of recounting history as an archivist, but rather chose to write his history through the eyes of its central participant.

Thus, the reader of Sandburg's Lincoln volumes experiences events much as Lincoln did. There is great advantage to this method. It allows both Sandburg and the reader free access to Lincoln's motives without the imputation or suspicion they are the biographer's. Such a method, however, demands an intense accumulation of detail, for it is out of this detail that the motive grows and takes command, forcing itself on the reader's attention.

Thus, when Sandburg talks of Chase's ambition, he describes that ambition as it affected the President, and in describing the assassination at Ford's Theatre, Sandburg calls John Wilkes Booth "the Outsider," so that we sense the irony of Lincoln's unawareness that death stalked the Presidential box.

The theme of *The War Years*, as Allan Nevins puts it, is "the theme of the folk hero of a great and terrible folk war." This is not a cerebral subject, but a tragic subject, and catharsis does not come because we understand but because we feel. In Lincoln, Sandburg found the terrible sorrow democracy enforces, the loneliness, the isolation; in the Cabinet and the Confederacy he found the ambitions; in the quibbling and backbiting of the States, the selfishness. And in the war, Sandburg found the ennobling qualities that justified the weaknesses of the raw and the coarse, the effete and the weak, the blunted and insensitive qualities. In its way, *The War Years* is as perceptive an analysis of the causes and effects of the equalitarian society as Alexis de Tocqueville's *Democracy in America*.

Sandburg's literature changed Lincoln from a historical personage into a moral force. It was against this background of political, economic, social, and personal forces that Lincoln kept making decisions to preserve his foremost goal—the Union—which, in its way, is the age-old goal of brotherhood.

Alfred Harcourt

"Be sure to put in your book," Carl warned, "how Alfred Harcourt proved himself a wonderfully game sport and truly great publisher when I was writing *The War Years*."

Mr. Harcourt was so sure *The War Years* was going to be a success that an initial printing of 15,000 sets was ordered and when the advance orders came, he ordered another 14,000 sets. All these 29,000 sets at $20.00 the set sold—within a few months.

"It must have been a bulky manuscript," I said to Sandburg.

"Bulky, yes, somewhat over thirty-four hundred typed sheets."

"Where is it?" I asked.

"In the Sandburg Room at the University of Illinois where it stands alongside of the eleven hundred typed sheets of *Abraham Lincoln: The Prairie Years*."

"A fact in crimson mist"

"Lincoln was in himself so large a mirror of mankind," wrote Lloyd Lewis for the *New York Herald Tribune* in 1939, "that every biographer finds in him the thing he admires most. Hence lawyers think Lincoln's legal side the thing that made him great, soldiers think his education at handling soldiers the main thing in his fame, preachers say it was his exalted moral sense, and Sandburg, the writer, while giving the most catholic evaluation to date would seem by his emphasis to feel that it was as a user of words that Lincoln shone the brightest . . . to read Sandburg's detailed description of how Lincoln wrote his most renowned papers, speeches and letters, of what was in the air at the moment, is as absorbing as it would be suddenly to come across the revelation of just how Shakespeare wrote *Hamlet*."

Lloyd Lewis was reviewing Carl Sandburg's four volumes, *The War Years*. He struck upon the central emphasis of Sandburg's biography, Lincoln's facility with words. Edmund Wilson remarks in one of his essays that Lincoln was our only President who could have been a writer (I think now we'll have to include President Jack Kennedy too). Sandburg never neglects to pay close attention to what Lincoln wrote—and how.

Sandburg understands Lincoln because he himself is a writer, but here let us consider another truth Lloyd Lewis does not touch upon.

Sandburg also understands Lincoln because Sandburg was a Socialist and knew the political ways and means of both government and society. The Socialist and the poet combined to understand Lincoln the President and the writer. This happy combination is best and happily evident in Sandburg's chapter, "Lincoln Speaks at Gettysburg."

There was a myth that had heavy circulation about how Lincoln wrote his Gettysburg address: on a train, on a piece of foolscap, in pencil, while his son was dying at the White House. For most people the myth may persist. I do not know that it was Sandburg who laid it to rest—I suspect it was Nicolay and Hay —but certainly the writer Sandburg understood no important writing is done on trains in four or five hours. And the Socialist Sandburg saw how important politically the speech was to Lincoln.

Sandburg's chapter is not only a day-by-day chronological account of the events preceding the speech, but it is an interpretation of the speech itself.

The battle of Gettysburg had left a huge crescent of corpses. "In the hapless onrush of the war, it was known, too many of the fallen had lain as neglected cadavers rotting in the open fields or thrust into so shallow a resting place that a common farm plow caught in their bones," says Sandburg.

On the day of the speech itself visitors to Gettysburg could see the still decaying remains of the mutilated horses dotting the meadows and the fields. Lincoln was aware of conditions at Gettysburg. He had been in constant touch with the men on the battlefield and afterward. Sandburg says Lincoln's personal touch with Gettysburg by telegraph, mail courier, and military dispatch and strong associations made it a place of great realities to him.

Carl describes in detail the wedding of Kate Chase, daughter

of the Secretary of the Treasury, Salmon P. Chase, to Governor
William Sprague of Rhode Island which took place in Washington shortly before the dedication of the Gettysburg Cemetery.
He also tells us of the resounding victory the Republicans scored
in the October elections.

Both of these happenings are the historian's way of inter-
relating the moods of the country. Washington, D. C., was not
thinking of the war—it considered the war won. The concentration of the nation, if focused at all, was focused on large faceless
armies and the big chessboard battles.

It is Sandburg's purpose to paint this in bold relief so that he
can analyze dramatically to what purpose Lincoln spoke.

It is with the printed invitation in Lincoln's hands that Sandburg begins.

The cemetery at Gettysburg was a State-inspired institution.
It was not until many years after Lincoln's death that the Federal Government nationalized the cemetery. The Union soldiers
who died there were buried in separate plots owned by each of
their respective States who subscribed on the basis of their Congressional representation. Illinois, for example, gave twelve thousand dollars although the State lost but six men at Gettysburg.
Each of the governors of the eighteen Northern States appointed
a special agent to attend the ceremony and the chairman of this
committee was David Wills, special agent of Governor Andrew
Curtin of Pennsylvania. Wills wrote Lincoln asking him for "a
few appropriate remarks." But the invitation to speak was an
afterthought. Lincoln was not always popular or universally respected with most of the governors.

But Lincoln wanted to go and the politician in Sandburg understands why. The election of 1864 was coming up and with
eighteen governors on the rostrum, Lincoln hoped to make a
good impression that would secure him political alliances. (His
stay in Gettysburg, Sandburg writes, helped cement a relationship with Governor Curtin, the leader of one of the two political
factions of Pennsylvania.)

Lincoln began working on his speech almost immediately after
he received the formal invitation to speak at Gettysburg. Sandburg includes the Alexander Gardner photograph of Lincoln sit-

ting on a chair beside a felt-covered table. At his right arm is
Everett's Gettysburg Oration, which he had brought with him to
study.

In this chapter Sandburg is trying hard to show what most
people imagined were the causes of the war. He includes the letter
John Murray Forbes wrote Lincoln in the early fall in which
Forbes claimed that an aristocracy ruled the South and that the
war basically was fought for the aristocratic class who wanted to
maintain slavery against the working people who wanted to
abolish it.

Lincoln did understand the war and understood it best of
anyone engaged in it. Abolition, the success of the Republican
Party, the possibilities of reconstruction were all issues, but
not central issues. The war was about Union and slavery, his
opening sentence, "All men are created equal," and maintaining
the Union involved personal sacrifice. Specifically this is all Lincoln
said at Gettysburg.

The Gettysburg Address was one of the supreme political
speeches ever made. It was brief, yet it cut away all side issues
and concentrated on the single issue the war was fought for.

It is Sandburg, however, who brings us to this realization by
his patient research, his narrative, judicious use of dialogue, and
apocrypha which create the existence of these side issues and
their seeming importance. Lincoln spoke exactly to the contrary
of the spirit of the State-supported cemetery.

"The poets have always understood Lincoln," wrote Henry
Steele Commager in his review of *The War Years* twenty-two
years ago, "from Whitman to Emerson to Lindsay and Benét
and it is fitting that from the pen of a poet has come the greatest
of all Lincoln biographies. One of the great biographies of our
literature."

Carl Sandburg did America a great intellectual service when
he published this monumental biography of Lincoln. It was not
so much that Sandburg rescued Lincoln the man from Lincoln
the martyr and myth, or that out of every available document,
letter, book, and diary he assembled Lincoln and his times; Sandburg's great gift was that he saw eye to eye with Lincoln. Sandburg, like Lincoln, understood it takes a politician to run this

country. This is a hard truth to grasp, and often even politicians don't grasp it.

In the spirit of Theodore Roosevelt

When Abraham Lincoln was shoveled into the tombs, he forgot the copperheads and the assassin . . . in the dust, in the cool tombs.

Put the question directly to Carl, "How did you happen to write that poem?" and Sandburg replies, "I did it in the spirit of Theodore Roosevelt and the Spanish-American War. T.R. said it wasn't much of a war but it was the only war there was. That's how it was with some of my books. There were things that no one else had tried for, so I tried."

"Blood on the Moon"

There are few in whom poet and historian exist in equal excellence. Sandburg is one. All his poetry manifests a strong sense of history, almost a predilection. His poetry, in fact, sometimes is just that—history; not a longing for the past, but an understanding and praise of it. So, too, is his history admixed with poetry, invested with tactile imagery, rhythms, and symbols.

The combination of the poet-historian has always been felicitous for literature. Greek prose reached its summit in Thucydides' *History of the Peloponnesian War* and in Plato's *Dialogues*, which respectively applied the principles of Greek tragic poetry to history and philosophy. Remember also Shakespeare's commitment to history.

Sandburg's supreme concentrate of poetry and history is in his *Abraham Lincoln: The War Years*, particularly in his chapter "Blood on the Moon," which narrates Lincoln's assassination in Ford's Theatre on the night of April 14 by John Wilkes Booth.

Sandburg takes his title for this chapter from *Macbeth* (Act III, Scene 5): "Upon the corner of the moon/ There hangs a

vaporous drop profound . . ." One suspects Sandburg consciously
or unconsciously uses *Macbeth* as a template for this chapter.
Like Shakespeare, he fills his opening with symbols of menace
and ominous brooding.

> Cold, raw weather, gusty and changeable met those who
> stepped from indoor comfort the afternoon and evening of
> this April 14. A ceiling of clouds hung low, mist and fog
> held the streets, and occasional showers had put a chill and
> pervasive damp on the air. In the daytime hours no one
> could throw a shadow from the sun and in the night time
> away from street lamps the walking men became blurred
> humps. The evening lighted windows and the corner gas
> jets formed vague lumps of light, dim agglutinates of light;
> the world between sky and ground lacked firm ceiling and
> had an uncertain floor . . . Had there been a full golden
> moon . . . door knobs would have been . . . less noncom-
> mittal and secretive, not so much like faces wearing a blank
> look of having nothing to say, nothing worth telling . . . The
> covering shawl of night was anonymous and indecisive.

Sandburg has created the night and now he begins to pen-
etrate it. He penetrates the night by finding its total meaning,
and he does this by literary convention; by conceit.

He asks, "And of what is Abraham Lincoln thinking?" But he
never quite answers that question.

Instead he follows with another series of questions which take
on an absolute and definitive shape in this blurred and foggy
night. These questions sum up everything he has talked about
in these six volumes:

> Who had gone farther on so little to begin with? Who
> else as a living figure of republican government, of democ-
> racy in practice, as a symbol touching freedom for all men
> —who else had gone farther over America, over the world?
> Yes, of what is Abraham Lincoln thinking? Draped before
> him in salute is a silk flag of the Union, a banner of the
> same design as the one at Independence Hall in Phila-
> delphia in February of '61 which he pulled aloft saying,

"I would rather be assassinated on this spot than surrender it," saying the flag in its very origins "gave promise that in due time the weights would be lifted from the shoulders of all men, and that all should have an equal chance."

This is Sandburg's heath and if no witches stir kettles, we still feel the moral structure of the universe is awry.

Instead of the cackling witches, Sandburg introduces John F. Parker who played an accidental but crucial role in history. He was one of four officers detailed from the metropolitan police force for White House duty guarding the President. The key to Lincoln's murder was Parker's dereliction of duty. He left the theater and his post outside the Presidential box to drink whiskey in a nearby saloon.

Parker was appointed to his duties by Mrs. Lincoln, yet his career had been filled with a history of inefficiency. He had been accused by the police of being found asleep on a streetcar when he should have been patrolling his beat; of living in a whorehouse for five weeks where it was alleged he had been drunk, had been put to bed, and had fired a revolver through a window; of using highly offensive language to a superior officer.

The chapter has an intense dramatic tension. For if it includes the villainy of John Wilkes Booth ("the Outsider") and the negligence of Parker, it also includes the heroism and idealism of Charles A. Leale, assistant surgeon, United States Volunteers, the first doctor to attend Lincoln in the box. The final action is seen through Leale's eyes. Whereas Parker deserted his post to drink liquor, Leale specifically came to the theater to see Lincoln whom he admired and respected. Leale is created as genuinely a sensitive figure as John F. Parker is created as genuinely a nothing. Leale held Lincoln's hand before the President died knowing that "just before departure recognition and reason return to those who have been unconscious caused me for several hours to hold his right hand firmly within my grasp to let him in his blindness know, if possible, that he was in touch with humanity and had a friend."

The chapter concludes with John F. Parker's realization of his act and Leale's final specific detail: "His eyes happened to fall on his [own] wrists and the detachable cuffs. They had been laundered stiff and immaculately white. Now they were limp, wet, blood-soaked. He decided he would keep the cuffs as long as he lived. To him they were 'stained with the martyr's blood.' "

Transitional passage

In his apologia to A *Lincoln Preface,* Carl writes: "After finishing *Abraham Lincoln: The Prairie Years,* I made an attempt at covering all the rest of his life by the device of an introduction. This introduction would begin at the death of Lincoln and work back to the day he left Illinois. The reader could then turn to the book and begin with the birth of Lincoln. When I decided to continue the Life into *The War Years,* I considered throwing away this piece of writing. But now, some thirty years later, for the benefit of a large circle of friends who would understand it, I am ready to let it go into publication."

A hard bound book of sixteen pages, A *Lincoln Preface* has enjoyed wide readership. Harcourt, Brace and Company issued the book in 1953, just before Carl published his one-volume *Lincoln.* The first edition of the *Preface* was limited to 2,850 copies, privately printed, and distributed to friends of the author and publisher as a New Year's greeting. Since then, however, it has become much more important than a significant greeting card.

Carl's public reasons for not including the *Preface* to *The Prairie Years* seem responsible enough, but (and here I speak for myself) he withheld it, too, because he had come to a deeper understanding of his own process of literature. If he was going to continue with the Life, he was also widening his method.

Let it be remembered Carl started his *Lincoln* as a children's book but found the materials of Lincoln's life took him along a more arduous journey. The process of writing itself changed his ideas, gave them more scope, made them more intense, commanded him more than he they. Carl became one of those writers who discover the idea they want in the act of writing itself.

So it was not until he had finished *The Prairie Years* that he real-ized what he was up to. The immense cost in labor and spiritual energy perhaps blinded him to his ultimate aim. But not for long. *A Lincoln Preface* is the transitional passage between what he set out to do and what he knew he could finally accomplish.

This accomplishment was to create an American myth.

Some people will tell you myths are lies; and indeed they are if the myths intend to describe existentially. More often a myth assembles a series of facts and felt impressions and so structures them and arranges them that they tell more than fact and feeling alone. A myth manages to express a moral truth in a way strict representation cannot. Or, as John Crowe Ransom more briefly and succinctly put it, a myth is a not a descriptive but a pre-scriptive exercise. It is a presentation of an exaggerated physical and historical configuration to suggest a more meaningful moral and spiritual configuration.

Which was what Sandburg did in his *Lincoln. The six volumes not only re-create what America was but what America could and morally ought to be.* The *Lincoln* focused on the fortitude with which terror, frightfulness, destruction, hard choice, and sacrifice must be borne to give life heroic dimensions.

By enigma and extremes *A Lincoln Preface* both prefigures and devises Carl's purpose. Never once throughout his sixteen pages does he use the surname "Lincoln" and only twice, and that in the same passage, does he use the name "Abraham." This enigmatic exclusion has this for its meaning: that Lincoln is more than a man and a President: he is also a quality.

Nor does the *Preface* have a narrative line as such. It is an anecdotal account. The book begins with a paragraph describing Lincoln's death and leaps to one describing his election. It re-produces Lincoln's comic and serious statements, his sense of play and his sense of politics, his mercy and his power, the rev-erence he elicited and the hate he inspired.

And, as he concludes, Sandburg confesses his role: "The facts and myths of his life are to be an American possession, shared widely over the world, for thousands of years, as the tradition of Knute or Alfred, Lao-tse or Diogenes, Pericles or Caesar, are kept. This because he was not only a genius in the science of neighborly human relationships and an artist in the personal handling of life from day to day, but a strange friend and a friendly stranger to all forms of life he met."

Who doubts that in his *Lincoln* Carl Sandburg was trying to articulate the American myth? The succession of names—Knute, Alfred, Lao-tse, Diogenes, Pericles, Caesar—are any of these bare historical figures? Is not Pericles the myth of Greece? Is not Caesar Rome?

Sandburg may not have captured all the Lincoln myth—in certain respects Sophocles did not capture all of Oedipus—but Sandburg caught as much of the Lincoln myth as we can expect to be caught in our time.

There is a part of America, Sandburg is saying, which is beyond reading, a part that cannot be explained or analyzed, only prophesied and felt. His Lincoln has remained for us a myth— a story which lends itself to constant retelling without ever becoming ototo verbalized and dissipated.

PART 9

A Final Lilt of Song

Forewords

There are at least twenty forewords written by Carl in plain sight on the bookshelves of Connemara. From correspondence and conversation I have learned there are at least another twenty, perhaps more.

One of his first forewords was for the autobiography of Oscar Ameringer, the famous Oklahoma Socialist editor. Oscar is the fellow who once observed, "Feudalism replaced cannibalism when man discovered that it was more profitable to exploit his fellow-man than eat him."

I sent Carl a copy of the manuscript of my own book, *Only in America*, for which he wrote the Foreword. He was the first to predict the book would be a success. When Carl sent me his Foreword he wrote, "This will be a famous book."

Set him alongside Carl XII

On his way home from the Soviet Union where he and Ed Steichen opened *The Family of Man* exhibit for the United States Government, Carl stopped off at Stockholm. Thousands and thousands cheered him at the Swedish-American Day exercises on August 6, 1959.

Carl read his mother's last letter in Swedish and he read it again three days later over the Swedish television. He visited his mother's birthplace at Apuna, southwest of Stockholm.

A few days later King Gustav V decorated Carl with a gold medal with the words, "Litteris et artibus," for accomplishments in fine arts. Few such medals are given out and rarely does a foreigner get one.

"I'll die at an age divisible by 11"

Governor Luther H. Hodges of North Carolina declared January 6, 1958, "Carl Sandburg Day." Authorities arranged a dinner for the poet at the State capital at Raleigh. Carl came and the newspapers were filled with his quotes.

"He felt no 'high anxiety' about taking on any heavy literary projects. He had 200 new poems to be published. "I'll keep on producing.

"I'll probably die propped up in bed trying to write a poem about America.

"Or a poem about a man who prayed to God that he live to be an age divisible by 11.

"It's inevitable, inexorable, it's written in the book of fate that I die at an age divisible by 11.

"Two of my great grandfathers and one of my grandmothers died at ages divisible by that number.

"It is fate I follow suit."

Pressed for details, Carl airily dismissed the subject: "The details are lost in the mists of Swedish antiquity."

As for the fear of death, Carl said: "There's health in nonsense of a certain kind." He said he liked to remember a passage from the journal of Ralph Waldo Emerson, "When Emerson recorded the fact that brother Charles . . . went away, he wrote: 'They took Charles away under restraint. They say it is a taint in the blood but I have no fear because I have an element of silliness in me.' "

On American youth: "Never was a generation that has been told by a more elaborate system of the printed word, billboards, newspapers, magazines, radio, television—to eat more, play more, have more fun. But General Robert E. Lee told a mother with a child in her arms: 'Teach him to deny himself.' "

On poetry: "The modern poets prefer to write about people like John Donne, Dante and Henry James. Lincoln? No. Washington, Jefferson, Jackson, Franklin, the sublime American figures? No."

On advertising: Carl said he had written a new poem called "Instructions for the Tomb of George Washington Hill." He said they could carve the words over the tomb: "Irritate 'em! irritate 'em! They'll forget the irritation and remember the name of your product."

A month later Carl appeared as a witness for Nathan Leopold, then fifty-three years old, who was pleading with the Illinois Parole Board in Joliet for freedom.

Sandburg asked the board to "perform a historic act" in freeing Leopold. "Those who perhaps won't like it are those who believe in revenge. They are the human stuff of which mobs are made. They are the passion ridden."

Asked what effect on teen-agers the release of Leopold might have:

"There has been a struggle toward light that any teen-ager could contemplate with healthy results."

Leopold was freed and when he flew from Chicago to Puerto Rico he changed planes at Idlewild—and phoned Sandburg from the airport. "It's strange," said Sandburg when Leopold told him where he would work as an X-ray technician, "but my old regiment—the Sixth Illinois Volunteers—slept on a rainy night in that same spot in Puerto Rico, sixty years ago."

Some things we buy, some not

A friendship with Carl Sandburg is like no other friendship. It involves more than mere pride of fellowship with a great literary figure.

Friendship with Carl Sandburg is a *complete* thing. It is so complete that at every stage of the relationship you feel yourself helpless because he gives so much more than he receives. He throws his whole personality and loyalty into it. Certainly there is nothing you can give Carl, so you find yourself at the receiving end constantly.

He sends you books, he responds to requests for encouragement or endorsement, and if you are his friend, it means that everybody associated with you, your family, your publisher, your editors, your friends, associates, and even your employees, none of whom he knows or has ever seen, are his friends, too, taken in in one fell swoop.

I have examined the exchange of correspondence with some of these close friends of Carl's, William O. Douglas, John Steinbeck, Archibald MacLeish, Mark Van Doren, Adlai Stevenson, and many others.

The letters reveal this *complete* commitment. If one of his friends writes that he is ill or is going to the hospital, Carl is deeply concerned and insists on knowing every detail. He follows it up. He keeps in constant touch.

I have studied him carefully at close range for the past ten years. And aside from a few pet peeves and his taking so seriously unfavorable critiques (which he rarely discusses outside his home), I doubt seriously whether Carl Sandburg is capable of a thoughtless act or an unkindness, and that goes for his politics in which he is so heavily involved.

During the Presidential campaign of 1960 he agreed to join me on the platform at several Kennedy meetings. When we returned to the hotel room on one occasion I expressed myself strongly against the Republicans. Carl raised his finger to his lips and said, "Shh-hh, they gave us Earl Warren, didn't they?"

A Foreword for the President

In August, 1961, Carl received a letter from John W. Gardner, president of the Carnegie Corporation of New York: "President Kennedy is going to put out a book based on his speeches and writings from the time of his Inaugural Speech to the closing of this session of the Congress. I have agreed to edit the book. Mr. Kennedy was very pleased with your kind comments on his Berlin speech and wonders whether you might be persuaded to contribute a Foreword to the book. Something between 500 and 1,000 words might be appropriate."

Carl's reply: "It will be a pleasure to write a Foreword to President Kennedy's book. He has style and content and the gleams of a great historic figure in his utterance. I hope to put color and high meaning in the Foreword."

Solitude and prayer

When young people ask for an autograph, Sandburg sometimes inscribes: "Remember Paganini when asked the secret of his accomplishments, saying: toil, solitude, prayer."

Sandburg has been fortunate throughout his life to have a wife and family grant him the solitude he needs. There are long stretches when he requires solitude pure and simple.

Mrs. Sandburg and the family have not only permitted him to be a free soul, to come and go as he found the need to come and go, but also they recognize immediately those hours when Carl needs to be alone with his books, his typewriter, his paper, and his pencils.

Carl believes all men need solitude: "I feel sorry for those who have never learned what Pascal meant when he said, 'The miseries of men come from not being able to sit alone in a quiet room.' Today they've got to have radio, gotta have everything besides books. Books were enough for Pascal. William James enjoyed presenting an Indian chief who said you had mastered the secret of life 'when you could sit in a chair and think about nothing.' Some of the psychiatrists think it is quite a trick, to sit quiet and 'empty your mind'; that's their phrase—'empty your mind.' Along with this emptying will go all your worries and anxieties. And this Indian had what it takes."

A breathing structure newly come to life

Six high schools and five elementary schools are named after Carl Sandburg. There is a Carl Sandburg High School in Mundelein, Illinois. There are Carl Sandburg Junior High Schools in Orland Park, Joliet, and Elmhurst, Illinois; in Levittown, Pennsylvania; and in Robbinsdale, Golden Valley, Minnesota. There are five Carl Sandburg Elementary Schools: Harvey, Wheeling, and

Springfield, Illinois, and Pontiac and Drayton Plains, Michigan.

Harcourt, Brace and Company, Carl's publishers for the last forty-one years, have placed in each of these schools a shelf of the complete Sandburg corpus.

Carl has spoken at several of the dedication ceremonies. In the high school in Robbinsdale, Golden Valley, Minnesota, a suburb of Minneapolis, this dedicatory address graces the main hallway on a bronze tablet:

> Old and tarnished sayings have it, "Time is a great teacher" and "Time will tell."
>
> This building as a tool and an instrument, as a breathing structure newly come to life, might speak for itself today and say, "I am a child of Time. I celebrate the dignity, importance and pathos of Time. Loving hands and thoughtful hearts have seen my foundations and walls rise to serve as best they may a young generation living in a time of world storm. Here to my rooms will come fresh generations, one after another, gazing out on the world in history, gazing in on themselves in reverie, some asking the ancient questions, 'While we live, what is worth looking at, what is worth listening to, and what might be worth dying for?'
>
> "Here they may study the guarded meaning of Lincoln opening his House Divided Speech: 'If we could first know where we are and whither we are tending, we could better judge what to do and how to do it.'
>
> "Always the path of American destiny has been into the unknown. With each new test and crisis it always cost and there were those ready to pay the cost, as an affirming character in *Remembrance Rock* says: 'Man is a changer. God made him a changer.' You may become the witnesses of the finest and brightest era known to Mankind. The nations over the globe shall have music, music instead of murder. It is possible. That is my hope and prayer—for you and for the nations."

"May all the gods go with you"

In an interview with Murray Schumach, the Hollywood reporter for *The New York Times*, Sandburg discussed his speech before the Eighty-sixth Congress:

> I've lived long enough to know that self-importance can be a terribly dangerous thing. Somehow, across thirty years, I have been writing short pieces, seldom more than a page long, and I called them nonsense wisdom for children and grownups. Nearly all the best things that came to me in life have been unexpected, unplanned by me.
>
> It was reported that only two private citizens of the United States were ever asked to address a joint session of Congress. I was one and I went on with the speech I had worked on for eighty-one years. The other man? Oh, he was George Bancroft, one-time Secretary of the Navy, a stuffed-shirt historian who delivered a eulogy on Lincoln.
>
> Delivering speeches is a sort of acting. All good politicians are actors. They all want to play Hamlet. No, I have never played Hamlet, but I did some acting. When I was in college, I played Mark Antony to a pretty girl from Missouri. She played Cleopatra and her final line to me was "May all the gods go with you and smooth success be strewn before your feet." And when she died five years ago, I gave a salutation to her shadow.

"For brave Amerikay"

"It seems like every day when I am at all in good health I've got to sing," Carl tells his audience. "I've got to find the guitar and pluck a little at it, go over old songs and new songs, and as long as I live I am going to be learning songs.

"There's a human stir throughout our songs with the heights and depths found in Shakespeare. The rich and poor, robbers, murderers, hangmen—fathers and wild boys, mothers with a soft word for their babies, workmen on railroads, steamboats, ships, wanderers, and lovers at home—they tell what life has done for them."

In a mellow voice, Sandburg rambles, establishing rapport with his listeners on the basis of personality rather than verbal skills or self-conscious dramatics.

Then, if you're lucky, he will sing one of his favorite ballads, "Amerikay."

> Torn from a world of tyrants
> Beneath this Western sky
> We formed this new dominion
> A land of liberty.
> The world shall know we're freemen here
> And such shall ever be
> Huzzah, huzzah, huzzah
> For free, free Amerikay
>
> Lift up your hands ye heroes
> And swear with proud disdain
> The wretch that would ensnare you
> Shall lay his snares in vain.
> Should Europe send invading force
> We'll meet her in array
> And fight and shout and fight
> For brave, brave Amerikay

Great work of the world

And so—my commentary on Carl Sandburg, and the Idea behind the man. Admittedly my facts are scant facts, but I was more interested in the quality of this man who lived through the most turbulent and terrifying history the world has ever known, and emerged from it as one of its most important men.

Whatever people realize from this commentary, there is one thing everyone should know about this man. They should know he has courage. They should know this because despite his early struggles to make his reputation as a poet, despite the race riots and the vicious labor wars he reported, despite the occasional breakdown of the democratic process he has seen, and despite the poverty he lived through and the cruelty and prejudice he knows others have suffered, the message of his books is: *Americans are really nice guys.*

One of the reasons Carl Sandburg was able to affirm his belief in people was that he did not look back to another time and wish vainly for it. He made the best of the time he lived in. He came from the small town of Galesburg, Illinois, but he saw quite clearly that the future of America was in its big towns—its Chicagos, New Yorks, San Franciscos, and eventually its Charlottes —the places that kept growing with people.

The word "people" had no terror for him, nor did even the word "mob." Sandburg knew he was a person and part of the mob. He has written, "I am the people—the mob—the crowd— the mass. Did you know that all the great work of the world is done through me?"

Sandburg has roamed America listening to people talk, watching them work, hoping they made the money they had to make or got the bushel yield per acre they had to get, or the shorter workday they agitated for. His instincts are with the people. He believes they have an infinite capacity for good.

Not only is this a hard belief for many people to hold, but if they do, it is a harder belief to make articulate. There are politicians who swear to it, ministers who preach it, orators who shout it over the gossiping audience, and television personalities who praise it. But none of them are able to say it as simply as Carl Sandburg said it: "The people, yes."

No end in sight

In 1904, a young stereoscopic-view salesman published from a campus basement his first poetry—*In Reckless Ecstasy.* For a 1962 book of the *National Geographic,* a patriot writes of the hope for pilgrims to learn anew "Landmarks of Liberty."

These two different pieces exist at the opposite ends of a career that has spanned fifty-seven years and included two Pulitzer prizes: the first in history for *Abraham Lincoln: The War Years*, awarded in 1940; the second in poetry for the *Complete Poems of Carl Sandburg*, awarded in 1951.

Yet this career is all of one piece. Describing the monuments of Washington, Carl Sandburg remembers that it was sixty-four years ago that he rode into Washington with twelve hundred other recruits of the Sixth Illinois Volunteers and bivouacked that night in nearby Falls Church, Virginia.

The college boy who rolled the press and hand-pulled the galleys of his first poetry became the first private citizen to address a joint session of Congress, just as he was one of the first American poets to surrender his hard-earned leisure and risk his laurels to involve himself in every political controversy and social problem of America.

Carl Sandburg believes the past is a prologue to the present and the present a prologue to the future. So it is with the privately printed *In Reckless Ecstasy* and in the forthcoming *National Geographic's* widely printed *Landmarks of Liberty:* each a prologue to the present and an ever more hopeful prologue to this poet's future.

Everybody writes about Napoleon

I go annually to several Southern writers' conferences. In the seminars and symposia we discuss our work, and controversy always rages over whether or not to retain a literary agent. Every year, there are a couple of fellows who approach me and, in muted awe, tell me, "I am writing a biography of Napoleon," or "My manuscript on Napoleon's Women is almost finished."

Next time I hear this, I am going to shield my face and laugh. Anyone can write a biography about Napoleon or Napoleon's women. I do not mean to insist that the materials are any more tractable, I mean it is easy to write a biography about Napoleon for the simple reason that he is dead.

Imagine old Bonaparte reading the galleys and erupting with, "What the hell do you mean on page 41 I was nervous. I was never nervous. Anxious, maybe; maybe a little concerned, but nervous—never."

But Napoleon isn't around, and because he isn't around is the reason he has been the subject of innumerable studies.

To attempt a commentary about someone who is not only living but a close friend is to understand finally what writing a biography is all about. The fellows who use Napoleon, or Stonewall Jackson, or Tiberius are literary naifs.

I am leaving for my heirs and literary executor several envelopes which contain Sandburg's and my correspondence, as well as notes of our discussions, regarding this book. With the envelopes go the instructions that they may not be used for twenty-five years or at such time as both Sandburg and I are standing on some parapet *up there*, I hope.

Carl Sandburg represents the best effort I could muster. The book represents everything I know about Carl and everything I think about his work. Whether it is the whole truth or not, I cannot say. Carl himself wrote in *The People, Yes*:

> Do you solemnly swear before the ever-
> living God that the testimony you are
> about to give in this cause shall be the
> truth, the whole truth, and nothing but
> the truth?
> No, I don't. I can tell you what I saw
> and what I heard and I'll swear to that
> by the everliving God but the more I
> study about it the more sure I am that
> nobody but the everliving God knows the
> whole truth and if you summoned Christ
> as a witness in this case what He would
> tell you would burn your insides with the
> pity and mystery of it.

Amen. So be it.

Works of Carl Sandburg

Privately printed by Philip Green Wright (Galesburg, Illinois, Asgard Press)
In Reckless Ecstasy, 1904
The Plaint of a Rose, 1905
Incidentals, 1905

Published by Social-Democratic Publishing Co. (Milwaukee, Wisconsin)
You and Your Job, 1908

Published by Henry Holt and Co.
Chicago Poems, 1916
Cornhuskers, 1918
   Reprinted in one volume, Poems of the Midwest, by The World Publishing Co., 1946

Published by Harcourt, Brace and Co.
The Chicago Race Riots, 1919 (Harcourt, Brace and Howe)
Smoke and Steel, 1920
Slabs of the Sunburnt West, 1922
Rootabaga Stories, 1922
Rootabaga Pigeons, 1923
Selected Poems (with Intro. by Rebecca West), 1926
Abraham Lincoln: The Prairie Years (2 vols.), 1926
The American Songbag, 1927
Good Morning, America, 1928
Steichen the Photographer, 1929
Potato Face, 1930
Early Moon, 1930
Mary Lincoln: Wife and Widow (with Paul M. Angle), 1932
The People, Yes, 1936
Abraham Lincoln: The War Years (4 vols.), 1939
Storm Over the Land, 1942
Home Front Memo, 1943

The Photographs of Abraham Lincoln (with Frederick Meserve),
   1944
Remembrance Rock, 1948
   The Fiery Trial (taken from Remembrance Rock), Dell Pub-
   lishing Co., Inc., 1959
Lincoln Collector, 1949
   Reprinted by Bonanza Books, 1960
Complete Poems, 1950
Always the Young Strangers, 1952
A Lincoln Preface, 1953
Abraham Lincoln: The Prairie Years and the War Years (1 vol.),
   1954
   Reprinted as Carl Sandburg's Abraham Lincoln (3 vols.) by
   Dell Publishing Co., Inc., 1960
Prairie-Town Boy (taken from Always the Young Strangers),
   1955
The Sandburg Range, 1957
Harvest Poems: 1960 (1960)
Wind Song, 1960
World of Carl Sandburg (Norman Corwin, Collaborator), 1961

Published by Broadcast Music, Inc.
The New American Songbag, 1960

Published by U. S. Government Printing Office
The 150th Anniversary of the Birth of Abraham Lincoln, 1959

Index

Abraham Lincoln: The Prairie Years, 41, 68-69, 80, 90, 93, 96, 116, 121, 204, 239, 240, 241, 244, 251, 258, 259; *The War Years*, 97, 116, 174, 216, 229, 240, 241, 248, 249, 250, 251, 254, 255, 258, 272
"Abraham Lincoln Walks at Midnight," 182
Abramovitz, Bessie, 133, 135, 136
Addams, Jane, 45
Addison, Joseph, 37
Ade, George, 203
Algren, Nelson, 214
Allen, Gay Wilson, 159
Altgeld, John Peter, 72, 74, 140, 152
Always the Young Strangers, 45, 46, 53
Amalgamated Clothing Workers, 133-36
America First Committee, 217
American Academy of Arts and Letters, 56
American Dilemma, An, 210
American Federation of Labor, 115, 195
American Language, The, 162
American Mercury, 165
American Milk Goat Record Association, 106
American Protective Association, 49
American Society of Composers, Authors, and Publishers, 149
American Songbag, 56, 82, 100, 169, 187, 204, 240
American Tragedy, An, 34
"Amerikay," 270
Ameringer, Oscar, 263
"Anarchists of Taste, The," 177

Anderson, Sherwood, 81, 223, 239, 244
Angle, Paul, 245
"Anna Imroth," 154
Anne Sullivan Macy—The Touch of Magic, 61
Anti-Semitism, Sandburg's hatred of, 109
Arbeiter Zeitung, 73
Arnold, Isaac, 242
Asgard Press, 67, 69
Asheville, N. C., library at, 107-08
Atkinson, Brooks, quoted on Sandburg, 108
Atlanta *Constitution*, 206
Atlantic Monthly, 86, 245
Auden, W. H., 168

Babbitt, 231
Baer, Bugs, 59
Barlow, Samuel Kossuth, 50
Barrett, Oliver R., 206, 245
Barzun, Jacques, 226, 227
Basketball, played by Sandburg, 60
Beal, Fred, 115
Benét, Stephen Vincent, 34, 116, 176, 177, 181, 182; quoted, 41-42
Bennett, James Gordon, 199
Berger, Victor, 27, 28, 87, 89, 99, 119, 120, 129, 132
Bible classes attended by Sandburg, 63
"Billy Sunday," 122, 164
Bitter Summer Thoughts, 23
"Blow the Man Down," 169
Bodenheim, Maxwell, 207
Bonfield, "Black Jack," 73
Booth, John Wilkes, 250, 255, 257
Borodin (Berg-Gruzenberg), 137, 138

Bowers, Claude, 213
Bowes, Major, 54
Breit, Harvey, 56, 171, 172
Brisbane, Arthur, 198
Brocade (goat), 106
Brooks, Van Wyck, 168, 244
Brown, Athol, 67, 68
Brown, John, 140
Browning, Robert, 37, 89
Bryan, William Jennings, 51, 129, 130
Buchwald, Art, 171
"Buffalo Sinners, The," 80-81
Butcher, Fanny, 228

Cannibal, The, 59-60
Cantos, The (Pound), 160
Carl Sandburg Association, 41
Carlyle, Thomas, 39
Carolina Israelite, The, 104
Casey, Daniel Vincent, 201
Cather, Willa, 152
Catholic Worker, The, 93
Century Magazine, 68, 239
Chaplin, Ralph, 139, 143
Chapman College, 40
Chase, Kate, 252
Chase, Salmon P., 250, 253
Chicago, 46, 50; corruption in, 45; Haymarket riot in, 72-73; race riots in, 209-12
"Chicago," 153, 163, 164, 202
Chicago American, 196, 198, 205
Chicago Daily News, 27, 32, 81, 144, 173, 174, 183, 189, 193, 194, 197, 198, 205, 208; Sandburg on staff of, 39, 96, 163, 202, 203, 204, 209, 213
Chicago Daily Socialist, 118, 191
Chicago Daily World, 189, 191
Chicago Dynamic, 38
Chicago Examiner, 197
Chicago Movement, 28
Chicago Poems, 98, 115, 136, 143, 152, 157, 163, 164, 172, 242, 246
Chicago Race Riots, The, 131, 209-10, 212
Chicago Record, 203
Chicago Socialist, 134
Chicago Sun-Times, 228
Chicago Times, 216

Chicago Tribune, 228
Chicago University, 87
Chicagoan, The, 80
Child of the Century, A, 81, 202
Churchill, Winston, 151
Civil War, 116, 249
Clapper, Raymond, 94
Clark, J. Scott, 37
Clay, Henry, 39
Clough, Arthur Hugh, 151
Cochran, Negley D., 191, 192, 201
Cochrane, Witt, 62
Cold War, 145
Collier's magazine, 165
Commager, Henry Steele, 254
Communists, Sandburg's opposition to, 145
Complete Poems of Carl Sandburg, 66, 272
Complete Works of Abraham Lincoln, 68
Compton, Charles, 31
Conant, James B., 249
Connally, Tom, 108
Connemara Farm, 94, 95, 97, 98, 99, 108, 263
Cooper, Fred, 195
Cornhuskers, 157
Corwin, Norman, 215, 236
Cottage Hospital, Galesburg, 61
Cozzens, James Gould, 223
Crane, Stephen, 50, 116
Crashaw, Richard, 181
Crime and Punishment, 230
Cummings, E. E., 150
Curley, Bill, 197, 198
Curtin, Andrew, 253

Darrow, Clarence, 134, 135, 136, 140
Daughters of the American Revolution, 40
Davidson, Jo, 193
Davidson College, 98
Davis, Bette, 40, 215, 236
Davis, Jefferson, 240
Davis, Richard Harding, 58
Day, Dorothy, 93
Day Book, 84, 96, 124, 135, 195; Sandburg's association with, 191-93, 201, 202

Deadlines, quoted on Sandburg, 204-05

Debs, Eugene V., 119, 120, 122, 129, 130, 163; last days of, 138-40

Debs, Theodore, 120

Defoe, Daniel, 37

Degan, Matthew, 73

De Leon, Daniel, 128

Delineator, 189

Democratic Party, 31, 144

Depew, Chauncey M., 47

Depression, Great, 159

Dewey, John, 45

Diary of Anne Frank, The, 34

Dickens, Charles, 29, 230

Dill Pickle, 207, 208

Donne, John, 181, 264

Dos Passos, John, 168

Dostoevski, F. M., 230

Douglas, Stephen, 47

Douglas, William O., 75, 93, 140, 266

Draper, Theodore, 137

Dreamer, The, 69

Dreiser, Theodore, 34

Dubinsky, David, 135

Duke, Charles S., 211

Duke, James B., 119, 121

Duke University, 119, 120

Dunne, Finley Peter, 58

Eastland disaster, 122-23

Eastman, Max, 65, 160, 164

Eddy, Sherwood, 121

Einstein Award, received by Sandburg, 66, 128

Eisenhower, Dwight D., 117

Eliot, T. S., 28, 65, 150, 154, 168, 181

"Elizabeth Umpsteadt," 215

Elmhurst, Ill., 96

Emerson, Ralph Waldo, 37, 39, 264

Engel, George, 73

Engels, Friedrich, 155

Erikson, Leif, 215

Evjue, Bill, 188

"Fables in Slang," 203

Family of Man exhibit, 111, 112, 224-27, 263

Fascists, Sandburg's stand against, 28

Fathers and Sons, 230

Faulkner, William, 231

Feiker, F. M., 201

"Fellow Citizen," 157

Ficke, Arthur Davison, 163

Field, Eugene, 202, 204

Fielden, Samuel, 72, 73

Fifer, Joseph W., 106, 107

Finley, John Huston, 47

Finnish Revolution (1918), 136-37

Fischer, Adolph, 73

Fishbein, Morris, 80

Fiske, Jim, 117

Fitch, George, 47

Fitzgerald, F. Scott, 231

"Fog," 109, 149, 165

Foote, A. K., 212

Forbes, John Murray, 254

Ford, Worthington C., 245

Fortune, 165

"Forty Years of Friendship," 163

Francis, Arlene, 101

From Whitman to Sandburg in American Poetry, 174, 245

Frost, Lesley, 170

Frost, Robert, 26, 28, 163, 168, 225; and Sandburg, 169-71

Furuseth, Andy, 123

Galesburg, Ill., 36, 37, 41-42, 46-53 *pass.,* 243

Gannett, Lewis, 228; quoted, 235-36

Garden, Mary, 207

Gardner, John W., 266

Garrets and Pretenders . . . , 205

Gary, Judge, 74

Gastonia, N. C., 115

"General William Booth Enters Heaven," 163, 181

George, Adda, 41

George, John E., 41

Gettysburg Address, 24, 176, 252, 253, 254

Ghent, William J., 120

Gibbon, Edward, 248

Goat farm, Sandburg's, 105-06

Golden, Harry, as Sandburg's friend, 99

Gompers, Samuel, 115, 130, 189

Good Morning, America, 157, 165, 169, 204

Gould, Jay, 117
Graffis, Herb, 228
Grant, Ulysses S., 60
Grant, William C., 53
Great Gatsby, The, 231
Greatest Story Ever Told, The, 33, 35
Greeley, Horace, 199, 240
Griffith, D. W., 34, 235
Guitar, played by Sandburg, 79, 80, 82, 83, 98
Gustav V, Sandburg decorated by, 263

Hand, Augustus, 131
Hanks, Nancy, 46
Hansen, Harry, 206, 208; quoted, 173-74, 203
Harbert, Mich., 85, 96, 97, 98, 105, 142, 248
Harcourt, Alfred, 65, 66, 141, 142, 163-64, 197, 240, 243, 244
Harcourt, Brace and Company, 35, 96, 163, 221, 258, 268
Harding, Warren G., 138
Hardy, Thomas, quoted, 115
Harlan County, Ill., coal strike in (1917), 194-95
Harriman, Edward, 126
Harris, Bernard, 121
Harrison, Carter, 193
Harshbarger, Allen, 60
Harvard, John, 197
Harvard University, 69, 121
Hawthorne, Nathaniel, 28, 37
Hay, John Milton, 68, 239, 242
Haymarket riot, 72-73
Haynes, George Edwin, 212
Haywood, William D., 27, 122, 143, 193; interviewed by Sandburg, 193-94
Hearst, William Randolph, 121, 135, 158; Sandburg's obituary on, 196-200
Hecht, Ben, 205-09 *pass.*; quoted, 81, 202
Hegel, Georg W. F., 248
Hemingway, Ernest, 168, 171, 172, 183-84
Herbert, George, 181
Herndon, William, 242

Herodotus, 248
Hickok, Lorena, 61-62
Hill, Jim, 117, 136
Hillman, Sidney, 134, 135
Hillquit, Morris, 120
Hirsch, Emil, 64
Hoan, Daniel W., 120, 131, 189
Hobos, 54-57
Hodges, Luther H., 32, 264
Hoffman, Clare, 143
Hokanson, Nels M., 242
Hollander, W. K., 204
Hollywood, 34, 103, 203
Holmes, Oliver Wendell, 152
Holt, Henry, 65, 66, 163
Holt and Company, Henry, 65, 163
"Home Fires," 150
Home Front Memo, quoted, 214, 217
Hoover, Herbert, 242
House of Intellect, The, 226
How the Other Half Lives, 149
Howe, Jim, 188
Hubbard, Elbert, 59
Hull House, 45
Humphrey Barbershop, 49-50
Hunter, Robert, 120
Hurst, Fannie, 121
Hutchins, Robert M., 98

Ickes, Harold, 134
Illinois, democratic spirit of, 107
Illinois, University of, 86-87, 91, 251
Imagist School, American, 182
"In a Back Alley," 246
In Reckless Ecstasy, 67, 69, 271, 272
In the Cool Tombs, 227
Incidentals, 67, 69, 70-72
Industrial Workers of the World, 55, 131, 143, 193, 194
"Instructions for the Tomb of George Washington Hill," 265
International Socialist Review, 122, 123, 124, 125
Intolerance (film), 235
Irving, Washington, 37

James, Sidney, 142
James, William, 267
Jenifer II (goat), 105
John Brown's Body, 116
Johnson, Gerald, 46

Johnson, Samuel, 181
Jones, Jack, 207
Jones, Mary Harris, 122

Karsner, David, 138
Kazin, Alfred, 179, 180
Keller, Helen, 61
Kelly, Gene, 25
Kenna, Michael, 193
Kennedy, John F., 35, 40, 144, 145, 206, 252, 266
Kerr, Charles H., 122, 125
Kestnbaum, Meyer, 32
Kilmer, Joyce, 227
Kirkus, Virginia, 228
Knox College, 47, 59, 69, 187
Kolbe, Henry, 66
Kramer, Leon, 119
Kreymborg, Alfred, 165
Kroll, Lucy, 30
Ku Klux Klan, 145-46

Labour Party, British, 29
La Follette's Weekly, 117
Laidler, Harry W., 121
Lamb, Charles, 37
Landis, Kenesaw Mountain, 119, 143
Landmarks of Liberty, 272
Landon, Alfred, 144
Lang, Harry, 115
Lang, Lucy Robbins, 115
Larsen, J. Austin, 62
Last Adam, The, 223
Last Essays of Elia, The, 37
Lauer, Howard, 67, 68
Lawson, Victor, 203, 208
Lazinskas, Charles, 134
Leach, Paul, 209
Leale, Charles A., 42, 257
"Leave Her, Bullies, Leave Her," 135
Lee, Algernon, 98
Lee, Robert E., 264
Lenin, Nikolai, 137, 138
Leopold, Nathan, 94, 265
Lerner, Leo, 94
Letter to the American Workingman, 138
Letters, received by Sandburg, 103-04
Letters and Speeches of Lincoln, 239
"Letters from Lindlahr," 138-39
Levinson, Helen Haire, 164

Levinson, Salmon O., 164
Lewis, John L., 144
Lewis, Lloyd, 84, 107, 144, 197, 208, 239, 252; quoted, 80, 81, 251
Lewis, Sinclair, 80, 81, 139, 223, 224, 231
Library, Sandburg's, 91, 100
Life, 142
Ligon, Margaret H., 108
Lincoln, Abraham, 24, 25, 28, 42, 205, 206; assassination of, 255, 257-58; biography by Nicolay and Hay, 68, 239, 242; biography by Sandburg, see Abraham Lincoln; at Galesburg, 47
Lincoln, Robert Todd, 47
Lincoln, Thomas, 45
Lincoln Book Shop, in Chicago, 93
Lincoln Collector, 206
Lincoln penny, 246-47
Lincoln Preface, A, 258, 259
Lincoln Room, at Galesburg, 42
Lincoln Studies, 68
Lindbergh, Charles A., 217
Lindsay, Vachel, 28, 163, 180, 181, 182, 225
Lingg, Louis, 73
Lippmann, Walter, 120, 131, 210, 215
Little Review, The, 165
Little Rock, Ark., 214
Lombard College, 46, 47, 58-60, 62, 63, 67, 69; Glee Club at, 79
Lombard Review, The, 60, 61
London, Jack, 122, 126
"Long Shadow of Lincoln, The," 165
Longfellow, Henry Wadsworth, 150, 151
Lost Lady, A, 153
Lovejoy, Owen, 24, 25
Lowell, Amy, 163, 164, 181, 182
Luce, Clare Booth, 144
Luce, Henry R., 142, 165
Lunn, George R., 131
Lutheran Church, 63

MacArthur, Charles, 205, 206, 207
MacArthur, Douglas A., 60
McCarthy, Catherine, 141
McCarthy, Joseph, 94
McClure's Magazine, 68, 239

MacDonald, J. Ramsay, 120
McGill, Ralph, 94, 206
McGirr, Thomas Leslie, 57
McKees Rocks, Pa., 55
McKinley, William, 60
MacLeish, Archibald, 94, 143, 165, 168, 266
Madison *Capital-Times*, 188
"Mag," 153
Maier, Henry W., 132
Main Street, 80, 223
Maine (battleship), 57
Malloy, Jack, 202
Manitowoc *Daily Tribune*, 188
"Many Hats," 164
March, Fredric, 24
Markey, Gene, 207
Marshall, S. L. A., 93
Marx, Karl, 36, 68, 126, 155
Masses, The, 65, 164, 165
Massey, Raymond, 206
Masters, Edgar Lee, 28, 47, 163, 181, 182, 225
Measure My Love, 90
Medill, Joseph, 240
Melville, Herman, 28
Memminger, Christopher G., 98
Mencken, Henry L., 59, 162, 164; quoted, 208-09; on Sandburg, 227
Merrill, Gary, 215
Message to Garcia, The, 59
"Micrometric Mirrors," 165
Midwest Portraits, 173, 206
Miller, Joseph, 84
Miller, Perry, 228
"Million Young Workmen, A," 122
Milwaukee, Wis., 89, 130; Socialist mayors of, 90, 120, 131-32, 189
Milwaukee *Daily News*, 188, 246
Milwaukee *Journal*, 133, 189
Milwaukee *Leader*, 90, 119-20, 165
Milwaukee *Sentinel*, 188
Mitchell, Billy, 111
Monroe, Harriet, 162, 163, 164, 166, 176
Monroe, Marilyn, 34
"Moonlight and Maggots," 165
Moore, Garry, 153, 154
Moore, Marianne, 168
Morgan, J. Pierpont, 126

Morris, William, 67
"Mr. Longfellow and His Boy," 165
Murphy, Carroll D., 200, 202
Murray, Phil, 38
Murrow, Edward R., 101, 106; quoted, 108-09
Muste, A. J., 121
"Muzzling the Machines," 200
Myrdal, Gunnar, 210
Myths After Lincoln, 208

Nagrekis, Frank, 134
Nathan, George Jean, 108
Nation, 165, 180
National Book Awards, 171
National Geographic, 271, 272
National Institute of Arts and Letters, 56
National Republican Club, Lincoln Dinner at, 121
Native Son, 214
Nazis, Sandburg's stand against, 28, 217
Neebe, Oscar, 73
Negro, in Sandburg's poetry, 215
Never Come Morning, 214
Nevins, Allan, 250
New Criticism, 175; Sandburg's views on, 175-76
New Deal, 74, 120, 125, 169, 249
"New Hampshire Again," 169
New Leader, 165
New Poetry Movement, 227
New Republic, 46
New York *Call*, 65, 164, 165; quoted, 138-39
New York *Herald*, 199
New York *Herald Tribune*, 83, 142, 217, 251; quoted, 84
New York *Times*, 46, 56, 84, 93, 164, 245, 269
New York *Times Book Review*, 171, 179, 228
New Yorker magazine, 56, 59, 228
Newman, Ralph, 93
Newspaper Enterprise Association, 136, 203
Nicolay, John George, 68, 239, 242
Nixon, Richard M., 117
Nobel prize, 171, 172
Nuorteva, Santari, 138

Oklahoma, Socialists in (1910), 129
Olander, Victor, 123
Older, Fremont, 197
Olson, Swan, 52
Olson, Will, 52
Only in America, 105, 263
Oppfer, Ivan, 177
Others magazine, 165
Oursler, Fulton, 33
Owens, Mary, 246
Owl's Roost, The, 90

Pack Memorial Public Library, 107-08
Page, Kirby, 121
Palmer, A. Mitchell, 131
Palmer, John M., 47
Parker, John F., 257
Parry, Albert, 205, 207
Parsons, Albert, 72, 73
Parsons, Geoffrey, 142
Pascal, Blaise, 267
Patterson, Joseph Medill, 45, 141
Pegler, Westbrook, quoted, 38
Penknives, Sandburg's fondness for, 103
Peoria Journal Star, 45
Petersham, Maude and Miska, 221
Pictorial Review, 90, 96, 165, 244
Place in the Sun, A, 34
Plaint of a Rose, The, 67, 69, 88
Playboy magazine, 30
Poe, Edgar Allan, 181
Poems by Sandburg, quoted, 25, 26, 57, 65, 66, 115, 150, 153-58 *pass.*, 160, 161, 162, 169, 202, 215, 247, 270
"Poetical Circuit Rider," 174
Poetry magazine, 162, 163, 164, 166, 167, 171, 176
Poetry Review, 164
Polk, James K., 247-48
Poor Writers' Club, 67, 68
Populism, 129
Possessed, The, 230
Potato Face, 204
Pound, Ezra, 28, 150, 159, 166-68, 182
"Prayers of Steel," 66
Prejudices, 227
Prince, George W., 60
Pulitzer Prize, 232, 272

Quigley, Martin, 189
Radek, K. B., 137
Radford, A. W., 111
Rand School, 98
Ransom, John Crowe, 175, 259
Rascoe, Burton, 207
Rayburn, Sam, 23
Red Badge of Courage, The, 50, 116
Red Special campaign train, 130, 131
Redbook magazine, 229
Redfield, William C., 123
Religion, Sandburg's views on, 64, 65, 66
Religion and Life, 66
Remembrance Rock, 64, 102, 108, 109, 180, 228, 229, 231, 232-35, 269
Republican Party, 121, 141-42
Rickover, Hyman, 93
Riis, Jacob, 149
Robinson, Edwin Arlington, 163, 225
Rockefeller, John D., 126
Rockwell, Norman, 165
Rogers, Will, 194
Roosevelt, Franklin D., 74, 117, 120, 121, 125, 140, 144, 151, 158, 165, 169, 242, 247, 249-50
Roosevelt, Theodore, 127, 130, 255
Rootabaga Stories, 90, 91, 96, 187, 204, 221-24, 239
Roots of American Communism, The, 137
Rosenberg, Ira, 83
Rosenwald, Julius, 212
Ruskin, John, 37
Russell, Bertrand, 145
Ruth, Babe, 32, 189-90
Rutledge, Ann, 244, 245

St. Louis Public Library, 31
Sandburg, August, 41, 45, 46, 48, 49, 52, 53
Sandburg, Clara Matilda, 48
Sandburg, Helga, 90, 96, 97, 105; quoted, 91-93
Sandburg, Janet, 90, 93, 95, 96, 100, 164
Sandburg, Margaret, 90, 91, 93, 95, 96, 100, 139
Sandburg, Mart, 58, 62
Sandburg, Mary, 41

Sandburg, Paula, 35, 42, 70, 85, 86, 87, 89, 90, 94, 95, 96, 97, 105, 106, 189, 249; love letter from Carl, 87-88; *see also* Steichen, Lillian

Sandburg Birthplace, 41

Sandburg Collections, 187

Sandburg Day, 32, 264

Sandburg Range, The, 180, 235

Sandburg Room, at University of Illinois, 187, 251

Santayana, George, 71

Saturday Evening Post, The, 47, 132, 165

Saturday Review, 228

Schaffner and Marx shops, 133, 134, 135

Schelling, Felix, 166, 167

Schlesinger, Arthur, 249, 250

Schlogl's Restaurant, 207

Schools, named after Sandburg, 267-68

Schumach, Murray, 269

Scripps, E. W., 191, 192, 193, 195, 199

Segovia, Andres, quoted, 83

Seidel, Emil, 90, 120, 131, 189

Selected Poems of Carl Sandburg, 152

Sercombe, Parker H., 69

Sevareid, Eric, quoted on Sandburg, 108

"Sharps and Flats," 203

Shaw, George Bernard, 29, 120

Sheil, Bernard J., 214

Shelley, Percy Bysshe, 87

Sherwood, Robert, 46, 241; quoted, 101

Simmons, Skeets, 54

Simpson, Kenneth, 141, 143

Sinatra, Frank, 40

Sinclair, Upton, 120

Singing, public, by Sandburg, 79, 80, 82

Siwasher, Knox College, 68

"Slabs of the Sunburnt West," 164, 204

Slang, Sandburg quoted on, 162

"Sleeping Mortgage, The," 53

Smith, Henry Justin, 198, 202, 203, 205, 207, 208; quoted on Sandburg, 204-05, 208

Smoke and Steel, 80, 204

Smythe, Ellington Adger, 98

Social Democratic Party, 75, 87, 89, 116-19, 129-30, 189

Socialist Party of America, 119, 120, 125-28

Socialists, Christian, 64, 124; in Oklahoma (1910), 129; in Wisconsin, 129-32; during World War I, 27, 120

South Atlantic Quarterly, The, 159

Soviet Union, 263

Spanish-American War, 27, 46, 55, 57-58

"Special Starlight," 165

Spencer, Harry, 205

Spies, August, 72, 73

Spoon River Anthology, The, 182

Sprague, William, 253

SSIIP, 40

Starrett, Vincent, 203, 207

Steffens, Lincoln, 173; quoted, 193

Steichen, Edward, 42, 70, 86, 89, 105, 224, 225, 226, 227, 263; Sandburg quoted on, 110-11

Steichen, Lillian (Paula), 48, 70, 86, 87, 118; *see also* Sandburg, Paula

Steichen the Photographer, 110, 204, 225

Steinbeck, John, 93, 166, 179, 180, 266

Stereoscope views, sold by Sandburg, 61

Stevens, George, 33, 34, 35, 36, 203

Stevenson, Adlai, 93, 107, 266; quoted, 106-07

Stong, Phil, 223

Strachey, Lytton, 181

Study of English Prose and Writers, A, 37

Stump, Felix, 111

Sunday, Billy, 65, 164

Supreme Court, U.S., 74, 75, 213

"Sweet Bye and Bye, The," takeoff on, 136

System magazine, 200-01

Taft, William Howard, 130

Tagore, Rabindranath, 163

Tales of the South Pacific, 232

Tarbell, Ida M., 68, 239
Tate, Allen, 175
Taussig, F. W., 69
Teillard, Dorothy Lamon, 242
The People, Yes, 33, 50, 143, 158, 159, 160, 161, 229, 236, 273
Theory of the Leisure Class, The, 45
"They Ask: Is God, Too, Lonely?", 66
Think magazine, 165
Thomas, Norman, 120-21, 130; Sandburg's open letter to, 218
Thompson, Wallace, 42
Thoreau, Henry David, 28, 101
Thucydides, 248, 255
Thurber, James, 56, 61; quoted on Sandburg, 109
Time magazine, 228
"To a Contemporary Bunkshooter," 65, 66, 164
Tomorrow magazine, 69
Towne, Charles Hanson, 227
"Training Workers to Be Careful," 200
Treasury Hour, The, 216
Trilling, Diana, 180
Truman, Harry S., 144
Turgenev, Ivan S., 230
Twain, Mark, 28, 29, 30, 86, 154, 159, 181
Twentieth Century-Fox Studios, 36

Van Buren, Martin, 160
Van Doren, Irita, 228
Van Doren, Mark, 94, 266
Vance, Arthur T., 165
Vanderbilt University, 175
Vanity Fair magazine, 177, 179
Veblen, Thorstein, 45, 87
Vetlugin, Valdemar, 229
Village Tale, 223
Vogue magazine, 86

Waldman, Louis, 121
Warren, Earl, 75, 140, 266
Warren, Robert Penn, 175
Wasteland, The, 182
Webb and Knapp, 35

Webster, Daniel, 38, 39
Weigel, John C., 68
Weirick, Bruce, 174, 245
Wells, H. G., 120
West, Jessamyn, 93
West, Rebecca, 152, 153
West Point, Sandburg's failure at, 27, 60
WEVD Radio Station, opened by Socialists, 120
Wheel of Earth, The, 90
When Death Came April Twelve, 1945, 158
White, William Allen, 141
Whitman, Walt, 28, 79, 87, 117, 173, 176
Williams, Roger, 234
Willkie, Wendell, 141, 144, 151
Wills, David, 253
Wilson, Edmund, 251; quoted on Sandburg, 177-79
Wilson, Woodrow, 69, 120, 140, 158
"Windy City, The," 153, 164
Winesburg, Ohio, 223
Wisconsin, 35, 129-32, 200
Wobbly, 139
Wolcott, Representative, 247
Woman's Home Companion, The, 165
World of Carl Sandburg, The, 40, 215, 236
World War I, 27, 120, 132, 158
World War II, 34, 150, 158, 177, 232
Wright, Chester, 188, 189
Wright, Frank Lloyd, 33
Wright, Philip Green, 67, 68, 69, 70, 124; quoted, 67-68
Wright, Richard, 214

Yerkes, Charles, 45
Yeshiva College, 66, 128
You and Your Job, 125-28
Young, Brigham, 97

Zeckendorf, William, 35, 36, 179
Zeidler, Frank T., 132

Prairie State Books

1988

Mr. Dooley in Peace and in War
Finley Peter Dunne

Life in Prairie Land
Eliza W. Farnham

Carl Sandburg
Harry Golden

The Sangamon
Edgar Lee Masters

American Years
Harold Sinclair

The Jungle
Upton Sinclair

Free Public Library
Paterson, New Jersey

GAYLORD MG